GREAT IRISH
HOUSES AND CASTLES

JACQUELINE O'BRIEN

GREAT
HOUSES AND

WEIDENFELD

AND DESMOND GUINNESS

IRISH CASTLES

AND NICOLSON

C O N

TENTS

FIRST PUBLISHED IN 1992 BY
GEORGE WEIDENFELD & NICOLSON LTD
ORION HOUSE, 5 UPPER ST MARTIN'S LANE,
LONDON WC2H 9EA

FIRST PUBLISHED IN PAPERBACK IN 1993

BRITISH LIBRARY CATALOGUING-IN-PUBLICATION DATA
A CATALOGUE RECORD FOR THIS BOOK IS AVAILABLE FROM THE BRITISH LIBRARY

DESIGNED BY HARRY GREEN
HOUSE EDITOR: SUZANNAH GOUGH
MAP: PEARTREE DESIGN ASSOCIATES

TITLE PAGE
CASTLE COOLE, CO. FERMANAGH.

PAGE 4
ABOVE LEFT THE MASTER BEDROOM AT MARINO CASINO, CO. DUBLIN.
ABOVE RIGHT THE LIBRARY AT LEIXLIP CASTLE, CO. KILDARE.
BELOW LEFT THE TOPIARY GARDEN AT CASTLETOWN COX, CO. KILKENNY.

PAGE 5
THE GOTHIC BALLROOM AT BIRR CASTLE, CO. OFFALY.

PHOTOTYPESET BY KEYSPOOLS LTD, GOLBORNE, LANCS
COLOUR SEPARATIONS BY NEWSELE LITHO LTD
PRINTED IN ITALY BY PRINTERS SRL, TRENTO
BOUND BY L.E.G.O., VICENZA

× DUNLUCE

GLENVEAGH

MUSSENDEN TEMPLE

DONEGAL

LONDONDERRY

ANTRIM

Bann

NORTHERN

BARONS COURT

TYRONE

MOUNT
STEWART

IRELAND

BELFAST ●

BALLYWALTER

CASTLE COOLE

Bann

DOWN

CASTLE WARD

LISSADELL

Sligo

LEITRIM

FERMANAGH

MONAGHAN

ARMAGH

FLORENCE COURT

LOUTH

BELLAMONT
FOREST

SLIGO

ROCKFLEET

Shannon

CAVAN

Clew Bay

MAYO

ROSCOMMON

CARRIGGLAS

STACKALLAN

× SLANE

● BEAULIEU

STROKESTOWN

LONGFORD

× TULLYNALLY

Drogheda

Roscommon ●

MEATH

WESTMEATH

Boyne

× TRIM

Dublin

NEWBRIDGE

MALAHIDE

KYLEMORE

× ASHFORD

Mullingar ●

DUNSANY ×

HOWTH

BELVEDERE

LUTTRELLSTOWN

×

Lough Corrib

LEIXLIP

MARINO CASINO

GALWAY

CARTON

ÁRAS AN UACHTARÁIN

Galway ●

OFFALY

CASTLETOWN

DEERFIELD

STRAFFAN

LUCAN

KILMAINHAM

LYONS

KILDARE

CHARLEVILLE

KILLRUDDERY

PORTUMNA ×

× BIRR

CASTLEMARTIN

POWERSCOURT

EMO

LAOIS

LUGGALA

Shannon

HUMEWOOD

RUSSBOROUGH

CLARE

ABBEY LEIX

WICKLOW

MOUNT
IEVERS

*Lough
Derg*

CARLOW

DROMOLAND ×

TIPPERARY

Kilkenny

Slaney

ADARE

Limerick

Barrow

× GLIN

LONGFIELD

KILKENNY

WEXFORD

LIMERICK

CASHEL

KERRY

SWISS COTTAGE

CASTLETOWN

Suir

DONERAILE

BURNTCOURT

CARRICK-ON-SUIR

WATERFORD

Waterford

Blackwater

LISMORE × ● DROMANA

Killarney

KILSHANNIG

● Cork

■ FOTA ISLAND

CORK

BANTRY

× CASTLE

■ HOUSE

0 ————————— 50 Miles

0 ————————— 70 Kilometres

ACKNOWLEDGEMENTS

The authors would, first of all, like to thank all those who have so generously allowed their houses and castles to be photographed, who endured the inconvenience and disruption of assembling lights and equipment, rolls of background paper and re-positioned furniture; who arranged flowers, set tables, provided endless hospitality with generosity and warmth, and who even said 'come again if it isn't right'. We are also sincerely grateful to the museum curators who helped us so patiently.

We would particularly like to thank John Derby of Cashel in Co. Tipperary, who assisted with nearly all the photography and taught us so much about Ireland and its history during the miles we drove, as well as spending many hours on the text. Thanks also to John Slater, David Davison and Ronnie Norton for their help.

Dr Edward McParland, Professor Kevin B. Nowlan and the Knight of Glin undertook the thankless task of reading the manuscript, for which we are indeed grateful. Dr McParland also helped with the List of Architects. In addition, David Griffin, Anne Henderson and the staff of the Irish Architectural Archive were unfailingly cooperative.

Our book has been a work of many hands and the following are among the people for whose help in various ways we are deeply indebted: *An Taoiseach*, Charles J. Haughey, T. D.; Captain F. B. Barton; Douglas Bennett; Dr and Mrs Nicholas Bielenberg; Alice Blake; Ian Burns; Ray Carroll; Maeve Casey; Alec Cobbe; Sybil Connolly; Col. Con Costello; Crawford Art Gallery; Luke Dodd; Dr Patrick Doran; Dublin Co. Council; Mairead Dunlevy; The Earl and Countess of Dunraven; Audrey Emerson; Gail Fahey; Lingard Goulding; Penelope Guinness; Robert Guinness; Peter Harbison; Jonathan Hill; Hunt Museum, Limerick; Harry Hutchman; Ben Jellett; Jim Kelly; Peter Lauritzen; Limerick City Museum; Mr and Mrs Terence Mack; Matthew McNulty; Arthur Montgomery; Commissioner Brian Murphy, O.P.W.; Rory Murphy; The National Trust; Catherine O'Brien; Charles O'Brien; Frederick O'Dwyer; Brian O'Halloran; Dr Ciaran O'Keeffe; Eleanor O'Neill; Sean O'Reilly; Office of Public Works; Nicholas Prins; Alan Rapier; John Redmill; Nicholas Robinson; Deidre Rowsome; Peter Ryan; Father Shiel, S. J.; Edward Smyth; Trinity College, Dublin; James Villiers-Stuart; Waterford Corporation, Waterford Glass; Westmeath Co. Council; Hugh and Grania Weir; Jeremy Williams; Richard Wood and Dean Woodworth.

Last, but not least, our thanks to David O'Brien for many corrections and suggestions as well as for compiling the index; to our patient and skilful editor, Suzannah Gough, and to Harry Green for his handsome design.

For Vincent O'Brien

INTRODUCTION

The countryside of Ireland, renowned for the picturesque beauty of its natural landscape, is richly endowed with a fascinating array of houses and castles. The image of Irish architecture abroad has consisted of the ruined abbey, round tower, castle fortress and thatched cottage. This romantic idea of our heritage has until recently ignored the great Classical buildings which are equal to anything comparable in Europe, or indeed the world. Because of a hundred years of peace from 1690 to 1798 a golden age flourished in the eighteenth century which produced some of the finest architecture in existence today. Besides the great Palladian buildings of the late eighteenth century there are many others of equal fascination from the early castle stronghold through to the emergence of domestic architecture and concluding with the multi-turreted dream castles of the Victorian era.

The purpose of this book is to chronicle these buildings and examine the various architectural styles as they developed from the arrival of the Normans to the end of Queen Victoria's reign. It was not easy to select the houses and castles. It seemed appropriate to balance key masterpieces like Castletown and Carton in Co. Kildare with less famous places such as Lyons in Co. Dublin and Humewood in Co. Wicklow, and to arrange them in chronological order to present an overall picture. Every house has a story to tell or a legend of some kind attached to it, and each makes its individual contribution to the story of Irish architecture. The interiors provide a dazzling visual feast and our final chapter is devoted to the fine and decorative arts which would have been, and are to this day, found in them. It shows a minute selection in order to illustrate the amount of talent that existed in Ireland in a variety of fields. The choice of subjects has been a personal one. For example, in the sculpture section we have included our favourites that have probably never before been illustrated in colour, such as the O'Brien, Conolly and La Touche monuments. These have been chosen not only for their beauty but also because they are so little known, being either remote or locked away from view. We make no apology for not having included one single portrait bust or statue adorning a public building.

It is a sobering thought to consider the quantity of Irish art and artefacts – silver, glass, furniture, bound-books and so on – that have left the country since Ireland's golden age. Very few of its great houses have been able to retain their original contents. Fortunately, the wonderful stucco interiors have remained intact even if, sometimes, the furnishings are of a later period. It is encouraging, therefore, that in many houses we have come upon in the course of our travels we have found that the owners have brought back to Ireland objects of beauty, often of great historical interest, that were made here.

The 'Big House' has a long-established place in Irish literature and has become familiar through the fiction of

Somerville and Ross, Elizabeth Bowen and Molly Keane among many other writers. However, when it comes to fact rather than fiction, there is a surprising dearth of literature on the subject. In 1953 Sacheverell Sitwell was writing in *Truffle Hunt*: 'In spite of the craze for Georgian buildings, no one has yet written a book on Irish country houses. It is a theme which could be tackled with fire and enthusiasm, for it would embrace such extraordinary characters, and not only the houses that they lived in.' Another twenty years was to elapse, however, before a book on the subject emerged, *Irish Houses and Castles* by Desmond Guinness and William Ryan, now for long out of print and, worse, out of date. Of the thirty-nine houses and castles described, twelve have since changed hands, four have lost an important part of their contents, and two have suffered from disastrous fires. In the current work nearly twice as many buildings have been included.

Ireland's heritage of houses and castles spreads throughout the land and is unaffected by the border. Its value from the cultural, historical and educational standpoint is self-evident. Now that many of these buildings can be seen by the public a great tourist attraction has opened up for the first time. We found 700 visitors at Glenveagh Castle in Co. Donegal on a wet Thursday in September, and nowhere could be more remote than Glenveagh. Some of these properties that are open to visitors are protected from the outside world such as the gardens and Telescope Museum at Birr Castle in Co. Offaly, which are hidden behind massive Gothic gates and crenellated walls, up to thirty feet high in places. Others display themselves with pride like Russborough in Co. Wicklow which, thanks to a courteous dip in the demesne wall, is visible in all its beauty to anyone travelling past along the public road. The tourist load will spread to parts of Ireland which have never benefited from it before. As these places have such a universal appeal an opportunity has been opened up for co-operation between the Tourist Boards north and south of the border to work in tandem.

The future of this heritage is in danger. Apart from the ever-present threat of fire, which reaps its grim annual toll, there is the cost of upkeep – repairs, maintenance, wages, insurance and so on – which ascends in a constant spiral from year to year. Fortunately, a National Heritage Council was established in 1988 by *An Taoiseach* (the Prime Minister), Charles J. Haughey, under the chairmanship of Lord Killanin, for the purpose of giving financial assistance to the built heritage of the Republic, often on a basis whereby the council matches the amount raised by the owner. In Northern Ireland a Historic Buildings Fund and a flourishing branch of the British National Trust already exist but there is no effective legislation as yet to prevent the export of Irish works of art. Moreover, there is still a pressing need for the establishment of proper conservation workshops where repair and restoration work can be both taught and carried out. Under proper supervision conservation work could help provide jobs for the youth of the country and even in schools children could be taught the value of their visual heritage.

So much has been lost from Ireland over the last 150 years that it is, in our opinion, vital to ensure that the present generation learns to take care of the best of the past so that it can be handed on to posterity. If this book stimulates an interest in, and a concern for, Irish art and architecture, it will have served its purpose.

EARLY RUINS
AND
PALE CASTLES

The Irish countryside is rich in picturesque ruins of all kinds, particularly those of ancient tombs, ring forts, abbeys, churches, tower houses and castles, reflecting in turn Ireland's sometimes splendid, sometimes troubled history. At the coming of Christianity in the fifth century the country was governed by provincial kings who were subject to the High King at Tara in Co. Meath. Great dedication to religion, learning and culture came from the monasteries, reflected in the beautiful artefacts which survive. This 'Island of Saints and Scholars' was shattered at the beginning of the ninth century by the arrival of the fierce Vikings in their longboats. They murdered, plundered monasteries and homes and carried off valuable booty. Thomas Barrington in *Discovering Kerry* quotes the poem of a lonely monk:

> Bitter and wild is the wind tonight
>
> Tossing the tresses of the sea to white;
>
> On such a night as this I feel at ease
>
> Fierce Norsemen only cross the quiet seas.

Eventually, finding little resistance, they settled at the mouths of rivers, establishing the important Norse settlements of Dublin, Wicklow, Wexford, Cork and Limerick. After 200 years the Irish united under the High King Brian Boru, and in 1014 the Vikings were defeated and driven out. Some had intermarried with the Irish and remained peacefully.

In spite of the fact that the *Annals of the Four Masters*, a seventeenth-century history of Ireland, recorded seven castles of stone as existing prior to the Norman invasion of 1169, it is generally agreed that stone strongholds were introduced to Ireland by the Normans. Initially they erected earthen mounds surrounded by palisades and ditches known by the name of 'motte and bailey', often with a timber keep covered in hides. Eventually these were replaced in stone. The Irish, on the other hand, lived mostly in ring forts; the remains of some forty thousand of these can still be seen throughout the countryside. The dwellings within these ring forts were built of wattle and clay and have since disappeared.

The finest Norman castle is also one of the earliest, being completed in about 1224. The great stronghold at Trim in Co. Meath was partly protected by the River Boyne and a moat. Massive curtain walls, punctuated by circular towers, enclose an area of three acres, towards the centre of which rises the gigantic, twenty-sided keep or 'donjon' that can be seen for miles around. Trim Castle was an important military outpost, whereas its offspring, the thousands of lesser castles, were intended as safe places to live in a warlike countryside. An agent sent to Ireland by Philip II of Spain reported that 'Every petty gentleman lives in a stone tower, where he gathers into his service all the rascals of the neighbourhood (and of these towers there is an infinite number)'.

Castles generally had a bawn attached, a fortified enclosure where livestock could be herded in at night for safety against wolves, as well as marauding neighbours. These minor castles would not have withstood a large army but were built with petty warfare, raiding and personal safety in mind. Inside, conditions were primitive and only a few castles would have boasted elaborate tapestries and furniture of quality. The walls were usually plastered and whitened to make the rooms lighter. Luke Gernon, a seventeenth-century writer, described the interior of an Irish tower house in 1620 as follows:

> When you come to your bedchamber do not expect a canopy and curtains, the wild Irish have no candles on their tables – What! Do I speak of tables? Indeed, they have no tables, but set their meat upon a bundle of grass and use the same grass to wipe their hands.

Edward Willes (1702–68), the Lord Chief Baron of the Irish Exchequer, tells an interesting tale of an invitation from a local clan chieftain, possibly one of the Joyces, to his house:

> ... a Magnificent palace, where there were two long Cabins, Thatched, opposite to one another, the one was the kitchen and apartments for the family, the other was the Entertaining room, neatly strewn, according to the Irish Fashion, with Rushes. A bottle of Brandy was the whet before dinner, and the entertainment was a Half Sheep Boiled on top, Half Sheep roasted at Bottom, broiled Fish on one side, a great wooden bowl of Potatoes on the other, and a heaped plate of salt in the middle. After dinner pretty good claret, and an enormous Bowl of Brandy Punch, which, according to the old as well as the Modern Irish hospitality, the guests were pressed to take full share of ... When the Chief began to grow mellow, he called his Favourite Girl to sing, which she did very well ... and was a neat handsome jolly girl. Before he called her in, he stipulated with his guests that they were welcome to any liberty with her from the Girdle upwards but he would not permit underhand doings. Later a bagpiper and a Bard sang about the glorious deeds of the Chief's illustrious and warlike ancestors.

The ring of castles originally built to protect the rich flat land to the north and west of Dublin was known as the Pale, Trim Castle being its standard bearer. The expression 'beyond the Pale' has passed into the language as a derisory expression. It was never a static line of defence, however, and changed constantly with the fortunes of the Anglo-Normans. A constable was appointed by the Crown and given charge of a fortress. He would have been forbidden to speak the Irish language or wear Irish dress and discouraged from becoming too familiar with the local populace. Some Pale castles fell into ruins such as Maynooth in Co. Kildare, the massive stronghold of the Geraldines, who rebelled against Henry VIII.

The middle years of the seventeenth century were turbulent in Ireland. Risings of both Irish and Norman lords were fiercely suppressed and Cromwell's brutal campaign brought an end to all resistance and ushered in a period of relative peace. Castles were continuously lived in and towards the end of the seventeenth century large windows were pierced through the old walls admitting daylight for the first time. Now that defence was less of a priority gardens were planted within the bawn and sometimes new bedrooms were added for greater comfort. These new rooms were attached to the massive stone keep, like some incrustation on the sea bed, while the great hall and kitchens continued in use as before. Additions of this kind did nothing to enhance the architectural harmony of the building, but were essential to its continued occupancy and ensured its survival as a dwelling. The need for large fortified castles had passed and people began to look for comfort instead.

DUNLUCE CASTLE
Portrush, Co. Antrim

Dunluce Castle stands dramatically astride its rock, surrounded by the angry northern sea. A narrow bridge once connected the mainland to the castle which would have made it easy to defend, although the danger of siege and starvation must have been ever present. This precarious site was used as a stronghold since the Viking invasions in around 800 and pottery from this period has been found in a souterrain beneath the present ruins.

Dunluce is mentioned in the fourteenth century as one of the properties of the de Burgo earldom of Ulster, but none of the existing remains can be dated to earlier than the sixteenth century. The castle was seized from the McQuillans by the McDonnells after the Battle of Orra in 1565. The McDonnells had covered a bog with rushes and stationed men on the few pieces of firm ground with the effect that the McQuillans charged straight into the bog and sank. Since that day there has been a local saying, 'There's been nobody fooled by a rush bush but a McQuillan'. The McDonnells adorned the castle with a battle standard captured after a victory over the English and four cannons salvaged from the *Girona*, a ship from the Spanish Armada which foundered nearby. They also held there 'St Columkill's Cross', which was described as a 'god of great veneration by all the people of Ulster'. By 1610 Randal McDonnell, the first Earl of Antrim, had restored the outside defences and built a three-bay, mullion-windowed manor house within the castle walls. The second Earl married the widowed Duchess of Buckingham, and in the late 1630s Dunluce was their principal residence. They added buildings on the mainland to the complex.

An inventory dating from this period shows that Dunluce was crammed with furniture and fittings of the highest 'London' quality. The young Earl and Countess of Antrim would have acquired these in England, where they were at Court, and when they left brought them to this remote Irish eyrie. There were tapestries amounting to three-quarters of a mile in the castle, including a set which had belonged to Cardinal Wolsey at Hampton Court. The inventory lists six sets of chairs of state, each of which would have been placed under an elaborate canopy, with lesser chairs and stools in attendance. No fewer than sixty other elaborately upholstered chairs and stools were at Dunluce, besides enormous quantities of linen and a small library of books. There were saddles worked with gold and silver, finely inlaid cabinets and valuable objects such as telescopes, celestial and terrestrial globes, travelling four-poster beds and a sedan chair. Both the Antrims were Catholic, and the priest's vestments are the most costly listing in the inventory. The Antrims also embellished the local Protestant church with a blue ceiling studded with gold stars.

In 1639, while the second Earl and his Countess were here, part of the castle including the kitchens fell into the sea; seven cooks went with the kitchens, but an itinerant cobbler, surrounded by the half-mended shoes of the vanished cooks, survived in a corner which miraculously did not subside. Three years later the castle was seized by a Scottish covenanting army and despoiled. The second Earl reoccupied Dunluce after 1666 and lived on there until his death in 1683. Oliver Plunkett, the Archbishop of Armagh who has been recently canonized, was a visitor during this period and described it as a 'palace washed on all sides by the sea'.

After the Battle of the Boyne in 1690, which led to the impoverishment of the McDonnells because they had adhered to the cause of James II, Dunluce Castle was abandoned. Ballymagarry, a house nearby, was adopted as the Earls of Antrim's main residence and part of its structure and garden walls are still standing. A barn survives with a massive oak roof said to have come from Dunluce when it was deserted. In 1745 the main house at Ballymagarry was destroyed by fire, after which Glenarm became the principal seat of the Earls of Antrim and remains so to this day.

Dunluce Castle was built between the fourteenth and seventeenth centuries by the McDonnells, Earls of Antrim, and abandoned before 1700.

ROCKFLEET CASTLE
Newport, Co. Mayo

It seems strange that this relatively small tower house should have been the principal residence of the great Pirate Queen, Grace O'Malley, whose power in these parts was undisputed during the sixteenth century. It was an ideal choice for her because it dominated a sheltered inlet which could be guarded by her faithful followers, besides which there was deep anchorage for her fleet of ships.

Granuaile, as she was known in Irish, was born in about 1530, the daughter of the Chief of the O'Malley clan whose family motto was *Terra Marique Potens* (Powerful by Land and Sea). She was married at the age of fifteen to Donal O'Flaherty, heir apparent to the chieftaincy of the O'Flaherty kingdom of Connemara. His incessant quarrels and disputes with his neighbours brought war and famine on his dependants; it was not long before Grace was to emerge as the leader of her husband's clan. She organized the trading of hides, tallow and wool, exporting produce as far afield as Spain and Portugal. Her business was supplemented, in the time-honoured manner, with piracy at sea. Her knowledge of the rocks and inlets around the Irish coast stood her in great stead and the English administration in Dublin had no means of taking her fast and manoeuvrable ships.

Grace's husband was killed in a dispute with the Joyce clan over possession of a castle on Lough Corrib. After his death the Joyces assumed that the castle was theirs for the taking. Grace, however, defended it with such bravery that its name was changed from Cock's Castle to Hen's Castle. In 1566 she married Sir Richard Burke (Richard of the Iron), the owner of Rockfleet Castle on the northern shore of Clew Bay, and made it her headquarters. She drew up her own marriage contract and once established in the castle she invoked the divorce clause that she had included. With the words 'I dismiss you' she rid herself of a husband who was proving difficult and proceeded to take possession of his property. Later on, however, she relented and bore him a son named 'Toby of the Ships'.

In 1574 the Sheriff of Galway sent a large seaborne expedition to capture Rockfleet Castle but the attack was successfully repulsed by Grace's band. After the death of Sir Richard she lived on alone at the castle with 'all her own followers and one thousand head of cows and mares'.

The castle, which is four storeys in height, has a small rectangular corner turret rising above the parapet; the principal room is at the top where there is a fireplace, affording the best view of the surroundings. Outbuildings and walled enclosures once extended well beyond the site of the castle itself but they were torn down over the years and the stone used to build the road and houses in the vicinity. In 1950 the castle was restored by Sir Owen O'Malley, a direct descendant of Grace. Mr and Mrs Walter J. P. Curley of Pittsburgh and New York, purchased the castle and the house beside it in 1957; he was appointed Ambassador to Ireland in 1975.

Grace O'Malley, the legendary Pirate Queen,
established her fleet here in 1566
when she married Sir Richard Burke.

PORTUMNA CASTLE
Portumna, Co. Galway

The finest Jacobean ruin in Ireland is Portumna Castle, at the northern end of Lough Derg in Co. Galway, built in 1618 for Richard Burke, fourth Earl of Clanricarde. He was Lord President of Connaught and from the powerful Norman family that ruled over this part of Ireland for four centuries. Brought up partly in England and educated at Oxford, Lord Clanricarde had fought with the English at Kinsale. He and his wife, who had previously married the ill-fated Earl of Essex, lived near Tonbridge in Kent, and there is no evidence that they ever visited their splendid Irish house. However, it owes its importance in the history of Irish architecture to its strong English links and to the high position held in society by its builders who were evidently abreast of the latest stylistic trends. Given the uneasy situation for English settlers in Ireland at this time, Portumna Castle was provided with essential defensive elements such as firing holes round the doors, and a machicolation above the front door.

In its day, Portumna was unequalled in terms of scale, grandeur and beauty, and it was here that Italian Renaissance ideas were first introduced to Ireland. The gateway which leads to the second

This Jacobean ruin is situated at the head of Lough Derg, and is being gradually restored by the State; it was built in 1618 for the fourth Earl of Clanricarde.

forecourt is said to be the earliest Classical archway in the country. The house, or castle, is symmetrical and consists of three storeys over a basement with square projecting corner towers; the front doorcase has elegant obelisks and strapwork. There was a long single-storey hall which extended the full length of the four central bays of the entrance front, with a drawing room of similar size above. The dining room, which enjoyed views of the lake, was situated at the back of the house, approached by a staircase of dark oak.

In 1826 the house was gutted by fire and never rebuilt. The second and last Marquess of Clanricarde who succeeded in 1874 was a notorious miser and eccentric who lived in London and presented a beggarly appearance in his ancient, tattered great-coat. When he died Portumna was left to his great-nephew, Viscount Lascelles, afterwards sixth Earl of Harewood, the only one of his relations who took the trouble to visit him.

BURNTCOURT
Burncourt, Co. Tipperary

Burntcourt derives its peculiar name from the sad fact that the immense building, with all of its twenty-six gables and seven tall chimney stacks, was burnt down before even being completed. The interior would have been lit by countless two- and three-mullioned windows and the wide corbels below the gables on the entrance front must have once supported a defensive timber walk. It is one of the largest and also probably the last of the gabled semi-fortified early seventeenth-century houses.

Burntcourt was built on land granted to Sir Richard Everard by Charles I in 1639. He was given the right to enclose and impark one thousand acres of plain, valley and mountain 'where he shall elect to keep horses, mares, stags, deers, hares, rabbits, and other wild beasts for hunting, so that none other except Sir Richard Everard, his heirs

Burntcourt was begun in 1640 by Sir Richard Everard but burned down by his wife when still unfinished in 1650 to prevent it falling into Cromwellian hands.

and assigns, shall enter into the aforesaid Manor of Everard's Castle to chase, hunt etc.'. The date of the building of Burntcourt Castle, 1641, is recorded on a stone above the doorway of a nearby farm building.

Sir Richard was a prominent Catholic, a Royalist and a member of the Kilkenny Federation. In 1650 when the Cromwellian troops approached his still unfinished house, Lady Everard set it on fire in order to prevent it falling into their hands. This gave rise to the saying: 'It was seven years in building, seven years in living, and fifteen days in burning.'

TRIM CASTLE
Trim, Co. Meath

Three years after the Norman invasion of Ireland in 1169, a Norman, Hugh de Lacy, erected a motte with a timber tower at Trim as a first step towards the conquest of Co. Meath. Roderic O'Conor, King of Connaught, believing he was threatened by its presence, equipped an expedition to destroy it. Hugh Tyrell, the constable in charge, set fire to the wooden castle which he then deserted before the Irish King reached it. By the time that King John visited Trim in 1210 it had begun to take on its present formidable aspect as the first and largest stone castle in Ireland. It was completed in around 1224.

When it came to warfare the disciplined Norman soldiery, clothed in armour and with the support of their archers, were vastly superior to the Irish. When Giraldus Cambrensis, a Welshman writing from Ireland at the time of the Norman invasion, described the Irish going 'naked and unarmed into battle' he was pointing out the disparity between the two sides. The principal weapons of the Irish were the spear, the dart and the axe. According to Giraldus the Irish were 'quicker and more expert than any other people in throwing . . . stones as missiles [which] do great damage to the enemy in an encounter'. De Lacy, the original builder of Trim, was himself felled by an Irish axe at Durrow in 1186. Until the end of the Cromwellian era the castle was

OPPOSITE The River Boyne which flows past Trim Castle gave it added protection.

BELOW Trim is the largest and most dramatic Norman castle in Ireland; it was begun in 1172 and completed *c.* 1224.

taken and retaken many times but by the end of the seventeenth century it became obsolete and was allowed to decay.

Trim Castle covers an area of three acres with curtain walls and battlements to defend the keep; the River Boyne and a manmade moat add further protection. The massive keep, now partly ruined, is seventy-five feet high and basically square in plan with four smaller squares, originally abutting, giving it twenty sides in all. The walls are eleven feet thick in places and at one time it contained a great hall and a chapel besides numerous other apartments. The present owner of the castle is Randal Plunkett, nineteenth Lord Dunsany, who describes Trim as 'Blockhouse Number One of the British Empire'. Today it is in the care of the Office of Public Works.

LEIXLIP CASTLE
Leixlip, Co. Kildare

Leixlip Castle, built on a rock, is a twelfth-century fortress that dominates the town. It stands at the confluence of the Rye Water and the Liffey a few hundred yards downstream from the Salmon Leap once so beloved of painters and engravers. A hexagonal boat house or fishing pavilion marks the angle where the rivers join. King John, when Prince John and Lord of Ireland, is supposed to have stayed here in 1185. The castle is haunted by a many-headed dog who peers in through the diamond-shaped window panes to terrify its denizens.

It was originally a Norman defence fortress and became one of the ring of castles and earthen ditches later known as the Pale that were built by the Normans from 1172 onwards, starting with Trim Castle, to protect the rich flat land they had conquered to the west and north of Dublin. Leixlip was granted to the eighth Earl of Kildare, taken away from the tenth Earl, the rebel 'Silken' Thomas, and given back to the eleventh Earl. The Earl of Kildare was the head of the FitzGerald family and ancestor of the Dukes of Leinster.

In the sixteenth century Leixlip Castle became the property of the Whyte family and one 'Sir Nicholas Whyte of Leixlip' succeeded the next until 1732 when William Conolly of Castletown, nephew of 'Speaker' William Conolly, bought the property, just downstream from the great house he was to inherit. His son Tom 'Squire' Conolly was born and brought up at Leixlip Castle and it was not sold by the

ABOVE The front hall is dominated by a black Kilkenny marble mantelpiece flecked with white fossil shells, originally made for Ardgillan Castle in Co. Dublin in 1740.

OPPOSITE An early painting of Leixlip, before the windows were gothicized, sits on the dining-room mantel in an eighteenth-century frame from Dromoland Castle. The German chinoiserie tapestry was made in 1750.

LEFT Leixlip Castle bestrides a rock at the confluence of the Rye Water and River Liffey; it was begun in the late twelfth century.

Conollys until 1914. They let it to a variety of tenants – Archbishop Stone, the Protestant Primate; the Viceroy Lord Townshend; Lord Waterpark; Baron de Robeck and others.

The earliest part of Leixlip Castle comprises the present front hall and dining room; it was originally an oblong-shaped keep measuring approximately fifty feet by thirty with massive walls and, of course, without window apertures. Soon after, the round tower which faces down the drive was added; it has a batter at its base so that stones flung down from above would bounce off and hit any assailant.

In the seventeenth century accommodation was built on to the south side and in about 1720 part of the courtyard was filled in when the main staircase and landing were added, providing access to each bedroom without having to go from one room directly to the next. This uncomfortable arrangement was commonplace in the seventeenth century and is said to account for the general use of four-poster beds with curtains to provide some privacy.

In about 1760 some of the windows were Gothicized and no doubt more would have been, had the thickness of the walls not made it such a difficult task. In the eighteenth century a library and drawing room were built on to the north-east side with twelve Gothic windows diminishing in size, and in the nineteenth century battlements were added at roof level in line with the Picturesque style fashionable at that time; the wheel had come full circle and what was once a castle had turned into a house and then back into a castle.

LEIXLIP CASTLE

Leixlip was originally a Viking settlement and *Lax Hlaup* means Salmon Leap in that language. The Irish name for the town is *Léim an Bhradáin* which means Leap of the Salmon. The leap consisted of a series of pools and cascades in the River Liffey about eleven miles west of Dublin and was one of the wonders of Ireland. It was submerged when a dam was built to generate electricity in 1947 and a manmade lake was created which is now part of Dublin's water supply.

Archbishop Arthur Price, who died in 1752 and is buried in the Protestant church at Leixlip, left the recipe for a dark beer and the sum of £100 'to my servant Richard Guinness'. Richard established a brewery in Leixlip in 1752 and his son Arthur, who also benefited from the Archbishop's will, purchased an existing brewery in Dublin in 1759 that bears his name to this day and was for a time the largest in the world.

ABOVE Mid eighteenth-century dolls' house in the drawing room, originally made for Newbridge, Co. Dublin where it stood in the nursery.

LEFT The library is decorated with a set of engravings by Massé after the paintings by Lebrun in the *Galerie des Glaces* at Versailles, representing the triumphs of Louis XIV.

HOWTH CASTLE
Howth, Co. Dublin

Howth Castle dates back to Norman times and recently celebrated eight hundred years of continuous occupation by the same family. The St Lawrences were Earls of Howth until the title died out, and Howth Castle descended through the female line to the Gaisford-St Lawrences who are the present owners. The Hill of Howth surmounts the tip of a promontory forming the northern arm of Dublin Bay. Until one hundred years ago, the harbour at Howth was one of the principal ports of entry on the east coast of Ireland.

A bird's-eye view above the mantel in the drawing room, painted around 1740, gives a wonderful idea of the picturesque surroundings which have miraculously changed so little since. The castle is shown with a broad terrace at the top of a generous flight of steps which lead to the front door and also Classical urns on the parapet. Twin clusters

The Norman castle with Howth Harbour and Ireland's Eye beyond; the Protestant church can be seen in the castle grounds.

of fifteenth-century towers, crow-stepped in the Irish fashion, frame the composition. An inscription, now hidden behind the plaster, on a plaque beside the main door reads: *The Castle was rebuilt by the Right Honourable William, Lord Baron of Howth, Anno Domini 1738*. Formal tree planting and hedges can be seen on either side and at the centre a pond and formal canal. The great elm tree planted in 1585 beside the free-standing gatehouse tower, which slightly detracts from the overall symmetry of the layout, could not be removed because of a family legend; it was said that when a branch fell, it signalled the death of a St Lawrence.

Of all the legends that have grown up around Howth over the years, the best known is the story of Granuaile, or Grace O'Malley, the Pirate Queen. While on her journey home from a visit to Queen Elizabeth I,

her vessel ran short of supplies and put into the harbour of Howth to replenish. While her men were stowing provisions aboard, Grace O'Malley knocked at the gates of Howth Castle (according to some versions, disguised as a beggar woman), in search of hospitality. The family sat at meat, and she was refused admittance. In a fury, she snatched the infant son and heir of Lord Howth from his wet-nurse, and sailed off with him to Rockfleet Castle in the wilds of Co. Mayo. The child was eventually reunited with his parents, but only on the strict understanding that the gates of the castle should always be open at mealtimes, and a place be set at table for the head of the O'Malley clan. This custom is rigidly adhered to, even down to the present day.

The architect Richard Morrison worked here and is likely to have designed the entrance gates which are so similar to his gates to Lismore

OPPOSITE A portrait of Dean Swift,
a friend of the family, by Francis
Bindon has pride of place in the
dining room, with its fine Lutyens
interior.

RIGHT The drawing room has a
monumental Kilkenny marble
mantel, and above it a bird's-eye
view of the castle in its formal
setting; the round-headed panelling
and heavily enriched plaster ceiling
date from 1738.

Cathedral. Some designs of various dates for improving Howth Castle and the stables, by Morrison, are preserved at Howth but only his proposals for the south-west wing were carried out: 'To the south front of this he added a shallow gable, a crenelated parapet with finials, flimsy buttresses, a large single-story bay window lighting the drawing room and a smaller slightly projecting window lighting the library beside it' (*The Architecture of Richard Morrison and William Vitruvius Morrison*, Irish Architectural Archive, Dublin, 1989).

Sir Edwin Lutyens, who had also worked at Lambay Island for Lord Revelstoke, designed the western tower, which contains the remains of the famous Gaisford Library. Most of the best books were sold in 1890 at Sotheby's, the sale lasting five days. Here he installed a curious early eighteenth-century Irish mantel, whose inverted shells became the source of some Lutyens detail on a bank he built in Liverpool. This mantel came from a house named Killester that stood on the Howth property, and was being dismantled at that time. Lutyens also designed a loggia, a Catholic chapel in the south-east range, and the present dining room, formed out of three small panelled rooms off the hall. At the time of these renovations an old stone fireplace came to light in the entrance hall. Lutyens had it opened up, and framed it with a pilastered timber surround that had originally been a Venetian window at Killester. A curious weathervane was installed, the wings sprouting out of the chimneypot. Mr McDonald Gill was commissioned to paint a map of Howth above the fireplace, with the names of the Gaisford-St Lawrence children on the sailing ships.

DUNSANY CASTLE
Dunsany, Co. Meath

Two great castles of the Plunkett family, besides Trim Castle, stand close to one another, Killeen (now a ruin) and Dunsany, both guarding one of the approaches from Dublin to Trim. It was not until 1738 that the twelfth Baron Dunsany conformed to the Protestant church. Considering the difficulties faced by those who remained loyal to the Catholic faith, it is remarkable that the Plunketts have survived at Dunsany to the present day.

The present Lord Dunsany is the nineteenth to live at Dunsany Castle, and the history of his family is indicative of the violence that has beset Ireland over the last five hundred years. The wife of the eighth Lord Dunsany, for example, was murdered in 1609, for which crime a hired servant named Honora Ny Caffry was burned at the stake. She was the victim of a fearful miscarriage of justice for, not long after, a man who was being executed for another crime confessed to the murder.

The ninth Lord Dunsany was imprisoned in Dublin Castle in 1641, where he remained for several years; his only crime, apparently, was being elected from among the Catholic lords as the one to assure the justices of their attachment and loyalty, and to beg leave for them to be allowed to retain their arms. In 1653 he was permitted 'at his earnest prayer' to plough his forefathers' fields, as tenant to the State, while awaiting transportation to Connaught. His wife and children refused to leave until they were physically dragged out of Dunsany Castle. This they were, and are said to have perished from the hardships of the journey west. At the time of the Restoration, Lord Dunsany regained his property and took his seat in the House of Lords, where he continued to sit until the year 1666. At the Battle of the Boyne, in 1690, the tenth Lord Dunsany fought on the side of James II and was outlawed. On his death in that very year he was succeeded by his brother who was a Jacobite, and also outlawed, but being included in the Treaty of Limerick, his estates were restored.

The ground plan of Dunsany shows the extent of the original four-towered Pale castle, clothed now in the additions and alterations of successive generations. The drawing room and library are the principal reception rooms, and they are reached by the elegant, late eighteenth-century staircase with its delicate Gothic tracery ceiling. The drawing room has plasterwork of about 1780 by Michael Stapleton and must have been decorated during the lifetime of the thirteenth Baron (1739–1821). The windows had attenuated Gothic glazing, and on the back of Dunsany where they were not altered they still do. Wooden

LEFT Dunsany is the great Pale castle of the Plunketts and has remained in their possession until the present day; successive Lords Dunsany have added to it according to the prevailing fashion.

OPPOSITE The library was created in the nineteenth century by James Shiel who also worked extensively at Killeen Castle, a now ruinous Plunkett stronghold next door.

ABOVE The Winter Queen, Elizabeth of Bohemia, with a lady in waiting, by Van Dyck. The Queen, who was the sister of Charles I, is on the right.

OPPOSITE The drawing-room ceiling is the work of Michael Stapleton, the Irish Adam, and dates from 1780.

mullions have been inserted in the windows on the front, presumably at the time the nineteenth-century library was made. Of all the rooms the library has the most character; it contains unusual Gothic decoration with graining to simulate wood. This room and the dining room on the ground floor were designed by James Shiel, who is known to have worked extensively next door at Killeen and must have designed the alterations at Dunsany at the same time.

Among the family relics is the plain gold ring of the great Catholic General Patrick Sarsfield, Earl of Lucan, with his arms, crest and initials. There are also – most prized possessions of all – the watch, cross and ring of St Oliver Plunkett, Catholic Archbishop of Armagh, who was hanged, drawn and quartered in London on 11 July, 1681. The famous Irish martyr was beatified by Pope Benedict XV in 1920, and was canonized in 1975 with all the Dunsany family present.

The late Lord Dunsany was the poet and author whose contribution to the Irish literary revival is well known. Oliver St John Gogarty once dedicated a volume of his poems to his friend Dunsany 'from one who loves the Muses to one the Muses love'. Many of his curiously modelled clay figures are still at Dunsany, and he seems to have collected almost the entire *oeuvre* of Sime, a contemporary of Beardsley.

The fascination of some Irish houses lies in the purity of their architecture, of others it is their association with a great family, or, in rare cases, it might be their contents in particular which attract attention. In the case of Dunsany it is the indefinable atmosphere which is imparted to a place when the same family has lived in it for many hundreds of years. Each generation of Plunketts has left its mark, whether in terms of art, literature or architecture.

MALAHIDE CASTLE
Malahide, Co. Dublin

Malahide Castle remained in the Talbot family from 1174 when the Lordship, lands and harbour of Malahide were granted to Richard Talbot by Henry II, until 1976. As a result of this continuity of ownership, combined with exceptional taste and the zeal for collecting works of art, the Talbots had an amazingly interesting and complete collection of paintings and furniture of Irish interest. A visit to the castle in the late Lord Talbot's day was an extraordinary experience because everything was still there, and so much of the country's history was written on those walls.

For a short time during the Cromwellian era, Malahide was wrested from the Talbots, then a leading Catholic family. The castle was granted by Cromwell to Miles Corbet, the regicide. Fortunately for the family Corbet had signed the death warrant of Charles I and was duly

OPPOSITE The Oak Room, probably used at one time as a family chapel; the Talbots remained Catholic until 1779.

LEFT Malahide Castle with the sea beyond; the Talbot family were hereditary Lord High Admirals of Ireland and lived here from Norman times until 1976.

hanged after the Restoration. The Flemish carving of the *Coronation of the Virgin* which had vanished from the Oak Room (no doubt to save it) miraculously reappeared when the Talbots were restored to their property.

The Oak Room is reached by a winding stone staircase inside the front door. It is an ebony-coloured room, lit by a row of five nineteenth-century Gothic windows. The elaborately carved panelling represents biblical scenes and as the Talbots retained the old faith until 1779 this room may well have been the chapel during the penal times when the Catholic faith was suppressed.

The great hall is medieval in aspect and dates from the reign of Edward IV. It has a beamed ceiling and minstrels' gallery but the mantels are nineteenth century and the great collection of Irish furniture and pictures mostly seventeenth and eighteenth century. The general feeling of the room with so much of it black, even the mantels, is sombre and dignified. There is a vast painting of the Battle of the Boyne, 1690, lent by the National Gallery, and it is said that fourteen members of the Talbot family sat down to breakfast on the day of the conflict, but none returned.

The two Georgian drawing rooms, each with a corner turret, are cheerful by contrast; both have retained the magical orange paint colour and unique khaki-beige ceilings and gold trim. The magnificent cornices with ferocious-looking birds are attributed to Robert West. The west side of the castle was destroyed by fire in 1760 and these drawing rooms subsequently rose from the ashes. Richard Talbot and his wife, Margaret O'Reilly (later created Baroness Talbot of Malahide in her own right), were responsible for these wonderful rooms.

The late Lord Talbot de Malahide died unexpectedly in April 1973 while on a cruise around Greece. He had been in negotiation with the Irish Government in the hope of making Malahide Castle the official residence of the Taoiseach (Prime Minister), leaving the contents intact but unfortunately no decision had been arrived at. He was unmarried with one unmarried sister; in the event she inherited the property and crippling death duties along with it.

Miss Rose Talbot was just as anxious as her brother that the contents of Malahide should be kept intact and was willing to spend the rest of

her days there, making sure that the transition to public ownership was sensibly and smoothly effected. The authorities were adamant, however, and insisted on the tax being paid. It all became to Miss Talbot an increasing worry and she went to live in Tasmania on the property, also called Malahide, which the family has owned since 1824. In the end everything had to be dispersed but at the eleventh hour thirty-five of the family portraits were bought by the National Gallery of Ireland and returned on loan to Malahide. The magical interiors were kept intact and a most sensitive restoration and refurbishment carried out.

The gardens were created by the late Lord Talbot who had the distinction of being a Fellow of the Linnaean Society, an old established group of botanical experts. He was a great plant collector and introduced many rare species to Ireland from countries as far afield as North and South Africa, South America, China, Australia and Mexico. The castle and the gardens are now owned and properly maintained by Dublin County Council and are open to the public.

The Talbot family still owns Malahide in Tasmania where Miss Talbot now lives and farms. The Irish Government saved Glenveagh Castle in Co. Donegal and at the same time nearly lost Malahide. Glenveagh is a wonderful place, but its importance to Ireland, both culturally and historically, does not compare with Malahide. Nothing could.

RIGHT The banqueting hall and the minstrels' gallery. Fourteen Talbot cousins, devoted followers of James II, are said to have sat at meat here on the morning of the Battle of the Boyne; none of them survived the day.

OPPOSITE The large drawing room, with a turret room off, was painted 'Malahide orange' in the nineteenth century; it contains much of the original contents.

THE EMERGENCE OF DOMESTIC ARCHITECTURE

The tenth Earl of Ormonde built a large manor house beside his castle at Carrick-on-Suir in 1568, now in State care and open to the public. It is the oldest major non-fortified house in Ireland still to have its roof intact and provides a link between fortified and domestic architecture.

The series of rebellions in the seventeenth century and their ruthless suppression had created an unsettled climate in Ireland which delayed the development of the finer things in life. After the Battle of the Boyne in 1690, there followed a century of peace during which time the Anglo-Irish became firmly established and prospered. Strong native traditions persisted, however, side by side with those of the settlers, so that the two cultures became to some extent intertwined and a golden age of art, architecture and artefacts dawned.

It was, however, one of the darkest epochs in the history of the Irish people. Although four-fifths of the population were Catholic, by the end of the seventeenth century they owned less than one-eighth of the land. They had suffered further extensive loss of their properties in the Munster, Ulster and Cromwellian Plantations. On account of the Penal Laws, some of which remained in place throughout the eighteenth century, Catholics could not vote, stand for Parliament or be a member of any municipal body. They could not operate a school or teach in one and Catholic parents were forbidden to send their children abroad to be educated. Freedom to practise religion was severely curtailed. Any Protestant could take away the horse of a Catholic, no matter how valuable, by paying him £5, and the child of a Catholic landowner who became a Protestant could at once take possession of his father's property. With the Flight of the Earls in 1607 and the Flight of the Wild Geese in 1691, Ireland lost many of her noblemen, leaders and soldiers. It is no surprise, therefore, that the attitude of the native Irish to the 'big house' was one of anger and resentment.

From 1700 onwards country-house building began in earnest, two hundred years or so later than in England. Owing to the troubled times not many Elizabethan or Jacobean houses had been built in Ireland. Myrtle Grove in Youghal in Co. Cork, Sir Walter Raleigh's house, and Rothe House, Kilkenny, built in 1594 for a rich merchant, both survive because they were built in walled towns. It is significant that most of the others such as Portumna in Co. Galway, Coppinger's Court in Co. Cork, and Lemaneagh in Co. Clare, are in ruins.

The Dutch influence in architecture became evident after the Battle of the Boyne and William of Orange has been credited with, in particular, the introduction of the sash window to Ireland. The Dublin streetscape in about 1700 was serrated like the teeth of a saw; little Dutch gabled dwellings with corner fireplaces and wooden panelling gradually took the place of the half-timbered houses. In the country also modest Dutch brick residences with tall chimneys and high-pitched roofs were quite simple by comparison with the great Palladian houses that were to follow. They are closely related to the brick houses in North America for precisely the same reason – the Dutch were there first.

In Ireland, even early eighteenth-century houses were sometimes built with security in mind and a cut-stone gun-port might look across the main door. A steep railed area, giving light to the basement, made a house more difficult to break into and the demesne wall was built as much to keep people out as animals in. Sometimes stone from an abandoned castle would be used for the foundations of a new house, which would sit beside the ruin like a newly-hatched chicken with its empty shell.

In the days before architecture was a closely defined profession these early houses were more often than not built by local builders or measurers. An anonymous eulogy on Thomas Ivory, which has been attributed to James Gandon, the great neo-Classical architect, declares:

> No sooner do these lads obtain a smattering of drawing but they please to call themselves architects and many gentlemen who have pretensions to taste in design and economy, give their scrawls to these tyros to make what they call drawings, which are afterwards produced, over the bottle, as their own. From these joint productions are the many medleys of country houses derived, that are scattered about to the disgrace of the taste of the country.

The Royal Hospital, Kilmainham, on the outskirts of Dublin, was, however, designed by one of the leading architects of the time, the Surveyor General Sir William Robinson (1643–1712). It was built for the accommodation of old and infirm soldiers and was a spectacular achievement. Happily, it has been saved from dereliction by the State and is now open to the public. The foundation stone was laid in 1680 by the Viceroy, James Butler, first Duke of Ormonde, thus pre-dating Sir Christopher Wren's Chelsea Hospital in London by two years, a matter of national pride. The Royal Hospital, Kilmainham, is the earliest major Classical building in Ireland. Although built by a professional architect, there is evidence that the craftsmen employed were not yet on familiar terms with the vocabulary of Classical ornament.

The Royal Hospital must have had a considerable influence on Thomas Burgh (1670–1730), who succeeded Robinson as Surveyor General in 1700. Burgh was a soldier and a country gentleman from Oldtown in Co. Kildare as well as a prolific architect. He designed the old Custom House on the Liffey in Dublin (since demolished), Royal (now Collins) Barracks, Trinity College Library and Dr Steevens's Hospital, all in Dublin. He also designed the Collegiate School, Celbridge, in Co. Kildare (now the Setanta Hotel). His buildings all have arcades not unlike those in the courtyard of the Royal Hospital and all except Trinity Library have steep roofs, dormer windows and pediments. Burgh may have designed Kildrought House, on the main street of Celbridge, which has extensive gardens that go down to the Liffey, a most elegant and sensitively designed house. Stackallan in Co. Meath is here attributed to Burgh on stylistic grounds. By about 1720 these 'Dutch' Palladian houses were beginning to become outmoded with the dawn of Irish Palladianism. The chief architectural inspiration was no longer to come from Holland but from Italy.

Gardens at this period were, like the houses, modelled on the Dutch pattern and sometimes, as at Burton Court in Co. Cork, enclosed in a high wall with pavilions like sentry boxes at the corners. The garden was an extension of the house with box hedges, herb gardens and knot gardens forming a colourful parterre. Beyond the garden wall formal tree planting and crow's-foot vistas would lead the eye to the countryside beyond.

CARRICK-ON-SUIR CASTLE
Carrick-on-Suir, Co. Tipperary

The fifteenth-century castle of the Butlers, Earls and subsequently Dukes of Ormonde, stands in the heart of the town of Carrick-on-Suir. In 1568 the tenth Earl of Ormonde, who had spent many years at the Court of his cousin Queen Elizabeth I, added a manor house to the castle of a type that is fairly common in England but otherwise non-existent in Ireland. The broad, many-gabled house with its curved-headed mullioned windows contains an Elizabethan long gallery on the *piano nobile* which has been beautifully restored. It was once hung with tapestries, perhaps of continental origin but more likely woven at the manufactory established in Kilkenny by the eighth Earl of Ormonde, employing Flemish artisans.

Carrick-on-Suir Castle, also known as Ormonde Castle, is noted for its plaster ornament. The long gallery has portraits in stucco of Queen Elizabeth I as well as the tenth Earl of Ormonde, 'Black Tom', who was one year older than the Queen. She was said to have borne him a son when she was twenty, but Court rumours have ever been rife.

ABOVE The long gallery, with its magnificent limestone mantel, was once hung with tapestries. Although most of the ceiling had collapsed, enough remained to enable the Office of Public Works to restore it at the eleventh hour.

RIGHT A contemporary portrait in stucco of Queen Elizabeth I flanked by figures representing 'Equity' and 'Justice' in the long gallery of the Ormonde Castle which stands by the banks of the Suir in Carrick-on-Suir.

OPPOSITE The castle of the Earls of Ormonde at Carrick-on-Suir dates from the fifteenth century, and the Elizabethan manor house grew up beside it in 1568.

Firing holes protecting the arched entranceway are the only indication of a need for defence in this apparently serene, domesticated dwelling. The tall castle stronghold, which makes the fourth side of a small courtyard with the Elizabethan manor house making up the other three, broods over the Tudor mansion in a protective manner. According to the historian Brian de Breffny, the hearth tax of 1663 lists thirty hearths here: he deduced from this that both buildings, old and new, were as one.

BEAULIEU
Drogheda, Co. Louth

Beaulieu is situated by the banks of the Boyne estuary, a few miles downstream from Drogheda and within easy reach of Dublin by sea, a great convenience in early days when communication and travel by land could be difficult and hazardous. While at Carrick-on-Suir a manor house was added to an existing castle, at Beaulieu an unfortified, domestic building was intended from the outset. The area that serves as a protective ditch for so many Irish houses is absent here; the castle has indeed by now been abandoned. 'Artisan Mannerist' houses of this type are often found in England, strongly influenced by the architecture of Holland; in Ireland, Beaulieu is unique. 'Artisan Mannerism' was a style that arose in the second and third quarters of the seventeenth century from the practical designs of master masons, joiners, carpenters and bricklayers quite separately from the Court style which was more sophisticated and 'correct'.

Mrs Nesbit Waddington is the ninth generation of her family to inhabit Beaulieu, her ancestor Sir Henry Tichborne, a prominent military commander in the Civil War, having purchased the land from the Plunketts. His son, William, built the house between 1660 and 1667. Few unfortified houses were built in Ireland in the seventeenth century, a time of widespread suffering with rebellion and counter-rebellion succeeding each other. Beaulieu is the most important one of its date to have survived intact and the fact that the original family is still living there is exceptional.

Of particular interest in the hall at Beaulieu is a painting of the town of Drogheda, set into the upper half of the great two-tiered seventeenth-century stone mantel, showing it with its defensive walls intact. The stone has been painted white here to match the early eighteenth-century carvings which decorate arched doorways in the hall, with coats of arms, military trophies and musical instruments beautifully carved in pine and likewise painted white. The Lincrusta frieze, with swags and ribbons, dates from around 1900 when such ornament was fashionable. The immense blackened horns of an Irish elk dominate the room, like a conductor leading an orchestra of ancestral portraits.

The drawing room and dining room have seventeenth-century panelling and door surrounds to match; the seventeenth-century plaster ceilings are of a type frequently found in England and Scotland but extremely rare in Ireland. In the drawing room the ornate oval frame in the centre contains an architectural *trompe l'oeil* painting, taking the eye up an imaginary storey with garlands of flowers and cherubs flying through clouds in the sky; the mantel is 1840.

Dr Edward McParland has found the following reference to the staircase and wainscoting at Beaulieu (Molesworth papers, National Library of Ireland). The son of the builder of the house, Sir Henry Tichborne, first and last Lord Ferrard, wrote to Lord Molesworth at Breckdenstown in Co. Dublin from Beaulieu on 4 September, 1722:

> ... yesterday I turn the joyners and carpenters out of the south end of my
> house I am now painting and hope in three weeks time to begin to furnish
> I have taken up the loft for my great stairs which I dayly expect from
> Dublin and then will have done till next year ... on Munday the carpenter
> tels me he will be with you his wages are twelve [?] and his victuals I will
> send by him Hackluit and your plan of which I have taken a Coppy and
> Curle and I have done something at itt which may be some help by takeing

OPPOSITE ABOVE Beaulieu was built from 1660 onwards and is one of the earliest houses in Ireland not constructed with an eye to defence. It has remained in the possession of the original family.

RIGHT The front hall, two storeys high, is dominated by the immense blackened horns of an Irish elk and is enlivened with elaborately carved white overdoors and sconces.

OPPOSITE BELOW The drawing room has elaborate seventeenth-century plasterwork framing an early eighteenth-century painted ceiling attributed to Willem van der Hagen (d. 1745).

out what you like and rejecting or altering the rest, as soon as he is able to travell we will wait on you . . .

John Curle was the architect of the old Castle Coole (1709) in Co. Fermanagh, a house with a steep roof and overhanging eaves not unlike Beaulieu in its general massing.

It is rare in Ireland to find such an excellent collection of modern pictures in an old country house; at Beaulieu they include works by Jack Yeats and Augustus John alongside the family portraits of Tichbornes, Astons, Tippings and Montgomerys. General Richard Montgomery of Beaulieu was one of the principal founders of the American army. Like Washington, he had been a British soldier, but after marrying the daughter of Judge Livingston, an important English settler who lived by the Hudson River, he changed sides. He was known as the Rebel General and lost his life attempting to capture Quebec in a snowstorm.

Mrs Waddington is an avid gardener, and the gardens at Beaulieu are testimony to her enthusiasm and knowledge. Thanks to her work this wonderful house will hopefully survive for many generations to come.

STACKALLAN
Navan, Co. Meath

Stackallan was formerly Boyne House, having been built by Gustavus Hamilton, first Viscount Boyne, in 1716. Hamilton was born in 1639 and was sworn Privy Counsellor to James II but resigned in disgust at the conduct of the King and Court, retiring to his estates in Co. Fermanagh. He was appointed Governor of Enniskillen by the Protestants in 1688 and took up residence in the castle there. He was witness to William and Mary being proclaimed King and Queen in that year and became a general, serving at the Battle of the Boyne, the Siege of Derry and the capture of Athlone where his heroism earned him a generous grant of forfeited lands beside the River Boyne. In 1710 he was sworn Privy Counsellor to Queen Anne and in 1714 to George I who created him Baron Hamilton of Stackallan and Viscount Boyne in 1717. He died in 1723.

The house is attributed to another Williamite soldier, the military engineer and architect Thomas Burgh (1670–1730) of Oldtown in Co. Kildare. He was appointed Surveyor General of Ireland in 1700, succeeding Sir William Robinson who had designed the Royal Hospital at Kilmainham. Burgh's major works, besides military installations, were the Royal (now Collins) Barracks, Trinity College Library and Dr Steevens's Hospital, all in Dublin. The foundation stone of the great library at Trinity was laid in 1712, four years before the building of Stackallan commenced.

Stackallan is a pre-Palladian house with no balustrade or parapet, and it provides the link between Beaulieu in Co. Louth and Castletown in Co. Kildare which was, incidentally, for long attributed to Burgh. The entrance front was changed at some stage after the painting of the house by Henry Brocas, Senior (1762–1837) and a walled, terraced garden was created on the south front. This was originally the entrance

LEFT The original entrance front of Stackallan is now the garden front, so that the present front hall is not the original but dates from the Regency period.

OPPOSITE Stackallan is a pre-Palladian house, dating from 1716, which has been attributed to Thomas Burgh, the architect of the great library at Trinity College, Dublin.

ABOVE The plaster ornament on the staircase ceiling dates from the time the house was built: it depicts the Hamilton arms and military trophies.

LEFT The drawing room, where the original front hall must have been, looks out across the garden to the statue of Eros.

BELOW Stackallan, painted by Henry Brocas *c.* 1820 before the entrance front was changed, showing the Gothic stable block in its original form (detail).

front and is therefore more embellished than the present entrance side; the window surrounds are heavier and more elaborate, and are clustered closer together, there being nine on this façade and only seven on the other. The stables can be seen to have resembled those designed by 'Capability' Brown at Slane Castle, a few miles away; although subsequently altered, those at Stackallan remain and are thought to be some sixty years later than the house.

The staircase ceiling is of great interest and depicts the Hamilton arms, surrounded by military trophies, enclosed in a stucco wreath of a type often found in England in the seventeenth century but rare in Ireland. The staircase itself appears to date from the rearrangement of the entrance fronts as the banisters are more delicate than would have been expected from a house built in 1716. A galleried landing has been created giving access to the bedrooms on the upper floor.

Since the last war Mrs Anthony Burke has lived at Stackallan, well known for the successful stud farm that she has established there. Her late husband was the great-grandson of Sir Bernard Burke, Ulster King of Arms and sometime editor of Burke's genealogical publications.

CASTLEMARTIN
Kilcullen, Co. Kildare

The Castlemartin estate was acquired in 1703 by Thomas Keightley for his daughter and her husband Lucius O'Brien, eldest son of Sir Donough O'Brien, first Baronet of Lemaneagh and Dromoland. When Lucius died of gout in 1717 his widow and her father sold Castlemartin. The present house was built in 1720 by a Dublin banker, Francis Harrison MP, using stone from the ancient castle of the Eustace family, seated here since the thirteenth century. In 1730 the house was sold to Captain Henry Boyle Carter, whose father commissioned Sir Edward Lovett Pearce to build him a magnificent house, No. 9 Henrietta Street, Dublin, which fortunately still stands.

Castlemartin forms three sides of a courtyard; thus unlike most Irish houses which have only one it has three properly balanced limestone façades. There is an elegant cut-stone front doorcase with bolection mouldings surmounted by a swan-necked pediment. Originally the house had dormer windows which have at some stage been removed. Dummy windows have been made use of here to preserve the rhythm of the fenestration on two fronts. Unfortunately the identity of the architect has been lost.

Castlemartin was commandeered during the rebellion of 1798 when it served as the headquarters of Lieutenant General Sir Ralph Dundas. Owing to the depredations of the troops stationed here the house was badly damaged. The fact that the original interior has not survived makes stylistic comparisons impossible. The front hall is panelled in plaster and ornamented with Corinthian pilasters; a generous opening leads straight into the staircase hall lit by a large window on the return. The property was purchased by T. S. Blacker in 1854 and descended to Sheelagh, widow of Lieutenant Colonel Frederick Blacker. It was he who closed the open side of the U-shaped house, adding bathrooms and completing the courtyard.

The magnificent set of wrought-iron entrance gates dates from the eighteenth century but has had the Blacker crest, an upstretched arm, inserted. It is said that Sheelagh Blacker sold these gates but that the purchaser did not have the heart to remove them. She left Castlemartin to her great nephew, the Earl of Gowrie, in 1967, who has happy memories of school holidays spent here in his youth when the front hall was full of stuffed animal heads and the roof was in a parlous state. In his poem *Easter 1969* Lord Gowrie wrote:

> Behind me, also rooted
> raptured to a corner,
> of earth and Ireland
> the eighteenth-century house.
>
> Grey face, dummy windows
> alternating with true,
> were in the northern dawn
> succinct at 6 a.m.

Taken from A Postcard from Don Giovanni

Lord Gowrie sold Castlemartin four years later to Dr A. J. F. O'Reilly, the chairman, president and chief executive officer of H. J. Heinz; his earlier claim to fame was won on the international rugby field.

Although his business commitments allow him to spend only a small part of the year at Castlemartin, in the twenty years that Dr O'Reilly has owned the house enormous improvements have been effected. Forty people can sleep here now in comfort, with the help of an annexe, so the house can be used for conferences as well as being a family home. Irish

Castlemartin has elaborate eighteenth-century entrance gates of wrought iron with the Blacker crest inserted.

ABOVE Castlemartin has three rough limestone façades of nine bays, made possible by the judicious use of dummy windows.

LEFT The front hall, paved in black and white stone, leads to the staircase through a generous opening flanked by clustered Corinthian pilasters. The horse painting by Jack Yeats is entitled *My Beautiful, my Beautiful*.

RIGHT The front door, surmounted by a naïve swan-necked pediment and sunflower rosettes.

The library has a portrait of
Dr A. J. F. O'Reilly by Derek Hill,
the Donegal artist, hanging over
the stone bolection mantel.

furniture and works of art adorn the rooms, with Walter Osborne and
Jack Yeats leading the field; the collection includes paintings by
William Ashford, William Sadler, Sir William Orpen, Camille Souter,
Sean Keating, William Mulready and Derek Hill.

At the suggestion of his father, in 1979, Dr O'Reilly, with the
assistance of the architect Percy Leclerc, undertook the restoration of
the small roofless church of 1490 dedicated to St Mary which stands on
an eminence above the river a short walk from the house. The tomb of
Sir Richard Portlester, a Norman knight, was restored and is now
safely housed in the little church. Dr O'Reilly said at the rededication
'The Christian message in this country has been used to drive people
apart. The restoration of this chapel is part of my contribution towards
reconciliation'.

The distinguished American landscape architect and garden designer Lanning Roper was given the task of creating a garden and of
altering the contours of the parkland to admit a better view of the
Liffey as the river makes a dramatic sweep towards the house, changes
its mind and flows away from it. Out of doors the sound of the Liffey, a
river that (in the words of Jonathan Swift) 'never roars but always
murmurs', is ever present. Among the many improvements he effected,
Lanning Roper planted a beech hedge 'forecourt' at the entrance, open
on the side of the magnificent formal lime avenue which was planted on
axis to the front door two hundred or more years ago.

Another of Dr O'Reilly's claims to fame is the creation of the Ireland
Fund through whose efforts millions of pounds are raised annually in
the USA, the UK, France, Canada and Australia, as well as in Ireland,
for programmes that generate peace and economic and cultural
development in Ireland, north and south.

MOUNT IEVERS COURT
Sixmilebridge, Co. Clare

A long, wild and hilly drive leading through beech woods ends at one of the most magical and appealing houses in Ireland, one whose beauty and mystery strikes deep into the heart of those fortunate enough to see it. Mount Ievers Court, still in the hands of the family for which it was built, has one front of limestone and the other of brick, faded over the years to an unbelievable shade of silvery pink. Tall, thin and ethereal it stands isolated from the world like a forgotten doll's house against the dark green of the trees.

Colonel John Ievers, MP for Co. Clare for sixteen years, died in 1731 and his son, Henry, demolished the old castle that stood here and built the present house; the architect was John Rothery who died in 1736. The house was completed by his son, Isaac, in 1737. Eleven masons and forty-eight labourers were employed – the masons received 5s. per week but the labourers only 5d.; however, they did receive food and clothing, even shoes and coarse linen woven at Mount Ievers. The massive roof timbers, made of oak from Portumna, were floated down the Shannon to Killaloe and hauled overland the remaining twenty-odd miles. The brick is not mentioned in the accounts and is traditionally said to have come from Holland in exchange for oil extracted from rape seed at a local mill. Building the new house cost Henry Ievers £1,478. 7s. 9d., a modest amount at the time. The walls are unusually thick and an added impression of height is gained by a curious architectural device: the house narrows by six inches at each string course.

The restrained panelling on the ground floor is in plaster, not timber as it appears to be. A handsome stone fireplace from the old castle has been re-erected in the hall with the date 1648 on it. One of the most striking features in the house is the staircase with its barley-sugar banisters suggesting an earlier period like so much else about Mount Ievers. It leads to a spacious landing with a handsome compartmented plaster ceiling. On the top floor there is a ballroom – a peculiar arrangement also found at another house by Isaac Rothery, namely Bowenscourt in Co. Cork, now sadly demolished.

In its overall massing, with the accent on a steeply pitched roof and tall chimneys as an integral part of the architectural statement, Mount Ievers looks much older than it really is and might easily belong to the seventeenth century. Because the house is isolated in the very west of Ireland it is understandable that the latest fashions had not yet arrived; however, according to Dr Mark Girouard the prototype for the design of Mount Ievers is Chevening House in Kent attributed to Inigo Jones and built in the mid-seventeenth century. Henry Ievers could have seen the design illustrated in *Vitruvius Britannicus* (1717). As well as similarity of design Dr Mark Girouard notes that 'a stone cornice with a pulminated frieze below the eaves is common to both houses'.

There is a painted panel on the ground floor with a primitive view of the house showing that it once had formal vistas behind and cascades with fish ponds in the foreground. Near the skyline can be seen Bunratty Castle and sailing boats on the Shannon estuary. Squadron-Leader Norman Ievers, who has devoted his life to this wonderful family house, has restored the fish ponds and given the house a new roof of slate. The windows are glazed in the manner of the early eighteenth century with heavy astragals and four panes across. The seven windows of the *piano nobile* on the stone front had been given delicate glazing in about 1850 which detracted greatly from the unity of the house. The present owner has rightly put them back as they must have been originally.

LEFT The staircase has alternating fluted and barley-sugar banisters; it leads up to the generous bedroom landing with its compartmented ceiling.

ABOVE A primitive mural depicting the formal garden and Bunratty Castle near the horizon.

OPPOSITE The red brick façade, with a stone string course at each floor level; the brick came from Holland as ballast.

DONERAILE COURT
Doneraile, Co. Cork

Doneraile and its park of 400 acres were purchased by the State in 1969 from the St Leger family, Viscounts Doneraile, for the purpose of creating a Wild Life Preserve for the people of Cork as well as for tourists. The park, with the River Awbeg, ancient trees, and formal water a quarter of a mile in length, is one of exceptional character; it has been restored to its former beauty by the State since its acquisition. The Court, however, was literally left to rot, abandoned to wind and weather and, worse still, plundered by vandals.

In 1627 the St Legers acquired part of the Doneraile property from the son of the poet Edmund Spenser and also part from the Synan family. The original date of Doneraile is uncertain, but it is likely that the date of 1725 over the porch refers to a major reconstruction undertaken in that year. This was commissioned by Hayes St Leger, the fourth Viscount Doneraile of the first creation, who was also responsible for landscaping the park with formal vistas and ponds at the time. The architect was John Rothery.

Later in the eighteenth century two end bows were added to the front and in 1805 a second bow was added to the garden front. A dining-room wing, added in 1869, has recently been demolished. When the balustraded porch with St Leger arms above the door was added in around 1820 the central three bays of the façade were removed and the immense weight of the front wall was supported by long wooden beams. Over the years these gradually sagged, causing the front wall to crack and making the upper windows lopsided; they have now been replaced with steel girders. A handsome cut-limestone cornice surrounds the house at roof level, supporting an ingenious system of lead guttering that is invisible from the ground. This was infested with ivy which has finally been eradicated and the lead has now been replaced.

Most of the principal reception rooms have been Victorianized and the windows on the garden front have been lowered to the ground. One small panelled room with a corner fireplace and a boxed wooden cornice has survived from 1725, with brown Victorian graining continued across the ceiling. The best feature of the interior is the late eighteenth-century staircase going right to the top of the house, with its attenuated banisters and Adamesque plaster ceiling almost certainly by the Cork architect, Abraham Hargrave. The original basement kitchen was replaced in about 1820 with a vast new vaulted one full of light and air, now restored as a tea-room; a freestanding octagonal meat-safe stands beside it.

The most famous incident to have occurred at Doneraile concerned the initiation in about 1710 of the daughter of the first Viscount, Elizabeth St Leger, who was later to marry Richard Aldworth of Newmarket in Co. Cork. She was found eavesdropping on a meeting of the Freemasons being held in the library at Doneraile. According to one version of the story, she hid in an alcove to read a book and fell asleep; apparently she was afraid to leave her hiding place when the meeting began. Another version insists that she hid in a grandfather clock. Both agree that, although women were excluded from Freemasonry, she was forced to take the masonic vows to preserve their secrecy.

The Doncaster St Leger was founded by Colonel Anthony St Leger of the English branch of the family. Another link with the turf is that the first steeplechase ever held was run from the steeple of Buttevant Church to the steeple of the church at Doneraile in 1752.

Doneraile Court was built *c.* 1725 by John Rothery for Hayes St Leger, fourth Viscount Doneraile; it is being restored by the Irish Georgian Society and will be open to the public in conjunction with the Wild Life Preserve established in the surrounding parkland.

The fourth Viscount Doneraile (of the second creation) died a terrible death in 1887. His hunting exploits were legendary and it was his passion for fox and hound that led to his tragic demise. He kept a pet fox which contracted rabies and bit his master, as well as the coachman. The two rabid men travelled to Paris where they went to see the great Louis Pasteur. The coachman took his treatment and survived but Lord Doneraile decided against it and had an agonising death, being suffocated by 'the gentlemen of the locality' at the last to put him out of his delirium.

For centuries there has been a herd of red deer at Doneraile, and it was said that when the doctor came out of the house after attending the

deathbed of the seventh Viscount in 1956, the herd was waiting, gathered into a great half-circle, for the news.

The last Lord Doneraile, Dick St Leger, was a truck driver from California who spent his life savings in trying to prove his rights to the property. Although he was given the full treatment as Viscount Doneraile in *Burke's Peerage*, it appears that he descended from an early nineteenth-century Lord Doneraile whose eldest son was born out of wedlock. The fact that this ancestor subsequently married the child's mother and that they had a large legitimate family apparently made no difference; the case went to the House of Lords but to no avail. Why he is listed in *Burke's* as Viscount Doneraile remains a mystery; he was

unable to prove his right to the title or the property that went with it and returned to end his days in California. The contents were dispersed, sold to a consortium of antique dealers, and the house and park went to the State.

Elizabeth Bowen, the writer, lived at Bowenscourt (now demolished), about seven miles from Doneraile. She was a friend of the St Leger family and a frequent visitor to the Court. It is hoped to establish a room dedicated to her memory at Doneraile, with reproductions of the Bowenscourt portraits as well as copies of her books and photographs of her house as it was when she lived there. Since 1976 the Irish Georgian Society has been restoring the Court.

THE
GOLDEN AGE OF
PALLADIANISM

Andrea Palladio is the only architect whose name has been immortalized in a style of building known throughout the world. He was born in Padua in 1508 and died in Venice in 1580. The influence of his architecture is found amid the snows of Russia, under the relentless Indian sun and as far afield as Australia and America. Palladio was one of many architects who, from the Renaissance onwards, looked to Classical antiquity for his inspiration. He went to Rome twice, to measure and draw the Imperial architecture, and in 1554 he published the results of his work in *L'Antichità di Roma*. His name is remembered at the expense of his contemporaries, working along the same lines, because he published *I Quattro Libri dell' Architettura* in 1570. Known in English as *The Four Books* this contained designs for town houses, country villas and advice on proportion, building materials and 'correct' Classical orders, porticoes, columns and other useful details. The publication was an enormous success; it was translated into many languages and spread Palladio's fame literally across the world. His life's ambition, which was to liberate Italy from the Gothic yoke, was amply fulfilled and not only in his native land.

Palladio had the fortune to be born at a propitious moment. Until the sixteenth century, the Venetians were discouraged from owning land or living in the country; their wealth was concentrated in Venice and in the maritime trading that made the city state so rich and powerful. However, Venice found herself totally at the mercy of inflationary grain prices and as a result the policy was relaxed. Venetians began to spend part of the year in the country and over the next 250 years a spate of villas was built in the Veneto; as many as 2,000 of them have survived. Palladio was in at the start. In *The Four Books* he gives advice to the 'gentleman farmer' to site his yard for threshing corn far enough from the villa so as not to be bothered by the dust, but not so far as to be *out of sight*. Farm buildings or *barchesse* were symmetrically arranged behind colonnades on either side of the villa creating an 'agricultural complex' with the master's house at its heart. The Villa Badoer, built by Palladio in 1554 and still standing, has curved *barchesse* stretching out to greet the visitor in a gesture of eternal welcome, an arrangement sometimes found in Ireland in both large and small houses.

The simple lines and satisfying proportions of Palladio's buildings appealed to the puritan spirit. Tranquil, symmetrical and serene, their lack of exterior ornament often concealed elaborately frescoed and stuccoed interiors. Protestant nations in particular took to Palladio, and although Ireland had a Catholic majority, it was governed by the Ascendancy who belonged to the Protestant church.

It is fitting that it should have been an Italian architect, two centuries later, who was destined to introduce the Palladian style to Ireland. Castletown in Co. Kildare, begun in 1722, was built to the designs of Alessandro Galilei

(1691–1737), best known for the façade he added to St John in Lateran in Rome. Without its quadrants and wings Castletown would resemble an Italian Renaissance town palace, a style of building that did not find favour in England and Ireland until the 1860s.

Russborough in Co. Wicklow, however, is the essence of Palladianism and would be so even bereft of its curved and colonnaded forecourt. Both houses are symmetrical and both have utilitarian yards on either side behind the wings. The agricultural complex, or economic Palladian layout, suited country life in Ireland just as it had in Italy 200 years before. Isaac Ware, author of *A Complete Body of Architecture* (1756), says: 'The plan may be so made that . . . it may appear much more considerable to the eye. The barn may now be a detached building . . . and the stable and cart house, answered by the cow-house and calf-house, separated from the principal building only by a gate on each side, may stand as two wings; which, with very little decoration from a judicious builder, will have a very pretty effect.'

Architectural pattern books such as those by Gibbs, Ware and Halfpenny have always played an important part in Ireland and in their lists of subscribers many Irish patrons are to be found. The earliest Irish architectural pattern book was published in 1754 by John Aheron (died *c.* 1761) and entitled *General Treatise on Architecture*. Aheron was a fine draughtsman and a copy of the album of his drawings for the old house that preceded Dromoland Castle is in the National Library in Dublin. Imported pattern books were used by the Dublin Society's outstanding Drawing School. It was here that in 1780 James Hoban (*c.* 1762–1831) of Co. Kilkenny was awarded a medal, now at the Smithsonian Institution, for 'Drawings of Brackets, Stairs, Roofs &.'. Twelve years later he was to win the competition for designing the White House in Washington, which, when built in 1792, was the most important stone Palladian building in North America designed by a professional architect. Thus it was that seventy years after the building of Castletown, Classical correctness reached the young United States setting a precedent that was widely followed.

In 1753 George Faulkner proposed publishing *Vitruvius Hibernicus* 'containing the plans, elevations and sections of the most regular and elegant buildings both public and private in the kingdom of Ireland, with a variety of new designs in large folio plates, engraven in copper by the best hands and drawn either from the buildings themselves, or the original designs of the architect'. Unfortunately for posterity the scheme was stillborn.

From about 1740 the great avenues and formal canals of the seventeenth- and early eighteenth-century Irish gardens began to be swept away and the taste for informal landscaped parks supervened. It became the fashion for sheep and cows to wander up almost as far as the windows, and both flowers and vegetables were banished from the house and locked up some distance away, in a walled garden. Although the great landscape designer 'Capability' Brown himself never came to Ireland it is said that he was invited over by the Duke of Leinster to remodel the park at Carton, but Brown is supposed to have replied haughtily 'I haven't finished England yet'. This was a brave refusal if it is true that the Duke offered him £1,000 upon landing in Ireland in addition to the cost of the work.

It seems odd that at a period when architecture was becoming increasingly formal and symmetrical the landscaping should take the opposite direction. The mid-eighteenth century ideal was a park where 'art and nature in just union reign'.

CASTLETOWN
Celbridge, Co. Kildare

'Speaker' William Conolly, Speaker of the Irish House of Commons from 1715, was a man of enormous wealth and power in spite of having, it is said, started from humble origins in Co. Donegal where he became an attorney. He amassed his great fortune by dealing in forfeited estates and in 1692 was elected Member for Donegal. He was appointed Commissioner of the Revenue in 1709 and never took an English title, proud, as were his descendants, to be known as 'Mr Conolly of Castletown'. It was essential for him to have a house within reach of the capital and he bought land near Celbridge beside the Liffey where he built the first and grandest Palladian house in the country, begun in 1722 and still unsurpassed in splendour.

Castletown was the first Irish Palladian house built to correct Classical proportions and designed by a professional architect, Alessandro Galilei (1691–1737). The massive silver-grey central block is flanked by wings of golden-brown Ardbraccan stone linked by curved colonnades so that they stretch forward to greet the visitor. The idea of creating utilitarian kitchen and stable yards behind the wings derives directly from Palladio himself. The hall and the magnificent staircase between them take up eleven of the entrance front windows facing south. This is one of the few Irish houses that does not blacken in rain and the source of the limestone with which it is built remains a mystery. Castletown was a hub of political and social life, as well as a seat of power and influence; it was admired by many people and the layout was copied in both large and small houses all over the country.

The design of Castletown can be said to have influenced that of the White House in Washington of which it has a strong claim to be the grandfather. Castletown was the first house in Ireland with a central front hall leading to an axial corridor dividing the rooms at the front from those at the back. The same arrangement is found at Leinster House, in Dublin (1745), which is acknowledged to be the father of the White House. The architect, Alessandro Galilei, was Italian and famous for the façade that he added to the old Basilica of St John in Lateran in Rome. The Duchess of Northumberland, an inveterate country-house visitor, was Vicereine in 1763 and wrote in her diary that year: 'to Castletown it stands on a flat the shell of the house is good it was designed by Gallini the Pope's architect who after built the Pope's palace on Mount Palatine at Rome'. This was the only house that Galilei designed in Ireland; who built it remains a mystery as he left Ireland in 1718 and building only commenced in 1722. Sir Edward Lovett Pearce, who was later to become the Surveyor General, was not in Ireland either at the time, but it is known that he designed some of the interiors, in particular the front hall which has survived the later eighteenth-century alterations to the house.

A vivid portrait of 'Speaker' Conolly's widow, Katherine, who had lived on at Castletown since his death in 1729, was drawn by the famous Mary Delany in 1752:

We have lost our great Mrs Conolly. She died last Friday, and is a general loss; her table was open to all her friends of all ranks, and her purse to the poor. She was, I think, in her ninetieth year. She has been drooping for some years, but never so ill as to shut out company; she rose constantly at eight, and by eleven was seated in her drawing-room, and received visits till three o'clock, at which hour she punctually dined, and generally had two tables of eight or ten people each; her own table was served with

RIGHT The front hall and the staircase are lit by eleven windows facing south, an imposing, albeit impractical use of space. The hall was designed by Sir Edward Lovett Pearce in 1724.

OPPOSITE Castletown was begun in 1722 to the designs of the Italian architect, Alessandro Galilei; it was the first and remains the greatest Palladian house in Ireland. The Conolly Folly, 1740, closes the vista to the rear.

seven courses and seven and a dessert, and two substantial dishes on the side-table; and if the greatest person in the kingdom dined with her, she never altered her bill of fare. As soon as dinner was over she took the ladies to the drawing-room, and left the gentlemen to finish as they pleased. She sat down in her grey cloth great chair and took a nap, whilst the company chatted to one another, which lulled her to sleep. Tea and coffee came exactly at half an hour after five; she then waked, and as soon as tea was over, a party of whist was made for her till ten, then everybody retired. She had prayers every day at twelve, and when the weather was good took the air, but has never made a visit since Mr Conolly died. She was clever at business, wrote all her own letters, and could read a newspaper by candlelight without spectacles. She was a plain and vulgar woman in her manner, but had very valuable qualities.

After Katherine Conolly's death Castletown was inherited by William, the nephew of 'Speaker' Conolly. He died after only two years and the house passed on to his only son, Tom, who became known as 'Squire' Conolly. He married Lady Louisa Lennox, daughter of the second Duke of Richmond, in 1758 when she was fifteen years old. In their day the staircase was put in with plasterwork by the Lafranchini brothers executed in 1759, by which time the Swiss-Italian stuccodores had been in Ireland long enough to become both fashionable and expensive; 'Mr Conolly and I' wrote Lady Louisa Conolly in 1759 'are excessively diverted at Francini's impertinence and if he charges anything of that sort to Mr Conolly there is a fine scold in store for his

honour'. Family portraits are incorporated in the plasterwork here, with the head of 'Squire' Conolly in pride of place, wearing a floppy hat. The banisters of the staircase are of brass, signed *A. King Dublin 1760*; this was the year after the plasterwork was executed which is the reason it does not follow the line of the staircase.

The Print Room dates from about 1765 and the drawing for laying out the prints is on display in the room. It was probably made by Lady Louisa Conolly with help from her sister Sarah and other friends as a wet-day pastime, and is the only period print room to survive in Ireland. The fashion originated in England in the 1750s so that, when the Castletown room was created, the concept was a novel one. Engravings and mezzotints were pasted straight on to the wall, framed by elaborate borders which were also engraved. No two print rooms are alike therefore, but for the subtlety and imagination of its arrangement, the Castletown print room rates high.

Eight windows at the back of the house, on the *piano nobile*, light the eighty-foot-long gallery that faces the obelisk on the skyline. Originally panelled in plaster, the panels were 'knocked off smack smooth' by 1776 and Pompeian grotesques were painted on the walls in that year, recently restored. A scheme for replacing the heavy, early ceiling was abandoned and instead it was painted in Pompeian colours to tie in with the newly painted walls. This wonderful room is sometimes used for concerts, and to hear chamber music in such surroundings is a memorable experience, in particular when the setting sun pierces the old glass windowpanes and fills the room with a reddening glow.

OPPOSITE Three of the brass banisters of the staircase are signed *A. King, Dublin, 1760*. The plaster decoration, was executed in the previous year by the Lafranchini brothers, and incorporates family portraits of the Conollys.

ABOVE The long gallery, one of the most beautiful rooms in Ireland, was painted in the Pompeian manner in 1776. Three vast Venetian chandeliers were bought for the room at that time and the colours in the glass are echoed in the ceiling.

Although the property often descended through the female line, Castletown never changed hands by purchase from 1722 until 1965 when it was put up for auction. The vendor was Lord Carew; he had inherited the property from his mother who was a Conolly. The great house, with six hundred acres of rich flat land beside the River Liffey, fifteen miles from Dublin, was bought by speculators who obtained permission from Kildare County Council to build on the land. As a result, a modern housing estate has sprung up beside the majestic lime avenue which leads from Celbridge to the house. In 1967 the empty and abandoned house and one hundred acres of land were bought by Desmond Guinness and made into the headquarters of the Irish Georgian Society which undertook its restoration.

Castletown became the first house in the province of Leinster to

OPPOSITE The superb eighteenth-century mahogany writing cabinet and the seat furniture with 'Chinese' fretwork are part of the original contents of the red drawing room; the Aubusson carpet was specially made for the room.

RIGHT The Print Room, created by Lady Louisa Conolly in the 1760s. The Louis XVI furniture with Aesop's Fables in tapestry was the gift of Mrs Douglas Auchincloss of New York.

BELOW A painting of the Drummond children hangs above a japanned lacquer cabinet in the green drawing room, inscribed *Mrs Conolly to Miss Burten* with Italianate views painted on the drawers. The chairs, from Headfort in Co. Meath have been copied by the Kindel furniture company.

open its doors to the public. It was in a terrible state; lead had been stolen from the roof, but fortunately the mantelpieces were still there, although the house had been empty and without a caretaker for two years. A great deal of work was accomplished by volunteers at weekends, and money was raised both at home and abroad for furnishing and repairing Castletown.

In August 1722, Sir John Perceval wrote to Bishop Berkeley as follows:

I am glad for the honour of my country that Mr Conolly has undertaken so magnificent a pile of building, and your advice has been taken upon it. I hope that the execution will answer the design, wherein one special care must be to procure good masons. I shall be impatient until you send me a sketch of the whole plan and of your two fronts. You will do well to recommend to him the making use of all the marbles he can get of the production of Ireland for his chimneys, for since this house will be the finest Ireland ever saw, and by your description fit for a Prince, I would have it as it were the epitome of the Kingdom, and all the natural rarities she afford should have a place there. I would examine the several woods for inlaying my floors, and wainscot with our own oak, and walnut; my stone stairs should be of black palmers stone, and my buffet adorned with the choicest shells our strands afford. I would even carry my zeal to things of art; my hangings, bed, cabinets and other furniture should be Irish, and the very silver that ornamented my locks and grates should be the produce of our mines. But I forget that I write to a gentleman of the country who knows better what is proper and what the kingdom affords.

The Irish Georgian Society and the Castletown Foundation, which has owned the house since 1979, have attempted to emulate Perceval's advice by filling the house with Irish furniture and paintings in the absence of the original contents.

THE OBELISK AT CASTLETOWN

Celbridge, Co. Kildare

The Conolly Folly is an obelisk mounted on arches and adorned with stone eagles and pineapples that closes the vista at the back of Castletown. It is 140 feet high, twice the height of the main block of the house, and was almost certainly designed by Richard Castle, the German architect who was working at Carton nearby in 1740, the year the folly was built. The winter of 1739 had been especially severe, and the work was undertaken in order to provide employment and relieve suffering in the neighbourhood. The obelisk was built by Katherine Conolly, widow of the 'Speaker', who lived on at Castletown in great state after her husband died in 1729 until her death in 1752. Her sister, Mary Jones, was writing, in March 1740: 'My sister Conolly is building an obleix to answer a Vistow from the bake of Castletown House; it will cost her three or four hundred pounds at least, but I believe more. I really wonder how she can dow so much, and live as she duse.'

In order for it to serve as an eyecatcher, the obelisk had to stand where it does, namely on the highest point of land at the back of Castletown, directly on axis to the house. In fact it was built on neighbouring land that belonged not to the Conollys but to the FitzGeralds, Earls of Kildare. In 1903, when Irish tenant farmers gained possession of their land, the obelisk, on an 'island' of five acres well outside the Carton demesne wall, remained the property of the Carton estate. Thus it came about that in recent years the owner of this remarkable structure was the late Lord Brocket, who acquired it when he bought Carton in 1949.

The stone was crumbling at the top and about to fall, causing a local wit to remark that if the top fell off it would lose its point. Dr Mark Girouard described it as 'the one piece of real architecture in all Ireland', and it was he who suggested that the Irish Georgian Society should undertake its restoration. A fund was set up and a firm of steeplejacks from Belfast were employed to secure the top. The vast stone pineapples lying on the ground were reset in place and two new ones were carved, as well as a limestone eagle to match the one that survived.

The Conolly Folly was built to close the view on axis to the rear of Castletown in 1740, and also to give employment after a severe winter had caused much hardship in the district.

STROKESTOWN PARK
Strokestown, Co. Roscommon

Those who hold dear the future of Irish country houses must forever be in debt to James Callery of Westward Garage Ltd. who has in every sense been the saviour of Strokestown Park. Originally the property of the Mahon family, later Hales-Pakenham-Mahon, the previous owner, Olive Hales-Pakenham-Mahon, lived on alone, bed-ridden, in the house so that essential maintenance and repair work were perforce neglected. Westward had bought the place in 1979 during her lifetime. The instant she died, the company carried out a massive restoration project which included repairing the roof. The saving of Strokestown at the eleventh hour created jobs in the locality. Above all the most important remaining country house in Co. Roscommon has been preserved as a focal point for tourists and local people proud of their cultural inheritance.

The main street of Strokestown, laid out by the second Lord Hartland, is so wide that during the Second World War a stray German aeroplane was able to land on it. Traces of interesting Palladian architecture can still be seen along its broad and stately length. At the

The façade is rendered still more splendid by triumphal arches each side of the wings in the same manner as at Carton in Co. Kildare and Russborough in Co. Wicklow, both designed by Castle. The stable wing has beautiful groin vaulting supported on Doric columns, also similar to the stables at Carton and Russborough. Strokestown may have the only original galleried kitchen left in Ireland, the balustrade of that at Russborough being a Victorian replacement. This is where the housekeeper, bunch of keys at waist, might have hovered, supervising those at work below. The staircase panelling appears to date from the early eighteenth century. At the back of the house the library, a late Georgian addition, with its fine Chippendale bookcases, has retained the magical brown and gold wallpaper dating from the early nineteenth century. A Regency porch and giant pilasters were added to the façade in 1819 by J. Lynn. When built, Strokestown was the focal point of a 30,000 acre estate.

Luckily enough Westward has also bought much of the contents so that, unlike so many restored Irish houses, Strokestown Park is

lower end an immense Gothic triumphal arch heralds the approach to Strokestown Park.

The architectural history of the house is poorly documented, but it would seem that part of the central block dates from 1696, the date carved on a stone beside the front door. Richard Castle is thought to have designed the Palladian wings connected to the house by curved walls. The blocked 'Gibbsian' doorcases have niches above, flanked by *oculi* and are also thought to have been designed by him in the 1740s.

The central block of Strokestown Park, dating from 1696, was incorporated into a Palladian design, probably by Richard Castle in the eighteenth century.

furnished with original pieces. The walled garden is being recreated with the help of a government grant and the advice of experts such as Helen Dillon and Jim Reynolds; when completed it will have the longest herbaceous border in Ireland.

ABOVE LEFT The old kitchen, which retains its original balustraded gallery, has been restored for use as a restaurant and tea-room.

ABOVE The library, added on to the back of the house, *c.* 1800, has retained its Regency wallpaper and important Chippendale bookcases.

LEFT The dining room has an old damask wallpaper that has faded to a magical shade of pinkish red.

OPPOSITE Palladian wings were built on in the eighteenth century with the kitchen to the left and stables to the right of the central block. The vaulted stables Richard Castle gave to Carton (1739) and Russborough (1741) are almost identical.

CASHEL PALACE
Cashel, Co. Tipperary

The Rock of Cashel was for seven centuries the seat of the Kings of Munster, and Cormac's Chapel built by the last king, Cormac McCarthy, in 1127–30, is an outstanding example of Irish Romanesque architecture. According to legend, the rock itself was bitten off a neighbouring mountain and spat out in the middle of the plain by the devil; the 'Devil's Bit' can be seen on the skyline.

The great Gothic cathedral was commenced in 1230 and finished by 1290. The first Protestant services were held in the reign of King Edward VI, in about 1550. In 1647, prior to the Cromwellian invasion, the cathedral was sacked and burnt by Lord Inchiquin and his army and as many as 3,000 people were reputedly slain. Theophilus Bolton became Archbishop of Cashel (1730–44) and offered £1,000 out of his own pocket to repair the damage – a huge sum in those days. Arthur Price who succeeded him in the Archbishopric (1744–52), however, removed the roof with the intention of building a Classical cathedral in the town. Opinions vary as to why the old cathedral was abandoned. It may have been too difficult to repair or the Archbishop too lazy to climb the steep hill to the rock, or he may have preferred the Classical style to the Gothic. At all events the last service was held in the great

cathedral on the rock in 1747, after which services were held in a room in the town until the new cathedral was completed in 1783–4. Church attendances were in any case remarkably low at that time. On Easter Sunday 1738, the number of communicants at St Paul's Cathedral in London failed to reach double figures.

At the foot of the rock stands the former Archbishop's Palace, now the Cashel Palace Hotel. It was designed by Sir Edward Lovett Pearce, Surveyor General of Ireland, in 1730. Theophilus Bolton commissioned the building at a cost of just under £4,000, and when he died in 1744 he bequeathed his library for the use of the clergy of his diocese. His books, many of them very rare, are now housed in a building beside the Georgian cathedral. A recent generous grant from Guinness Peat Aviation has enabled the Bolton Library to be restored and opened to the public.

The Cashel Palace has an entrance front of faded pink brick and beautifully cut limestone dressings. The Palladian windows to either side now have Gothic glazing and the blocking of the stone front door surround can be compared to that at No. 9 Henrietta Street in Dublin, also designed by Pearce. The garden front is more restrained and was

ABOVE The staircase with its twisted and fluted banisters has Corinthian newels similar to those at the Damer House, Roscrea.

LEFT The front hall has twin bolection mantels of black Kilkenny marble at either end, and a screen of Corinthian columns. The curved heads of the door surrounds are of a kind not found after 1740.

OPPOSITE Cashel Palace was designed by Sir Edward Lovett Pearce in 1730 for Theophilus Bolton, Archbishop of Cashel and is now a hotel; the garden front is built of limestone.

built of limestone. In this change of material from front to back the Cashel Palace resembles Mount Ievers Court in Co. Clare and Kilshannig in Co. Cork.

Pearce's pine-panelled entrance hall has a pair of black Kilkenny marble bolection mantels identical to that installed by him in the hall at Castletown in Co. Kildare but on a smaller scale. During recent restoration work traces of grey marbling were found on the panelling and on the elegant fluted Corinthian columns of the front hall. The rest of the interior on the ground floor is of later date as extensive damage resulted from the Palace being commandeered by the soldiery during the rebellion against the Government of 1798. Redecoration was carried out in the early years of the nineteenth century by Archbishop Charles Agar, afterwards first Earl of Normanton. The elaborate carved wood staircase has fortunately survived. It belongs to the same

family as those in the Damer House in Roscrea and at Dollanstown in Kilcock, with its twisted and fluted balusters. It could easily be twenty years earlier than the Palace. Slightly old-fashioned interior features are often found in Ireland, particularly in the provinces where craftsmen were slow to change their ways.

By 1956 the building was not in a good state of repair and was for sale with its garden for £4,000. Lord Brocket, the then owner of Carton in Co. Kildare, bought the Palace and made it into a hotel.

The tall chimneys were a vital part of the design of the Palace, but they were pronounced unsafe and taken down by the Church a short time before Lord Brocket bought the property. He had them rebuilt, although not to the original height as he considered they had been too tall – even so it was a great improvement. The Cashel Palace remains a hotel to this day and its preservation seems happily assured.

BELLAMONT FOREST
Cootehill, Co. Cavan

The Cootes of Cootehill are descended from a brilliant soldier, Sir Charles Coote, who was killed in 1642 'in a skirmish with the Irish'. His four sons were given land in different parts of Ireland; Sligo, Laois, Monaghan and Cavan, giving rise to the legend that you could walk across the country from one coast to the other without leaving Coote land. Colonel Thomas Coote created the town of Cootehill. His nephew, also Thomas, succeeded to the estate when a minor. He was called to the bar in 1684 and held many positions of authority. It is unlikely that he would have waited until 1730 to build himself a residence, as has been suggested, and more probable that he continued to live in the house by the town's bowling green, that he had inherited in 1671. He died in 1741 and it was more likely Charles Coote, Thomas's son by his third marriage, who built the new house in 1730, choosing an elevated site a mile from the town.

Charles Coote was born in 1695, became High Sheriff in 1719, MP in 1733 and died in Bath in 1750. He had seven daughters and a son Charles, born in 1738, who was eventually created Earl of Bellamont; the florid and conceited portrait of him by Reynolds, in his robes and plumes as a Knight of the Bath, hangs in the National Gallery of Ireland.

Bellamont Forest, as the house came to be called, was designed in

ABOVE The bedroom landing is lit from above by an oval lantern elegantly adorned with stucco ornament. A similar arrangement is to be found at Russborough in Co. Wicklow.

LEFT Bellamont Forest was designed by Sir Edward Lovett Pearce for the Cootes, Earls of Bellamont, *c.* 1730. It is the most perfect Palladian villa in Ireland. The portico does not have respondent pilasters which has led to the theory that it may have been an afterthought.

OPPOSITE The front hall of Bellamont, paved in black and white and adorned with busts of Roman emperors, has simple lines and noble proportions.

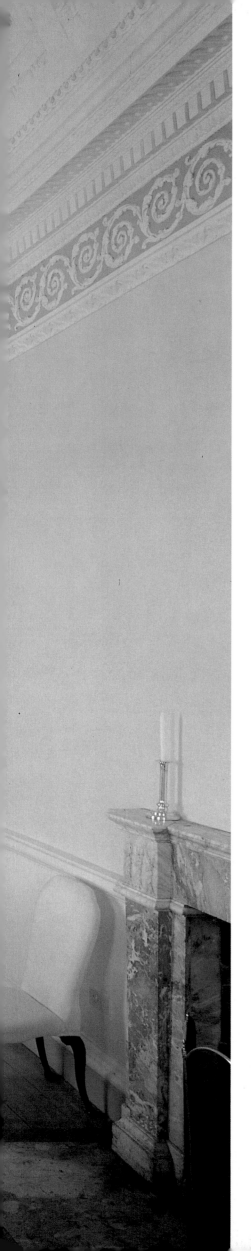

ABOVE The drawing room, panelled in plaster, has an elaborate ceiling dominated by a massive wreath of a type generally associated with the period of Charles II.

OPPOSITE The dining room with its coved and coffered ceiling has an Irish 'hunt' or 'wake' table and copies of a 'balloon' chair from Castletown, Co. Kildare made by the Kindel furniture company.

c. 1730 by Sir Edward Lovett Pearce, nephew of Mrs Thomas Coote and cousin of Charles, the builder. It stands four-square on rising ground built of red brick with a Doric limestone portico and pediments over the windows to either side. The portico may have been an afterthought because respondent pilasters are lacking. An early sketch by Pearce for Bellamont shows it with a recessed portico – an arrangement favoured in the Veneto but unsuitable to the Irish climate. It is the first and remains the purest example of a Palladian villa, as opposed to a country house, in Ireland and is loosely based on Palladio's Villa Pisani at Montagnana.

The beauty and simplicity of the entrance hall, with its black and white paved floor and marble busts of Roman emperors set in *oculi* high up in the walls, is eternal. The drawing room beyond has an extremely elaborate ceiling dominated by a bold circular wreath, almost a throw back in style to the seventeenth century. By contrast the library and dining-room ceilings are coved and coffered in a geometrical scheme. For such an important house the staircase seems modest but no doubt space was at a premium. It leads up to the bedroom landing which is lit by a cupola very similar to that at Russborough in Co. Wicklow with exquisite plasterwork in high relief. This wonderful house was bought in 1987 by Mr and Mrs John Coote from Melbourne in Australia.

POWERSCOURT
Enniskerry, Co. Wicklow

Powerscourt was built in 1731 for the Wingfield family, Viscounts Powerscourt, to the designs of the German architect Richard Castle, incorporating the massive walls of the ancient castle of the De La Poers that stood on the site.

The saloon and the main reception rooms were on the *piano nobile*, an arrangement not normally found in country houses. Other reception rooms, a library and the dining room were on the ground floor but these had low ceilings and were not as grand. It was a particularly odd way to plan a house that had a stupendous view from the ground floor and where there was no need to improve on this by climbing up to the *piano nobile*. Another strange fact was the absence until the last century of a fireplace in the saloon, an omission which must have rendered it unusable for much of the year. Giving up so much of its space to reception rooms seems to suggest that Powerscourt may have been built more as a villa for entertaining in summer than as a house to live in all the year round.

When George IV paid his state visit to Ireland in 1821 he was the first reigning monarch to have set foot on Irish soil since William of Orange in 1690. He very nearly did not make the journey because, as he was waiting for a favourable wind to take him across the Irish sea, news of the death of his wife reached him and he was urged to return to London. The Irish visit went ahead as planned, however, and a large luncheon party was given in his honour in the saloon at Powerscourt, one of the grandest country houses in Ireland at that time. The famous waterfall was dammed up beforehand to ensure a spectacular torrent on the great day. A road was specially built to bring the royal party from the house to the waterfall, and a viewing stand was put up for their greater comfort. In the event the King fell asleep after lunch and the stand was filled with estate workmen instead. When a bugle was sounded and the sluice gate opened, the torrent was so fierce that it swept all before it, royal stand included.

The gardens at Powerscourt are world famous and justly so. Nowhere is such a vast *théâtre de verdure* to be found with such a dramatic natural backdrop as the pointed Sugarloaf Mountain. A map of Co. Dublin in 1760 by Rocque, the great cartographer, shows that the terraces and round pond existed at that date and they must have been designed by Richard Castle, the architect. In 1843 reconstruction of the terraces began under the supervision of the architect Daniel Robertson. Supposedly inspired by those at Villa Butera in Sicily the plans show terraces, gardens and stonework. In his notes Lord Powerscourt says of Robertson:

> He was much given to drink and was never able to design or draw so well as when his brain was excited by sherry. He suffered from gout and used to be wheeled out on the Terrace in a wheelbarrow, with a bottle of sherry, and as long as that lasted he was able to design and direct the workmen, but when the sherry was finished he collapsed and was incapable of working till the drunken fit evaporated.

The sixth Viscount died in 1844 and work stopped until the seventh Viscount came of age fourteen years later. In 1854 Alexander Robertson, an accomplished gardener, from a well-known Scottish nursery family, came to Powerscourt and eventually took over the running of the demesne. Lord Powerscourt and he worked out a set of plans based on Daniel Robertson's design. A garden comparable with any in Europe was created; embellished and enlarged with statues, wrought-iron work and paving, and planted with rare and beautiful trees and shrubs. Today a wide terrace gives a vantage point from which to gaze down across the inlaid pebbled staircase to the urns and the prancing horses beside the round pond, its jet fountain spurting a single white plume.

The ninth Viscount Powerscourt found the cost of upkeep too heavy and sold the property with the original contents to Mr and Mrs Ralph Slazenger in 1960. One day Mrs Slazenger chanced upon an Indian statue made of stone, lying in the corner of a tractor shed in the farmyard. On enquiring about it she was told that it was attached to the harrow, to add extra weight at times when the ground was exceptionally hard. Although the statue was not to her liking, Mrs Slazenger thought it deserved a better fate than this, and had it put on a pedestal in the garden. Not long after, the Indian expert of the Victoria and Albert Museum in London happened to be in Ireland on holiday with his family and was surprised to stumble on a statue of a particularly rare period, whose artefacts are now jealously guarded by the Indian government. The expert asked to see Mrs Slazenger and made her an offer of £1,000 on the spot for the statue – had he suggested a lower figure she might have agreed but she decided to make further enquiries. Negotiations ensued which resulted in the statue eventually being bought by the Victoria and Albert Museum where it now lives in state, a far cry from its erstwhile resting place in the corner of a tractor shed.

In 1962, the Slazengers' daughter Wendy married Lord Powerscourt's son and heir, the present Viscount. All seemed set fair for the future of one of Ireland's most beautiful houses when in 1974 fate struck Powerscourt with a vengeance. With great public spirit, Mr and Mrs Slazenger had decided to open the house, until then private, to the general public as an added attraction to the famous gardens which had been open for many years. A major programme of decorating and picture-cleaning was instigated; when all was ready, a lunch party for forty was held to show off the newly renovated interior. A fire was lit in the morning room which had not been used for some time and the chimney caught alight. The brigade was summoned and the fire was, it was thought, put out. In the early hours of the following morning a small electric bell went off in the Slazengers' bedroom, not giving a proper ring but just enough to be heard. It saved their lives; the whole of the top floor of the house, and the roof, was ablaze.

The loss of the house is indeed a tragedy. The walls still stand, however, and as Powerscourt boasted a flat lead roof, it has been suggested that a reinforced concrete roof would look just the same from below. This could make the house watertight and give the internal walls a chance to dry out – some of them are up to thirteen feet wide in places and have by now been saturated by many years of soft Irish rain. A structural survey is being carried out at the time of writing by the National Building Agency, with advice on historical information from the Irish Architectural Archive.

Powerscourt, built in 1731 by Richard Castle for the Wingfield family, Viscounts Powerscourt, with its famous terraced gardens and round pond. The house suffered a disastrous fire in 1974 and is now a ruin.

CARTON
Maynooth, Co. Kildare

Carton is situated about fifteen miles west of Dublin beside the Galway road in a setting that is remarkable for its beauty in that dull, flat part of Co. Kildare. The Rye Water, by nature hardly more than a stream, meanders through the park disguised, with the help of judicious dams, as the River Thames. There is a manmade cascade beside Shell Cottage at the far end of the lake and the Rye flows on past lofty crags until it slips out unnoticed in the direction of Leixlip. A wall, five miles in length and pierced by five lodges, seals off this thousand-acre paradise which resembles an island, forbidden to ordinary mortals.

Carton was once the great country seat of the FitzGeralds, Earls of Kildare, who were in 1766 to become Dukes of Leinster; it was remodelled by Richard Castle in 1739 with a huge pedimented central block, curved colonnades and wings. Six years later the same architect built their town house, Kildare, now Leinster House, by far the grandest private residence in the city of Dublin, at present occupied by the Dáil, or Irish Parliament.

Emily, Countess of Kildare, and her husband removed the straight avenues and created a 'lawn'. In 1750 she wrote:

> We shall return to Carton in a fortnight. I believe, which I shall be mighty glad of; for besides that I long to be there, I am excessively impatient to see how the lawn looks now some of the hedges and ditches are taken away, which has been done since we left it. I am ridiculously eager about the alterations there. They tell me I can talk of nothing else, but I think I have never worry'd you much about them yet, but if I once cou'd get you there, I believe you wou'd hear a good deal of them.
>
> Did I ever tell you my passion for spotted cows? I believe not. You have no notion what a delightful beautiful collection of them I have got in a very short time, which indeed is owing to my dear Lord Kildare; who, ever since I took this fancy into my head, has bought me every pretty cow he saw. It's really charming to see them grazing on the lawn.
> (*Emily, Duchess of Leinster*, Brian FitzGerald, 1949.)

Only two of the rooms on the ground floor at Carton remain more or less as they were in the eighteenth century. The saloon, far the most important room in the house, has had its doors enlarged, its windows lowered and a Victorian pipe organ installed at one end, but

Carton was remodelled and enlarged by
Richard Castle in 1739 for the nineteenth
Earl of Kildare, head of the Leinster branch
of the FitzGeralds. The south front,
formerly the entrance, faces across
the park to the Prospect Tower.

fortunately the great eighteenth-century Baroque ceiling remains unaltered. This magnificent plaster ceiling depicting 'The Courtship of the Gods' was probably the first work in Ireland by Paul and Philip Lafranchini and dates from 1739. The saloon was originally the 'Eating Parlour'. A young lady who stayed at Carton in 1779 wrote 'I forgot to tell you the part you would like best – French horns playing at breakfast and dinner'. As there is also a contemporary report of French horns enlivening mealtimes at Castle Ward in Co. Down, there was evidently a fashion for this; for a time it may have been the Irish equivalent of the bagpipes played at meals in Scotland.

ABOVE The bridge over the Rye Water that flows through the park at Carton was designed in 1763 by Thomas Ivory, the Cork-born architect best known as the creator of the Blue Coat School in Dublin. The original balustrades have been replaced by solid parapets.

OPPOSITE The saloon has an important plaster ceiling dating from 1739 representing 'The Courtship of the Gods', the work of Paul and Philip Lafranchini. The organ was designed by Lord Gerald FitzGerald, son of the third Duke of Leinster, in 1857.

OPPOSITE Emily, Countess of Kildare, purchased a hand-painted Chinese paper depicting domestic scenes in 1759 and created the Chinese room at Carton with it; the arms of the gilt wood overmantel would have carried Chinese pots or statuettes.

ABOVE The Shell Cottage in the park at Carton was made for Emily, Countess of Kildare c. 1760 and originally had a thatched roof. Her husband, James, twentieth Earl of Kildare, was created Duke of Leinster in 1766.

The other room to have retained its eighteenth-century appearance is the Chinese room with panels of Chinese wallpaper purchased in 1759 and elaborate gilt wood embellishments made for the room. Emily, Countess of Kildare, imported the paper but when it arrived there was not enough to cover the walls. Accordingly she had borders made in a Chinese design, painted the room in the colours of a peacock, and cut out pieces of the paper into strange shapes to complete the decoration. The effect is not unlike that of a print room; moreover, like her sister Lady Louisa Conolly at Castletown, Emily did make a print room for Carton which has not survived.

In 1815 the third Duke of Leinster sold Leinster House in Dublin to the Royal Dublin Society and engaged the fashionable Cork architect, Richard Morrison, to make drastic alterations at Carton. The curved colonnades were squared off and new rooms added to either side of the central block. At the same time the entrance was moved to the north side of the house so that the wings no longer stretch forward to greet the visitor as they do at Castletown and Russborough. There was a good reason for this as the windows with the best view, facing south across the parkland to the prospect tower, originally belonged to the hall and staircase which, like the saloon, took up two storeys. Today the reception rooms on the ground floor and bedrooms above face south.

Had all things been equal Carton should now belong either to the FitzGeralds, Dukes of Leinster, who created it or to the Nall-Cains whose reign, though short-lived, was so exemplary. Today there is no family to give it life. Both the FitzGerald and Nall-Cain families departed for financial reasons, the first through its own folly and the second through the Wealth Tax which was introduced in 1975 and that robbed Ireland of so much capital. It was repealed in 1978.

It was the rash behaviour of the seventh Duke as a young man that ended the FitzGerald connection with the property. Lord Edward FitzGerald was an extravagant third son, with few prospects and trustees who were restrictive and old-fashioned. He soon found himself in debt. He was eighteen years old in 1910 and shortly afterwards he sold his birthright to a moneylender, stipulating that in the unlikely event that he inherited the Dukedom he would receive £1,000 a year for life, enough to subsist on in those days. To be fair to him, it was only his own life interest that he was putting at risk and had he died early he would not have brought down the rest of his family. Unfortunately he lived until 1979, being nearly ninety when he died. Maurice, the eldest brother, died unmarried in 1922 aged thirty-five, by which time the second son, Lord Desmond, had already fallen on active service in France in 1916.

There had been an immense amount of property, ground rents in Dublin and Athy, and 67,000 acres in Co. Kildare. This land consisted of prosperous tenant farms which were given to the tenants under the terms of the Wyndham Act in 1903. Compensation was paid to the Leinsters but the income from that compensation went to the moneylender and his heirs until the death of the seventh Duke. Carton was bereft of the funds necessary for its upkeep. So it was that in 1949 Carton was sold, with the agreement of all concerned, to Lord Brocket whose principal seat was the magnificent Brocket Hall in Hertfordshire.

BELVEDERE

Mullingar, Co. Westmeath

It is unfortunate that in these times of financial constraint in Ireland, houses boasting interiors of quality tend to be excessively large and that the smaller and therefore more habitable country houses seldom have interiors of particular refinement. The exception is Belvedere, a modest-sized fishing lodge of 1740, probably designed by Richard Castle, that stands by the shores of Lough Ennell in Co. Westmeath. A villa rather than a country house, Belvedere has delicate Rococo plasterwork believed to be by Bartholomew Cramillion who was also responsible for the Mespil House ceilings and the Rotunda Hospital chapel in Dublin. The stucco ceiling of the minute entrance hall represents 'Night'; the decoration is in such low relief that it is hardly noticeable. There is an owl and a flaming torch; clouds and stars are scattered about with carefree abandon, hemmed in by no orderly frame except the richly decorated frieze and cornice that surrounds the room. The dining room and the drawing room to either end of the

house also have delicate Rococo plasterwork of rare quality, liveliness and gaiety. They are most untypical of contemporary Irish stuccowork in their freedom and lack of over-crowding in the design. With their high ceilings and rich carving these are grand rooms, but they are not large.

The ground floor cornices are typical of the mid-eighteenth century and provide a perfect frame for the brilliant plasterwork. The joinery and panelling are of outstanding quality with beautiful carving which is most unusual in that it has never been painted.

Belvedere may be, according to Mark Bence-Jones, the earliest bow-ended house in Ireland. The rusticated front door of simple design is flanked by blocked 'Gibbsian' window surrounds but the frames of the Venetian windows on the projecting bays to either side are very plain by contrast. Above them there were curved Diocletian or therm windows which in the old photographs resemble eye-lids. These

Belvedere was built as a villa for entertaining and the dining room enjoys spectacular views of Lough Ennell. All the ground-floor rooms have delicate Rococo ceilings attributed to Bartholomew Cramillion.

OPPOSITE Belvedere was designed by Richard Castle in 1740 for Robert Rochfort MP, later created Earl of Belvedere. It has an interior of unequalled refinement; the stone balustraded terraces below the house are Victorian.

windows were squared off in the last century. Originally Belvedere would have looked down across natural parkland to the shores of Lough Ennell but in Victorian times three descending terraces were built with elaborate stone balustrades, steps and little pointed Irish yews.

In 1704 Lady Elizabeth Moore, daughter of the Earl of Drogheda, married George Rochfort, MP for Co. Westmeath, and in 1708 produced a son, Robert, who eventually took over his father's seat in parliament. Robert's first wife, Elizabeth Tenison, died and in 1736 he married Mary, the sixteen-year-old daughter of Viscount Molesworth. By this time he had been made Lord Belfield by George II whom he had impressed at Court with his 'handsome appearance and distinguished manners'. In 1740 he and his young wife began to build Belvedere, five miles away from the ancestral family home of Gaulston Park. Before long, however, the Earl of Egmont was writing in his diary as follows (2 May, 1743):

Last post several letters from Ireland gave an account of a most unhappy affair that lately passed in Dublin. Robert Rochfort, Baron Bellfield of that

kingdom, who some years ago married a daughter of Richard Viscount Molesworth for love, she being very handsome though no fortune, and used her in the tenderest manner, was privately informed that she cohabited unlawfully with his younger brother. Upon which he put the question to her, and she with consummate impudence owned the fact, adding that her last child was by him, and that she had no pleasure with any man like that she had with him. My Lord thereupon locked her up . . . and in his rage took a charged pistol with him with intention to find his brother and shoot him, but that very night he went on board a ship and sailed for England, where he now lies concealed if not fled abroad. My Lord Bellfield then went to Lord Molesworth and telling him his unfortunate case, asked his advice what he should do? My Lord replied he might do what he pleased; that having committed such a crime as incest and confest it, he should have no concern about, and the rather because she was only his bastard by his wife before he married her. My Lord Bellfield resolved to be divorced, is now prosecuting her as an adultress, and we are told that when separated, she will be transported to the West Indies as a vagabond.

The Jealous Wall, in Gothic arches, is a sham ruin built *c.* 1760 by Lord Belvedere to screen from view the house of his brother next door, with whom he had had a severe quarrel.

From 1743 onwards Lord Belfield locked his wife up at Gaulston where she was allowed to see nobody except the servants. If she went into the garden, she would be preceded by a footman, who was forbidden to speak to her, and who rang a bell to keep anyone from coming near her. After twelve years of strict confinement she managed to escape and reached her father's house in Dublin, but he refused to admit her and within twenty-four hours she was back in her prison. For the next eighteen years she was locked up, and is said to have walked in the gallery, gazing at the pictures as if conversing with them. The Earl of Belvedere never remarried, and found Belvedere large enough for his wants. He entertained there a good deal, however, and when he died in 1774 his estate was in considerable debt.

When her son came to release her, the Countess of Belvedere is said to have exclaimed, 'Is the tyrant dead?'. Her hair had gone white, she was dressed in the fashions of thirty years before, and she had acquired a wild, scared, unearthly look; the tones of her voice, which hardly exceeded a whisper, were harsh, agitated and uneven. A year or so later she left on a visit to Italy. There she became a Catholic, and not long after her return she walked behind the coffin of her eldest son. The second Earl had no children and the title of Belvedere became extinct.

The unfortunate Arthur Rochfort, the younger brother with whom she had been implicated, had managed to escape to Yorkshire but in 1759 he made the mistake of returning to Ireland. Hardly had he landed when he was imprisoned for life, being charged by the unrelenting Lord Belfield, now Earl of Belvedere, with £20,000 damages that were impossible for him to pay. He died in the Marshalsea, the debtors' gaol in Dublin.

The view from the house is interrupted at one point by a remarkable sham ruin that was built in about 1760 by the first Earl, to blot out the neighbouring house of another brother, George Rochfort, with whom he had also quarrelled. This large mid-eighteenth-century house, originally called Rochfort, and later Tudenham, is now itself a ruin, and the park has been carved up by the Land Commission. It is situated beside the lake about half a mile from Belvedere.

RUSSBOROUGH
Blessington, Co. Wicklow

A handsome Palladian archway flanked by curved sweeps and built of the local silver-grey granite stands at the head of the straight, formal beech avenue that leads to Russborough. Being approached from the side the house with its incredible façade of seven hundred feet suddenly springs into view. The central block, curved colonnades and wings embrace a forecourt the size of a parade ground. There is, however, nothing masculine or military about this most welcoming of houses, and no other Palladian house in Ireland equals it either for its architecture or its spectacular setting of natural beauty.

Russborough is the jewel in the crown of all Richard Castle's houses and the best preserved with every original feature still intact; stonework, statuary, inlaid floors, mantels and so on. It was built in 1741 by Joseph Leeson, first Earl of Milltown. Russborough is highly ornamented; the seven ground-floor reception rooms lead from one to the other, unrivalled in Ireland for the richness of their stucco decoration. Round each room, except the dining room, a mahogany

Russborough was designed by Richard Castle in 1741 for Joseph Leeson, first Earl of Milltown. The stable wing is to the left and the kitchen wing to the right. Utilitarian yards on either side help to create a façade 700 feet in length.

dado four feet high provides a sober anchor for these plaster flourishes. The very height of these dados is astonishing and completely dwarfs furniture of normal size. The lavish use of mahogany on the staircase, where the banisters are of elephantine proportions, is equally surprising. The white and gold front hall has a black Kilkenny marble fireplace; Richard Castle was fond of putting black mantels in the entrance halls of his houses, as he did for example at Westport House in Co. Mayo and at Leinster House in Dublin. The hall, which has a wooden floor, leads through to the saloon on axis to the front door. On stylistic grounds it is possible to assert that the plasterwork in the saloon, or principal drawing room, is by the Lafranchini. The rest of the very varied plaster decoration is probably the work of foreign craftsmen, or possibly Irishmen working alongside them. So that the saloon ceiling should not stand out as being very different from its neighbours the human figure, here in the form of cherubs, has a very subordinate part to play by comparison with the Lafranchinis' work elsewhere. The most astonishing plasterwork at Russborough is to be found on the staircase where the crowded effect caused one commentator to describe it as 'the ravings of a maniac', adding that he was sure the madman was Irish. The bedroom landing, lit by an oval lantern, is similar to that at Bellamont Forest in Co. Cavan.

Both the dining room and drawing room have coved ceilings and lavish Baroque plasterwork as well as mantelpieces made in Kilkenny by Mr Colles, who owned the marble-works there, to the design, it is believed, of the architect himself. The three rooms at the back of the house facing north, namely the music room, saloon and library, have

ABOVE The front hall has a black Kilkenny marble mantel – a type much favoured by the architect, Richard Castle, for the entrance halls of his houses. Above it hangs a painting by Oudry of an Indian buck and hounds straining at their leashes.

LEFT The dining room at Russborough has a monumental mantel of Irish manufacture with white marble adornments. The carpet was made specially for this room at the Royal Carpet Factory in Madrid.

OPPOSITE The walls of the saloon are covered in wine-red cut Genovese velvet dating from c. 1840, an ideal background for the paintings. The ceiling is by the Lafranchini brothers, and the mantel was made in London by Thomas Carter the Younger. Inlaid wood floors are seldom found in Ireland.

mantels of superb quality imported from England. In the little panelled boudoir there is a delicate mantelpiece of inlaid marble on a white background, made by Pietro Bossi, who worked in Dublin. It is of later date than the house. The inlaid wooden floor of the saloon is unusual for Ireland, being of a type found mainly on the Continent.

The detail of the panelling, coving and so on in the bedrooms is fastidious; the designs of some of the mantels on the upper floor are unusually modern but there is no question as to their being of the period. Russborough is somewhat more of a palace than a country

castle stronghold so that having the house surrounded by its farm buildings was a continuation of this arrangement. At Russborough the park is almost as symmetrical as the house. Leeson carved it out of barren territory beside the upper confines of the River Liffey and it is hard to imagine such an opportunity in England where old boundaries would intrude. One of the very few comments on record about Russborough in the eighteenth century refers to the lack of trees here at the time.

The series of grass terraces at the back of the house, framed now by

house; it is hard to imagine the customary jumble of walking sticks, gumboots and fishing rods in such rarefied surroundings. These would have been relegated to the colonnade passages with their stone floors.

Russborough is the most elaborate example of the agricultural complex in Ireland. Two utilitarian yards are to be found to either side of the house, creating a façade of 700 feet in length. This arrangement of wings and out-buildings derives from Palladio's recommendation that farm buildings be positioned far enough from the villa so as not to annoy with dust and noise but not so far as to be out of sight. Another factor that may help to explain the popularity of this arrangement in Ireland was that it served to lengthen the façade and make the house appear larger than it in fact was. For centuries farm animals for reasons of safety had lived within the confines of the keep or bawn beside the

magnificent beech trees, and the formal layout of the straight drive banked on either side, were the last gasp of the Classical garden layout in Ireland. The formal water at the back of the house is too high up to be visible even from the roof, let alone from the windows, and legend has it that the money had run out before the terraces could be adorned with steps, statues and balustrades. No such embellishments are likely to have been contemplated in 1741. In the nineteenth century flower beds were planted up outside the back windows of Powerscourt, Castletown, Carton, Lyons and many other places besides, but at Russborough the garden remained within its walls.

In 1951 Russborough came into the possession of Sir Alfred and Lady Beit. They had contemplated building a house in South Africa to house their great collection of paintings when Russborough came on

RIGHT Between the windows of the drawing room hangs an oval Irish mirror, complete with its glass candelabra, surrounded by an elaborate stucco frame with eagle atop.

OPPOSITE LEFT The stucco ornament on the staircase is as eccentric as it is elaborate. If there is a theme it is the chase; a music book is open at 'the early horn' and lugubrious hounds with floppy ears support the weighty plaster swags. Shields emblazoned with dogs' heads are surrounded by guns and bags for game. The Milltown crest is engraved on the landing window.

OPPOSITE RIGHT The bedroom landing is lit from overhead by an oval lantern in the same way as at Bellamont Forest in Co. Cavan.

the market and they came to Ireland instead; their choice was a happy one for this country.

Life amid such beauty during the Beits' regime at Russborough was suitably formal but never dull. Plans for a weekend were laid with loving care and precision long in advance, and the guests were drawn from artistic and intellectual circles as well as the *beau monde*. It was here, and in Ireland it could only have been here, that Kenneth Clark, Peter Quennell, Christopher Sykes, Gaston Palewski, Charles de Noailles and Diana Cooper would be found staying. A visit to Russborough during one of these weekends would provide an exciting change from Dublin society, rather like going abroad without all the bother of having to pack. All the latest books would be laid out on a table in the drawing room. Sometimes the candles on the chandelier in

the saloon would be lit, making the wine-red velvet walls glow with the softness of their light.

In 1974 a raid was carried out on Russborough by members of the IRA who stole the best paintings for ransom. Thankfully, the culprits were found and the paintings recovered. In spite of this experience the Beits have given the house and parkland to a foundation and opened Russborough to the public, moving into a wing of the house themselves. A second burglary in 1986 saw many of the best pictures leave under mysterious circumstances again, and at the time of writing only one has been found. Such problems would deter even the most intrepid benefactor, but not the Beits. Long may they remain at Russborough to make sure that everything is done as it should be – the house is an enduring monument to their munificence.

NEWBRIDGE
Donabate, Co. Dublin

The Revd Charles Cobbe came to Ireland in 1717 as Chaplain to the Viceroy, his cousin the Duke of Bolton, and enjoyed rapid promotion in the Church of Ireland, becoming Archbishop of Dublin in 1746. He had already purchased the land where Newbridge now stands, and in 1749 commissioned his friend George Semple to build the house. In the same year Semple added the 100-foot spire to St Patrick's Cathedral in Dublin.

The front hall has a paving of large black and white stone squares as at Castletown in Co. Kildare and an architectural mantel with the Cobbe coat of arms decorated with swans in carved stone. It is, also like Castletown, panelled in plaster and the general effect is sober tending towards the severe. Charles Cobbe, the builder of the house, died in 1765. He was succeeded by his son Thomas, who married Lady Elizabeth Beresford, the eighth and youngest daughter of the first Earl of Tyrone. Evidently bent on entertaining, they added a vast drawing room with a picture gallery to house the growing collection of old master paintings being purchased with the advice of Matthew Pilkington, Vicar of Donabate, author of the first English dictionary of artists in 1770, entitled *The Gentleman's and Connoisseur's Dictionary of Painters*. The new room, forty-five feet in length, was given an elaborate Rococo ceiling by Richard Williams. 'Williams the Stuccoer', as he is described in Newbridge account books, would appear to have

ABOVE The dining room has a black Kilkenny marble mantel of the architectural variety and 'Irish Chippendale' sideboards made specially for the room.

OPPOSITE The drawing room, which was added in 1765 for Thomas Cobbe, son of the builder of Newbridge. Thanks to the felicitous agreement between the Cobbes and Dublin County Council, the room looks the same as it always did.

LEFT Newbridge was built for the Revd Charles Cobbe, Archbishop of Dublin, in 1749 to the designs of George Semple. Since acquiring it in 1985, Dublin County Council has, to its eternal credit, replaced the glazing bars.

added some plaster flourishes to relieve the severity of the dining-room panels, besides which he almost certainly decorated the family pew in the little church of Donabate. The Cobbe family household accounts date back to the 1720s, before the building of Newbridge, and run almost continuously from then until the end of the nineteenth century. Purchases of pictures, furniture, china, statuary, trees and plants are all recorded. Much of the Regency furniture was supplied by the Dublin firm of Mack, Williams and Gibton who also made the curtains for the drawing room in 1828.

In the 1830s the finest picture in the collection, a large landscape by Hobbema, was sold by Thomas Cobbe's grandson Charles in order to rebuild all the houses on their mountain estates, now known as the Hobbema Cottages. The picture went into the Holford Collection at Dorchester House in London and fetched the sum of £3,000 – a staggering amount in those days. It is now at the Metropolitan Museum in New York. Charles Cobbe recorded his lengthy deliberations prior to the sale in his diary. He reasoned that the painting hung in a dark corner, hardly noticed and not appreciated by those who saw it. He felt that a much better picture would be presented to the Christian eye if he built warm, dry stone cottages for every tenant.

LEFT Newbridge has always had a museum; it is still intact with a fascinating wallcover, recently restored, of bamboo and Chinese paper resembling a print room.

BELOW The Lord Chancellor's coach made for 'Black Jack' FitzGibbon in 1790, was itself black until it was restored recently to its original state. Even the panels were painted out, probably for a royal funeral.

In 1986 Newbridge, complete with the loan of a great deal of the original contents, passed happily from the hands of the Cobbe family into the care of Dublin County Council. Glazing bars were replaced in the sash windows, missing since Victorian times, and the rooms on the ground floor and in the basement were arranged to show off the wonderfully robust but elegant interiors with their Irish furniture. The Cobbes still go there, by a unique arrangement that enables them to use what had been their own dining room for entertaining, and to stay upstairs in their own bedrooms.

FLORENCE COURT
Enniskillen, Co. Fermanagh

The best approach to Florence Court is to follow the winding drive that leads up to the front of this majestic house. To the left the ominous Cuilcagh mountains, shaped like a great basking whale, lie sleeping. The parkland is rough and appears to have escaped being tamed by man, although William King, a landscape designer and follower of 'Capability' Brown, did work here in 1780. It is thought that he also made plans for the landscaping of Castle Coole and Downhill. The original Florence Court yew, whose progeny swept the length and breadth of Ireland, is still alive and stands in a clearing in the woods. It can only be propagated by cuttings.

The house originally consisted only of the central block which is considerably earlier and cruder in its detail than the wings. The architect of this is unknown but it was probably begun by Sir John Cole (1680–1726) who had married Florence Wrey of Cornwall for whom the house was named. Their son was made Lord Mountflorence and his son, William, became the first Earl of Enniskillen.

In 1767 William inherited and is thought to have employed Davis Ducart, the Sardinian architect, to add the straight arcades and pavilions to the front of the house. This was a similar arrangement to the one that Ducart had given Kilshannig in Co. Cork two years earlier. These additions are well articulated and blend successfully with the central block; there is nothing amateurish about them and they are certainly the work of an accomplished architect.

The main feature of the interior is the lavish Rococo plaster

The central block may be as early as 1730 and the arcades and wings may date from 1770. The house remained in the Cole family until it was given to the National Trust in 1953, but little is known about its architectural history.

OPPOSITE A small room above the front door, known as the Venetian room, has the most elaborate Rococo plasterwork in the house.

ABOVE The Rococo plasterwork on the staircase walls appears to date from c. 1750; it was restored by the firm of the late Sir Albert Richardson after the fire.

OPPOSITE BELOW The dining-room ceiling was saved on the night of the fire in 1955 by the inspired action of Mr Bertie Pierce who drilled holes in it to let the water escape.

ornament which, if it had been made in Dublin, would date from around 1750 but here it could have been executed as late as 1767, Florence Court being so far from the capital. Besides, Ducart built two houses in the south during the mid-sixties, both with rich Rococo interiors. Perhaps if it was he who added the wings, he could also have found a plasterer to decorate the interior of the main block in the manner he was known to favour.

The house was given to the National Trust in 1953 by the fifth Earl of Enniskillen and his son, Viscount Cole, and an endowment was provided by the Government for its maintenance. Two years later a disastrous fire broke out that virtually gutted the main block. Fortunately it was restored; even the plasterwork was remade, using photographs taken in 1915. No record had been made of the plaster decoration in the nursery where drums, rocking-horses and other toys were originally incorporated in the ornament. The dining-room ceiling was saved by the quick thinking of a builder who drilled holes in it to allow the water from the fire engines to escape.

BANTRY HOUSE
Bantry, Co. Cork

Bantry House, with its southern, sleepy character and magnificent art collection, has all the magic and mystery that visitors to Ireland expect to find in a country house. Slightly *délabré*, it stands at the foot of a steep terraced garden overlooking Bantry Bay and Whiddy Island in the most dramatic and beautiful situation imaginable. The house today is mainly the creation of Richard White, second Earl of Bantry; the title is now extinct and the property has descended through the female line.

The first house to be built here was erected by the Hutchinson family in about 1710; it was called Blackrock and formed the nucleus of the present Bantry House. In 1739 the property was acquired by an earlier Richard White, a farmer who by continual acquisition became the largest landowner in the area.

During the 1790s a band of Irish patriots, the United Irishmen, encouraged by the American and French Revolutions, were planning to free Ireland from English rule. They sought and obtained help, as had the Americans before them, from the French Government. In December 1796, a fleet of forty-three ships and 16,000 men sailed from Brest to invade Ireland. A tremendous hurricane along the route caused the fleet to disperse, and only sixteen vessels and 6,000 men managed to rendezvous at Bantry Bay. After waiting several days for the remainder, and with no attempt to land in the face of strong northeasterly winds, the fleet sailed back to France. Bitterly disappointed Wolfe Tone, the Irish revolutionary leader, aboard the *Indomptable*, wrote in his diary, 'We were close enough to toss a biscuit ashore'.

It was quick thinking on the part of Richard White, grandson of the first Richard, that propelled his family into the limelight. White himself would hardly have claimed to have expelled the French fleet. He did, however, show great initiative in obtaining intelligence of the invading fleet's movements throughout the crisis, organized local defences, and placed his home, then called Seafield, at the disposal of the British General and his staff. In March 1797 he was raised to the peerage of Ireland as Baron Bantry, 'in consideration of the zeal and loyalty he displayed . . . during a period of great trouble . . . for having been the means of repelling the French fleet when they entered Bantry Bay in 1796'. In 1800 he was made a Viscount.

In 1816 Richard White was created Earl of Bantry and his son, also Richard, Viscount Berehaven, travelled all over the continent and as far afield as Russia where he purchased the furniture and works of art for which the house is famous. In 1820 a six-bay addition with bowed ends facing north across Bantry Bay was added. This provided two large drawing rooms and bedrooms above.

In 1845 the house was greatly enlarged and remodelled by Richard White, Viscount Berehaven and later second Earl of Bantry. He added two more wings which face south up the steep incline of the terraced gardens. To start with the five-bay central block which now houses the long library on this front was left empty and consisted of a one-storey conservatory. Soon, however, the library was built, over sixty feet in length, with four freestanding scagliola Corinthian columns supporting the compartmented ceiling. Thus the house dates from at least four different periods. It was given architectural unity by the giant brick pilasters that surround it and the stone balustrade with which it is capped.

In 1739, Richard White purchased an existing house on Bantry Bay which has been added to over the years by both himself and his descendants. The Whites became Earls of Bantry in 1816, and although the title is extinct the property has descended through the female line to the present owners.

LEFT The dining room is dominated by full length portraits of George III and his Queen in elaborately carved frames which hang above an immense sideboard made for the room.

ABOVE The Aubusson tapestries in the drawing room were brought back from France by the second Earl of Bantry, and are said to have been ordered by Louis XV as a wedding present for Marie-Antoinette.

LEFT The library, over sixty feet in length, overlooks the steep slope of terraces at the back of the house; it was built *c.* 1850 by the second Earl of Bantry.

OPPOSITE Twin yards with cupolas over the pediments were created by the second Earl of Bantry and placed symmetrically on either side of the house.

A generous porch over forty feet in width supported by six widely spaced Corinthian columns makes an unusual introduction to the splendours within. Every sort and kind of decorative motif has been employed by succeeding generations at Bantry. The blue dining room is dominated by life-sized portraits of George III and Queen Charlotte by Allan Ramsay, the Court painter, in lavishly carved frames. By command of the King these were presented to the first Earl of Bantry in gratitude for his efforts in helping to repel the French invasion of 1796. There are two drawing rooms with outstanding French tapestries from the Gobelin, Beauvais and Aubusson workshops brought to Ireland after the French Revolution by the second Earl of Bantry. The Aubusson tapestries in the rose drawing room were made for Marie Antoinette on her marriage to the Dauphin, later Louis XVI, and were commissioned by Louis XV; they represent a *Fête Champêtre*.

Since he inherited Bantry from his mother in 1978, Egerton Shelswell-White has extensively restored the Italian garden and the main house. Both wings, which had become so ruinous that their demolition had been seriously considered, have been restored to provide accommodation for tourists. The east stable block has been rescued from dereliction and houses an exhibition entitled *1796 Armada Trust*. Although Mr Shelswell-White 'shares' Bantry with 47,000 visitors annually, he continues to inhabit the house of his forebears with his wife and children and plays the trombone in the local band.

KILSHANNIG
Rathcormac, Co. Cork

Kilshannig is well sited, standing on a ridge, affording it spectacular views over the surrounding countryside. It was designed in 1765 by Davis Ducart, the Sardinian architect, for a Cork banker named Abraham Devonsher. The faded brick entrance front faces south, with wings projecting forward to create an elegant forecourt. The back of the house is of limestone with straight arcades similar to those designed by Ducart for the Limerick Custom House (1765–9) and Castletown Cox (1767). These arcades lead to one-and-a-half-storey pavilions, with *oeil de boeuf* windows above and arched windows below. These pavilions once had copper domes and may have been crowned with lanterns as at Castletown Cox.

The front hall has a grandiose stone mantel flanked by caryatids of bearded men. Ingenious use of columns in the corners of the hall give the illusion that it is elliptical. The black and white stone floor carries through along the axial corridors to either side, and there is a black star in stone at the foot of the circular staircase which forms a cardinal rose with North, South, East and West as well as the intermediate points, Northeast and so on. This star is not quite symmetrically placed, which mystified the owners until they understood that it was a compass.

The plasterwork executed by the Lafranchini is the great feature of the house, being more accomplished here than anywhere in Ireland. The coved ceiling of the hall is one storey high, and that of the saloon into which it leads is one and a half; this sudden change of height is breathtaking. Attention is at once drawn to the ceiling, dominated by the figures of Bacchus, Pan and Ariadne with putti, scrollwork and fruit surrounding beribboned ovals of the four elements. The modelling of the figures is a feat of delicacy and graceful movement. The library is to one side of the saloon and the dining room to the other, both have amazing ceilings; the dining room has representations of dead game and a fox in the coving.

Commander and Mrs Douglas Merry have lived here since 1962 and have done much to improve the house and the grounds.

Kilshannig was built for a Cork banker named Abraham Devonsher in 1765 to the designs of the Sardinian architect, Davis Ducart. One front is of brick and the other of limestone.

RIGHT The front hall has a black and white floor and a stone mantel supported by bearded caryatids. The Lafranchini plasterwork throughout the house is of superb quality.

BELOW The drawing room has a plaster ceiling by Paul and Philip Lafranchini, depicting Bacchus, Pan and Ariadne.

CASTLETOWN
Piltown, Co. Kilkenny

Castletown was built in 1767 for the Archbishop of Cashel, Michael Cox, whose arms are to be seen on the garden front. He was the fifth and youngest son of Sir Richard Cox of Dunmanway in Co. Cork, who was made Lord Chancellor of Ireland in 1703. The house is generally known as Castletown Cox to avoid confusion with Castletown in Co. Kildare.

Michael Cox came into possession of the property by his first marriage to Anne Cooke, who had inherited it from her brother. Cox's second wife was Anne O'Brien, granddaughter of the Earl of Inchiquin; she died in 1746 after two years of marriage and her disconsolate husband erected a magnificent statue to her memory, representing Piety leaning on an Urn, in Kilkenny Cathedral. Cox left an empty space beneath her epitaph for his to be inscribed, but when he died in 1779 his family did nothing about this, giving rise to a poem being penned by Edmund Malone, the celebrated wit:

> Vainest of mortals, hadst thou sense or grace,
> Thou ne'er hadst left this ostentatious space,
> Nor given thine enemies such ample room
> To tell posterity, upon thy tomb,
> A truth, by friends and foes alike confess'd,
> That by this blank thy life is best express'd.

LEFT Castletown 'Cox', was built in 1767 for Michael Cox, Archbishop of Cashel, by the Sardinian architect, Davis Ducart, whose masterpiece it is.

The architect of Castletown Cox was the Sardinian, Davis Ducart, and it is generally considered to be his masterpiece. Kilshannig in Co. Cork, Ducart's other great house, also had twin pavilions surmounted by domes, linked to the main block by straight arcades. Those at Castletown are still intact and form the apex of the twin 'L'-shaped yards, stables on the left, carriages on the right. The design is one of overall perfection and the cut-limestone with which the house is built is beautifully carved. An unusual feature is that the quoins at the corners are not indented as they normally are but make a straight vertical line as they frame the façade. The garden front with its giant fluted Corinthian pilasters and breathtakingly beautiful arcades is spectacular; moreover,

LEFT The library, on axis to the hall, has three windows that enjoy views to the south-west; it occupies the centre of the garden front. The decoration on the mantelpiece is echoed in the frieze.

LEFT The walls of the dining room are panelled in plaster and enlivened with Rococo ornament which is a particular feature of the house.

LEFT The main staircase leads up to one floor only; the bedrooms on the floor above this are approached by a service staircase that also serves the basement.

OPPOSITE The topiary garden and one of the domed pavilions at either end of the garden front. Straight arcades were also used by Ducart at the Custom House in Limerick.

it faces southwest, unlike many houses designed by southern architects which have their living rooms facing north.

The front hall is paved in black and white as at Kilshannig and a screen of monolith grey limestone columns supports the weight of the wall above. These are beautifully carved and fluted, with elaborate Corinthian capitals. The original stone mantel, with its twin female caryatids, is an echo of the stone hall mantel at Kilshannig supported by two bearded satyrs in profile. All the ground-floor rooms, and the staircase, have rich Rococo plaster decoration by Patrick Osborne of Waterford. The frieze in the library is closely modelled on the white marble carved leaves and flowers in the mantel.

The house stands well above the formal gardens, admitting plenty of light to the basement; a terrace or balcony, approached by curved stairs, is a central feature of the garden front.

Castletown was sold in 1909 to Colonel W. H. Wyndham-Quin, under whose regime the most attractive formal box gardens were laid out. The Colonel succeeded to the Earldom of Dunraven in 1926, and sold Castletown shortly afterwards to Major-General E. R. Blacque, the son-in-law of Admiral Lord Beresford. His son Charles sold the property in 1976 to Nicholas Walsh who was principally interested in the land and never moved into the house.

Baron and Baroness de Breffny bought the house from him in 1979;

the Baron died ten years later. Baroness de Breffny, by whose kindness it is illustrated here, was born in Finland. Her late husband wrote books on Irish castles, houses and churches. He founded both the *Irish Arts Review* and the *Irish Ancestor*, journals of artistic and genealogical interest.

The Irish Georgian Society has helped raise funds for restoring the adjacent Protestant church at Castlane, empty and abandoned like so many of its kind when isolated from a town or village. The saving of this fine building was undertaken in memory of Colonel E. Blacque, cousin of the Blacques of Castletown, by his widow who inhabited the former rectory beside it.

ÁRAS AN UACHTARÁIN
Phoenix Park, Dublin

Dublin is fortunate to have on its doorstep a public park of 1,752 acres extending along the northern bank of the River Liffey towards Chapelizod. It is an area of considerable natural beauty with glens and valleys galore; one of these, known as the Furry Glen, is presumably a misnomer for 'Fairy Glen'. Within this vast expanse of grass and trees several lesser demesnes have been created which are like islands, floating in the sea. The most important of these is the house of the President, or in Irish, *Áras an Uachtaráin*, formerly the Viceregal Lodge.

The Rt. Hon. Nathaniel Clements, MP, was appointed Ranger and Master of the Game in the Phoenix Park in 1751. For many years Clements had been involved in the development of Georgian Dublin with Luke Gardiner, who owned vast amounts of property on the north side. He had worked with Sir Edward Lovett Pearce and Richard Castle, both as a contractor and an amateur architect. In the year of his appointment, Clements designed and built for himself an elegant Palladian house of red brick with single-storey wings and curved sweeps, on an 'island' of ninety-two acres (extended to 160 acres) with trees and an informal lake. Thirty years later his son, Robert Clements, later first Earl of Leitrim, sold Phoenix Lodge and grounds to the Government as a summer residence for the Lord-Lieutenant, or Viceroy, who held court in Dublin Castle during the winter season.

Plate 1 of Thomas Milton's *Views of Seats*, 1783, illustrates Phoenix Lodge and describes it as a 'neat, plain, brick building, and the Rooms within, are conveniently disposed. The Offices project on each side, and are joined to the House by circular sweeps'. From time to time it proved necessary to add on to the Phoenix or Viceregal Lodge, now that it housed the King's representative instead of the Park Ranger, but Clements's original house is still virtually intact at the core of the building to this day.

A handsome Doric portico was added on to the front in 1808 providing additional entrance space as the hall must have proved too small when there was an official reception. Unfortunately, this obscures Clements's handsome *demi-lune* window above the door which can be seen in the engraving by Milton. The *demi-lune* was a feature sometimes found in other country houses attributed to Clements by the Knight of Glin; these include Newberry Hall and Lodge Park in Co. Kildare, and Colganstown in Co. Dublin.

The front hall has a coffered, barrel-vaulted ceiling and a screen of fluted Doric columns. It leads to a top-lit passage where copies of the Lafranchini plaster plaques at Riverstown House in Co. Cork are ranged on either side, representing gods and goddesses. The passage leads to the early nineteenth-century State drawing room where foreign diplomats present their credentials to the President on their arrival in Ireland. The ceiling of this room, representing 'Time rescuing Truth from the assaults of Discord and Envy' is also copied from Riverstown. The carpet, woven in Donegal, was designed by Raymond McGrath incorporating the 'Riverine Heads' representing

LEFT The residence of the President of Ireland was built in 1751 by Nathaniel Clements, Ranger of the Phoenix Park, to his own designs. The park is situated on the outskirts of Dublin and extends to 1,752 acres.

OPPOSITE The drawing room at the centre of the original house, facing the garden. The egg and dart door frames were originally shouldered; the twin marble mantels date from 1751.

RIGHT The dining room used for meetings of the Council of State, has a ceiling attributed to Bartholomew Cramillion representing Aesop's Fables that dates from 1751, and a superb eighteenth-century mirror from Russborough in Co. Wicklow, part of the Milltown Bequest to the nation.

OPPOSITE The ballroom, known as *An Seomra Mor*, where foreign envoys present their credentials, has copies of the plasterwork of 1745 in the dining room of Riverstown in Co. Cork, executed by the Lafranchini brothers. More Riverstown plaques can be seen in the passage beyond.

the principal rivers of Ireland, that adorn the façade of the Custom House in Dublin. Beyond is a State dining room with a minstrels' gallery.

The small dining room, used for meetings of the Council of State, has a gilded plaster ceiling with scenes from *Aesop's Fables* attributed to Bartholomew Cramillion; it has always been in the original Clements house. The vignettes on the long sides illustrate the Fox and Stork while the short sides show the Fox and Crow and the Fox and Grapes respectively. A superb mirror, part of the Milltown Bequest from Russborough, and portraits of former presidents, adorn the walls.

The drawing room, which is on axis to the front door, has its original ceiling of Rococo plasterwork enclosed in a series of compartments and the original pair of white marble mantels. The Donegal carpet was woven for the room, its design based on a French Empire *Savonnerie*. Tall windows open on to the garden front beneath a pediment supported by four giant Ionic columns. This was designed by Francis Johnston in 1815 to create a focal point for the garden front which had been extended by five bays to either side in 1802. At the same time the red brick was plastered over and painted white, unwittingly giving Ireland its very own White House. In 1840 Decimus Burton laid out the formal gardens to the southwest and designed several of the park lodges and gates. A wing was added to the east end of the garden front for Queen Victoria's visit in 1849.

The President's study contains the most extraordinary ceiling in the house, introduced here by the late Dr C. P. Curran, the great authority on Irish plasterwork. This was rescued from the demolished Mespil House in Dublin, which was built in 1751, the very date of its adoptive home. Attributed to Bartholomew Cramillion, it represents Jupiter at the centre with his thunderbolts and sitting on a cloud, surrounded by the four elements; the four seasons adorn the corners. It is remarkable for the lightness and elegance of the Rococo design and must inspire the President when at work.

After Ireland gained her independence in 1922 the Viceregal Lodge was occupied by the Governor General and since 1938 it has been the residence of the President of Ireland.

THE
ADAM STYLE
REACHES
IRELAND

The style of interior decoration associated with the work of the Scottish architect, Robert Adam (1728–92) and his brothers became popular in Ireland from the 1770s. Its chief Irish exponent was Michael Stapleton (*fl.* 1770–1801), who inherited the architectural practice of Robert West (d. 1790) and whose Adamesque interiors were executed with the utmost skill and imagination. Though he used moulds, much of his work was freehand and of a particularly high quality which was difficult for his imitators to achieve. They relied on moulds alone, a fact which was particularly regrettable in Ireland where the exuberance of the Rococo style had given such successful rein to a whole generation of stuccodores.

From 1771 Robert Adam created some magnificent interiors for Headfort in Co. Meath, a house designed by George Semple in the 1760s, and they are in fact more sophisticated than the architecture of the house itself. Adam never came to Ireland; his drawings for Headfort are at the Paul Mellon Center for British Art in Yale, Connecticut, all in colour. Sir William Chambers (1723–96) likewise never crossed the Irish sea, but he was an important figure in the story of neo-Classicism and had a powerful Irish patron in the Earl of Charlemont. Chambers would send samples of colour for painting the interiors he designed, although he feared that the colour might change if exposed to the sea air during the course of the Channel crossing.

James Wyatt (1746–1813) also had a considerable Irish practice. He designed the grandest neo-Classical house in Ireland, Castle Coole in Co. Fermanagh, giving it an interior of the utmost elegance and purity and a magnificent exterior of Portland stone. The style overlapped with the Gothic Revival and faded out at the end of the eighteenth century.

James Gandon (1743–1823) was head and shoulders above the rest of Irish architects that worked in the Classical tradition during the late eighteenth and early nineteenth centuries. A pupil of Chambers, he was brought over to build the new Custom House in Dublin in 1781 and made Ireland his home. Gandon was too occupied with the major public buildings that were entrusted to him to build up a very large private practice; however, drawings have recently come to light that confirm him as the designer of several private commissions. Emo Court in Co. Laois was begun, but not completed, by Gandon, who also designed the very fine small church of Coolbanagher and other buildings nearby for Lord Carlow who had largely been responsible for his invitation to design the Custom House ten years earlier. Unexecuted designs by Gandon for Slane Castle in Co. Meath showed him to be an accomplished if reluctant Goth, although they include a very theatrical arrangement of Classical garden staircases flowing from the base of the neo-Gothic castle down towards the River Boyne. Abbeville in Co. Dublin, the residence of Charles J. Haughey, Taoiseach of Ireland, has a superb interior with niches and plasterwork of great refinement in the delicate tradition of Robert Adam. Abbeville has a stable yard akin to that at Carrigglas in Co. Longford, also by Gandon, which is illustrated on page 212 in the Victorian section as the house itself is of a later date. Gandon's elegant designs for an unexecuted domed villa for Carrigglas, with an oval room on axis to the entrance door, still exist. Emsworth in Co. Dublin is a villa by Gandon, built in 1794, that has fortunately survived intact.

The Custom House and Beresford Place, the Four Courts, the King's Inns, the Royal Military Infirmary, Carlisle Bridge (now O'Connell Bridge) and the House of Lords portico, besides other alterations to the Parliament House (now the Bank of Ireland), constitute Gandon's major achievements in Dublin. His excursions to the provinces include a noble Court House for Waterford (demolished). Gandon died in his house at Lucan in Co. Dublin in 1823. It had been rumoured that George IV was to bestow a knighthood on the old man when the King drove through Lucan in 1821, but the royal *cortège* drove by without stopping and Gandon was wheeled back up to his house in his chair without the honour being conferred.

MARINO CASINO
Clontarf, Co. Dublin

In the eighteenth century it would have taken two days for the Earl of Charlemont to make the arduous journey from his Dublin house to his seat in Co. Armagh. In order to be able to enjoy the country air during the Dublin Season, he would repair to his 'marine villa' at Clontarf, whence he could admire views of both the sea and of the Dublin mountains to the south. He embellished the park at Marino, as it was called, with a lake, a rustic cottage and a Gothic seat; moreover, the public was allowed in to share in the appreciation of these improvements.

In 1762 he began to build the little house or 'Casino' which is the only one of his creations here to survive to the present day. The architect was Sir William Chambers, who had originally conceived the design as an end pavilion for Harewood House in Yorkshire that was never built. The Marino Casino at Clontarf is Ireland's first neo-Classical building. It is easy to see the influence it had on the Custom House in Dublin, designed by Chambers's pupil, James Gandon, twenty years later.

The Marino Casino is one of the most perfect buildings in Europe. An engraving of it was published in Chambers's *A Treatise on Civil Architecture* (1759) so that it soon became known beyond these shores. It cost £60,000 to build. The workmen, as they handed the valuable carved Portland stones from one to another, are said to have taken

OPPOSITE The Marino Casino, on the outskirts of Dublin, was designed by Sir William Chambers as an elaborate garden pavilion for the 'Volunteer' Earl of Charlemont in 1758; it is one of the most distinguished and original buildings of its date in Europe.

ABOVE LEFT Four attendant lions keep guard at the corners of the building; the sculptor was Joseph Wilton, who carved the gilded State Coach used at coronations in London, also designed by Chambers.

ABOVE CENTRE The front hall with exquisite plasterwork has a little fireplace, and three mahogany doors with egg and dart panelling which face the entrance.

LEFT The vaulted basement kitchen where the hollowed-out columns contain downpipes that carry the rainwater from the roof.

ABOVE The china closet has delicate leaves and tendrils in the stucco panelling as well as the coving on the ceiling.

RIGHT The Apollo room, with its coved and coffered ceiling, has an inlaid floor of intricate workmanship.

OPPOSITE The master bedroom, where the Greek key pattern is found both in the ceiling and in the inlay of the floor.

extra care 'because every broken stone is another townland gone'. The urns on the parapet were once functional chimneys, and on the flat roof, with its superlative view, a temporary awning or canopy could be erected on a fine day. The freestanding columns were hollowed out to conduct the rainwater down from the roof; no unsightly gutters or downpipes were allowed to sully the purity of the architecture.

The interior consists of a number of small but exquisitely proportioned rooms. The entrance hall, with its elaborately carved door frames, its geometric parquet floor of rare woods and its magnificent plasterwork prepare the visitor for the splendour to come. The intricate patterns on the floor of the saloon echo those of the hall and the coffered and compartmented ceiling has the head of Apollo emerging from a sunburst as its centrepiece.

The study, its domed ceiling ornamented with figures from the zodiac, occupies the east arm of the building. Opposite is a room originally designed as a bedroom until the second Lady Charlemont decided to use it as a china closet. Garlands link agricultural implements on the plastered ceiling and the walls are panelled. On the first floor is the main bedroom, sparkling with its gilded plasterwork; the kitchen in the basement has a vaulted ceiling.

On the death of the second Earl of Charlemont the title passed to his nephew and in 1881 the estate was sold. Owing to years of neglect and vandalism, the Casino fell into a state of serious disrepair and this unique treasure was almost lost to the nation. In 1930 a special Act was passed in the Dáil to enable a building of such a late date to be taken into the care of the Office of Public Works. Due to lack of funds, it was not until 1974 that any major restoration took place. The Casino has at last been beautifully restored and opened to visitors. It is an ideal place to stop, for those visiting architectural monuments, *en route* from Dublin to Malahide Castle, six miles further north.

ABBEY LEIX
Abbeyleix, Co. Laois

At the dissolution of the monasteries in the sixteenth century, 820 acres of abbey lands on the banks of the River Nore reverted to the Crown. Thomas Butler, Earl of Ormonde, was granted this land in 1562 but it is doubtful that he built a house here. In 1698 Thomas Vesey, the son of the Archbishop of Tuam, acquired the leasehold in a generous marriage settlement from his father-in-law, Denny Muschamp, a successful seventeenth-century property speculator who had bought land in some ten different counties in Ireland. However, it was twenty years before Thomas's attempts to buy the freehold from the Earl of Belfast were successful.

After his marriage, Thomas Vesey was created a baronet and subsequently, following the calling of his father and grandfather, took holy orders, becoming in turn Bishop of Killaloe and Bishop of Ossory. His son Sir John Vesey, the second baronet, was made Baron Knapton in 1769, and his son, Thomas, the second Lord Knapton, was the builder of the present house.

Work commenced in 1773 on a site due south of the former modest house. Drawings by the fashionable James Wyatt, then only twenty-seven years old, are in the collection of the National Library in Dublin and show the elevation and floor plans which were only slightly modified prior to execution. There is a painting hanging in the house today showing how it looked when first built with a plain three-storey, seven-bay façade surmounted by a low pediment. Wyatt also designed the plasterwork in the main rooms and his drawings for these, dated 1773, are in the Prints and Drawings Collection in the Metropolitan

Museum in New York. As Wyatt did not visit Ireland until 1785, he would have relied upon a local architect or builder and there exists in the family collection of papers some interesting correspondence from this period including a detailed contract from a William Colles of Co. Kilkenny 'For the stone cutting of a house for the said Lord Knapton'. One condition of the contract suggests that the work was not being carried out to the detailed specification and design of an architect since

ABOVE The terraced gardens were modelled on those at the Woronzow's Villa Aloupka on the shore of the Black Sea. The third Viscountess was the granddaughter of Count Simon Woronzow, Russian Ambassador to the Court of St James during the Napoleonic period.

LEFT Abbey Leix was built for Thomas Vesey, second Lord Knapton, in 1773 to the designs of James Wyatt. Three years later, Knapton was created Viscount de Vesci.

OPPOSITE The entrance front. The balustraded parapet and carved stone window surrounds were added to the façade by the second Viscount.

the contract continues '. . . it is agreed that the said Lord Knapton shall not be permitted to alter the cornice mould from a plain Tuscan cornice to any other mould without first agreeing with said Colles for the rate thereof: if a better mould, a larger, and if a worse mould, a smaller price'.

In 1776 the second Lord Knapton was created Viscount de Vesci, reverting to the old Norman version of his family name for the title. Towards the end of the eighteenth century, the marriage of his grandfather, Sir Thomas, the Bishop of Ossory, to Mary Muschamp paid further dividends when the second Viscount de Vesci inherited extensive additional properties. His son Thomas was even considered a worthy husband for Lady Emma Herbert, daughter of the Earl of Pembroke and granddaughter of Russia's Ambassador to the Court of St James, Count Simon Woronzow. With her flair and enthusiasm for design and his money, they were able to add a further storey of staff accommodation into the roof cavity of the house, effectively hiding the new dormer windows behind a balustraded parapet. At this time the house was given a new stucco covering with heavy blocking around the ground-floor windows and shouldered surrounds to those of the

The drawing room has an old William Morris wallpaper of vivid blue beneath a white and gold ceiling by Wyatt, whose design for it is at the Metropolitan Museum, New York.

floor above, with three balconies to emphasize the central windows of both the front and back of the house. Many improvements were made to the gardens at this time, most notably the laying out of the formal *parterre*, the design of which is based upon that at Count Woronzow's palace in the Crimea which Emma had visited. Emma's desire to leave her mark on Abbey Leix is evidenced today by the fact that she had her own monogram (rather than that of her husband) placed in so many positions, from the wrought-iron garden gates to the façade of the local school.

Originally the village of Abbeyleix was low-lying, situated beside the river. It was pulled down in about 1780 when the present town, with its wide streets and cut-stone houses, was built by the Veseys. The family was held in such high repute that it was not thought necessary to build a demesne wall to enclose the parkland.

The late nineteenth century saw Abbey Leix as the western outpost

of 'The Souls', that dazzling galaxy of friends which included some of the most brilliant men as well as the cleverest and loveliest women of the time. The library on the southwest corner of the house had been extended to treble its original size, and a succession of summer house parties included Arthur Balfour, J. P. Mahaffy, Detmar Blow, and Sibell Grosvenor. Embellishments of this time, very much in the taste of 'The Souls', include the wonderfully vivid blue wallpaper by William Morris which still hangs in the drawing room; additional Morris fabrics and wallpapers remain in some of the upstairs rooms.

Almost every carpet in the house today is a product of the Abbeyleix Carpet Factory, started in the main street of the town in 1906 by Ivo, fifth Viscount de Vesci. It provided sorely needed employment for many local girls who might otherwise have been forced to emigrate. The designs were of Turkish inspiration and such was the quality of materials used that these carpets can still be seen in many of the grander houses of Ireland and England today. Smart Edwardian visitors would be taken to the factory by way of an afternoon's entertainment, and having inspected and admired the work and signed the visitors' book they would be expected to make a purchase for their own house.

The front hall has a portrait of Archbishop Vesey, in a black frame surmounted by a mitre, above the mantel. The floor is paved in black and white stone.

Substantial orders were received from the United States and carpets were also made for many of the luxury ocean liners including the *Titanic*, on which, incidentally, a number of people from the town of Abbeyleix were lost when she went down.

The fact that Abbey Leix remains one of the few estates left relatively intact within its setting of estate cottages, parkland and woods is largely due to the high proportion of forestry land which, together with town property, was exempted from the Wyndham Act in 1903 whereby tenant farms were bought out by law. The oldest oak tree in Ireland has been standing for over a thousand years in one of the few remaining fragments of continuous primeval oak forest left in the country. Acorns from this forest are still regularly collected and planted to ensure the same degree of continuity in the woodlands that can be found in the gardens and the house, the result of one family's uninterrupted care since the time that it was built.

LUCAN HOUSE
Lucan, Co. Dublin

The demesne of Lucan is still known as Sarsfield's Demesne, because the great soldier, Patrick Sarsfield, leader of the Irish in the Williamite Wars, hero of the Siege of Limerick, owned it together with the castle which once stood here. When ennobled by James II in 1691, he took the title Earl of Lucan but left Ireland with the 'Wild Geese' and fell at the Battle of Landen in Flanders. The estate came to the Vesey family through the first Agmondisham Vesey marrying Charlotte, the Sarsfield heiress. The Binghams, Earls of Lucan of the second creation, descend from her, but the Lucan property was left by Vesey to a son by his second wife who, like his father, rejoiced in the remarkable christian name of Agmondisham.

Lucan House was built by the second Agmondisham Vesey in 1780 to a design of his own invention. He was named Professor of Architecture in Samuel Johnson's 'Utopian University' and appears to have been an amateur architect of considerable talent. The oval dining room was possibly the inspiration for the oval room at the White House. Both are on axis to the front hall, and Lucan was built shortly before James Hoban, the architect of the White House, emigrated from Ireland to make his fortune in the New World in 1784.

The delicate plasterwork at Lucan is the work of Michael Stapleton; the Wedgwood room has painted panels in *grisaille* and mauve *trompe l'oeil*, and an interesting ceiling pulled down at the corners like a tent. Drawings for the plasterwork here are in the National Library in Dublin but are not signed. The painted panels are by de Gree who also worked on Abbey Leix for a Vesey cousin, Viscount de Vesci. Artists were frequently passed on from one house to another in this way. The tent-like ceiling in the Wedgwood room was repeated by Stapleton in two Dublin houses: Powerscourt House, South William Street and No. 17 St Stephen's Green, now the Kildare Street and University Club.

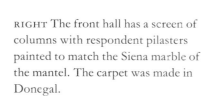

LEFT The monument to General Sarsfield, Earl of Lucan, designed by James Wyatt in the form of a triangle resting on the backs of three tortoises.

RIGHT The front hall has a screen of columns with respondent pilasters painted to match the Siena marble of the mantel. The carpet was made in Donegal.

OPPOSITE Lucan House, was built by Agmondisham Vesey in 1780 to a design of his own invention. This elegant Italianate villa is, suitably enough, today the residence of the Italian Ambassador to Ireland.

RIGHT The oval dining room has a pair of dummy mirrored windows matching the three real windows that look down to the river. There is a round sitting room above.

Before the days of photography it was easier for the stuccodore to get away with using the same design in more than one house. The use of moulds made this easier in the Adam period, but even the florid Baroque or Rococo Italian plasterers, the Lafranchini, repeated themselves. A smaller version of their great ceiling in the saloon of Carton can be found at No. 85 St Stephen's Green, and the staircase decoration they gave to Castletown is closely paralleled at No. 9 St Stephen's Green. Today, if an expensive decorator gave two clients the same interior it would be as dangerous for him as when two ladies of fashion find themselves dressed identically.

Lucan House is hemmed in between the Galway road and the River Liffey. By 1780 it would have been unthinkable to have a garden that could be seen from the house, and the land that surrounds it was laid out as parkland. The walled garden was the far side of the main road, approached by a tunnel. In the wood there is a Gothic hermitage with a cold bath fed by a natural spring. Sarsfield's Monument, designed by James Wyatt, a triangular pedestal of cut stone mounted on three tortoises and supporting an urn, has recently been moved from its

clearing in the woods and now stands beside the house. Two other similar monuments by Wyatt are in England.

Lucan descended through the female line to Captain Richard Colthurst who sold it to the O'Conor Don in 1932. The O'Conors lived in a very remote part of Ireland at Clonalis in Co. Roscommon. They had daughters to bring up and bring out, and needed somewhere nearer Dublin to launch them into society. Madam O'Conor belonged to an English Catholic family whose fortune had come from salt. Her father was responsible for the building of St James's, Spanish Place, in London, the fashionable Catholic church. Douglas Hyde, a Protestant and the first President of Ireland, was a friend and frequent visitor to the house.

The Italian government acquired Lucan as the residence of its Ambassador to Ireland after the Second World War. The Italians as a result have the finest embassy of any country and as Lucan resembles a villa in the Veneto, it was an appropriate choice. Successive ambassadors have added to the furnishings, and the house with its wonderful interior has been well cared for.

LEFT The Wedgwood room has a ceiling with its corners pulled down to give the effect of a tent, and panels painted *en grisaille* by Peter de Gree.

RIGHT The library has the original gold and white bookcases that were made for the room, with gilt chicken wire to discourage the borrowing of books.

BELOW The bedroom landing was once heated by an iron stove in the shape of an urn; light emanates from the generous Palladian window on the staircase which looks on to the River Liffey.

CHARLEVILLE
Enniskerry, Co. Wicklow

Built of a pale Wicklow granite, and standing as it does in incomparable surroundings, Charleville is a house of uncommon elegance and perfection. Fortunately it is in the hands of highly sensitive and understanding owners, anxious to collect Irish furniture and pictures for the house and bent on enlarging the already immense garden at a time when most are economizing. A series of 'rooms' formed by beech and yew hedges are approached down an ancient yew walk; at one end stands the temple-shaped conservatory with its grandiose frontispiece of Doric columns supporting a pediment. Beyond the potting shed a new circular plantation has just been established with *patte-d'oie* vistas leading to the semi-circular boundary garden wall.

The original Charleville was destroyed by fire in 1792 and the present structure was designed by Whitmore Davis to replace it. The estate had belonged to the Monck family since 1705 when Charles Monck married the heiress, Agneta Hitchcock. The builder of the present house was his grandson, also Charles, who was created Viscount Monck in 1801, as a reward for voting for the Union. This honour must have made for bad blood between him and his immediate neighbour Viscount Powerscourt who, when offered an Earldom as a similar bribe, replied by kicking the emissary down the stairs.

The imposing nine-bay front of Charleville is dominated by a handsome Ionic portico which takes the central three bays a storey higher than the rest of the house. As at Lucan House in Co. Dublin, this central feature is raised up on arched rusticated stonework although at Charleville the front door is pedimented whereas at Lucan it is in the shape of an arch. A stone string course divides the upper from the lower windows and the whole is finished with a handsome cut-stone frieze and cornice. The arrangement of the entrance hall, with its pair of fluted Ionic columns, is similar to the hall at Lucan except that here it leads through to the magnificent staircase with its brass banisters.

The end elevations have a pair of floor-length Wyatt windows at ground level similar to those given to Carton in Co. Kildare by Richard Morrison in 1817. Because they are Regency in character it is tempting to suppose that these windows were lowered twenty years after the house was built. It is possible that the finishing of the house was delayed by the rebellion of 1798 which would account for the interior being of a later style. The superb plasterwork at Charleville is bolder and more masculine than is usually found in a house built during the last years of the eighteenth century. Plaster musical instruments in the barrel-vaulted ceiling of the morning room probably indicate the room's original purpose. It has also been suggested that the interior may have been altered in anticipation of a visit from George IV when the King went to Powerscourt in 1821. Before the fire at Powerscourt, plasterwork similar to that at Charleville could be seen there also, for example, on the staircase.

LEFT The front hall, looking through to the staircase. The marquetry floor probably dates from the last century, when the tiles beneath the mantel were put in.

OPPOSITE Charleville was designed by Whitmore Davis for the first Viscount Monck in 1792. The formal gardens with beech and yew hedges can be seen beyond the house, with a conservatory in the form of a temple.

LEFT The dining room, hung with Irish landscapes by George Barret, has a heavy ceiling centrepiece with shamrock and foliage that dates from *c.* 1820; the acanthus frieze could have been added to 'strengthen' the cornice at the same time.

ABOVE The cantilevered Portland stone staircase, with its unusual brass banisters, can be compared to the staircase at Castletown in Co. Kildare.

LEFT The morning room has a barrel-vaulted ceiling with musical instruments in the plasterwork, as well as gardening implements and sheaves of corn.

OPPOSITE The magnificent set of seat furniture in the drawing room was made by Thomas Chippendale and was once in Lord Zetland's London house; the bill still exists.

LONGFIELD HOUSE
Goolds Cross, Co. Tipperary

Longfield is a handsome house overlooking the River Suir. The Long family who lived here had made their money in India and purchased 1,000 statute acres where in 1770 they built the present house. In 1846, by which time Captain Richard Long's father had been murdered, and the potato famine had done away with rents, he sold the property to Charles Bianconi (1786–1875), 'King of the Irish Roads', for £22,000. The story of Bianconi's life, of his arrival in Ireland as an itinerant pedlar from Italy selling prints in frames on the streets of Dublin and his rise to fame and fortune, is part of early nineteenth-century Irish history and has been written by his great-granddaughter Mollie O'Connell Bianconi. He established a web of long-cars transporting passengers and mail throughout Ireland; from

humble beginnings he soon dominated the country and even the advent of the railways failed to ruin him. The secret of his prosperity was caring for his horses as well as his employees, besides establishing a service that could be relied on. At the peak of his attainment his coaches were covering 3,000 miles a day. As a self-made man and a Roman Catholic he became a symbol of success, especially to the deprived, and could count Daniel O'Connell, the Liberator, among his friends. It was Bianconi who was eventually to erect the monument to O'Connell in Rome, where his heart is buried.

As an impecunious youth he had seen and fallen for Longfield and now that he was the owner he sent for experts from Italy. They laid out a formal Italian garden with yew hedges and installed urns and statuary

RIGHT The staircase ascends in a single sweep, clinging to the bow at the back of the house which balances the bowed front of the entrance hall.

OPPOSITE Longfield House was built in 1770 to a most ingenious plan; the identity of the architect is unknown. It was purchased in 1846 by Charles Bianconi, the transport pioneer and self-made millionaire. It is today part of Coolmore Stud Farms.

BELOW The drawing-room mantel, ornamented with dolphins and shells, was imported from Italy by Bianconi, together with sculptural ornaments for the garden.

that he had imported from Como. He planted a rose garden with white and yellow roses to represent the 'Joyful and Glorious Mysteries' and red roses for the 'Sorrowful Mysteries' of the Rosary. At Boherlahan Bianconi built a mortuary chapel as a last resting place for himself and his family. Without the help of an architect he and his head carpenter, Bob Noble, erected a solid, if unorthodox, little Italianate building in limestone, assisted by local artisans. A bell was hung in the *campanile*.

Longfield has a most ingenious, symmetrical ground plan with a curved bow front and back, and three-sided bows at either end. The rusticated front door leads to an oval hall and the staircase with its delicate balusters, which is the best feature of the house; the half landing is lit by two round-headed windows flanking a slender niche. The white marble mantelpiece in the drawing room with fluted columns, shells and dolphins was imported from Italy by Bianconi. In his day the walls of the dining room were hung with the scarlet cloth of Guardsmens' tunics, and there were Raphael tapestries on the staircase. He entertained lavishly and was entertained in return, even by the Viceroy, the Earl of Bessborough. His daughter, Minnie (1840–1908), married Morgan John O'Connell, MP for Co. Kerry, nephew of his old friend Daniel O'Connell.

Longfield House has for many years been a successful stud farm, and fortunately the house is well cared for.

EMO COURT
Portarlington, Co. Laois

After 1922, when the Irish Free State was founded, it became virtually impossible to dispose of country houses in Ireland and a number of those that came on the market were acquired by religious institutions. Many a Georgian niche was adorned by an Italian-made plaster statue of a saint, wearing a halo of coloured lights. With the passage of time, and a fall in the numbers of those giving their lives to the Church, some of these houses have come back on the market and are once again in private hands. Emo Court, for instance, was bought from the Jesuits in 1969 by Mr Cholmeley-Harrison and turned back into a private house – a courageous venture.

Emo was an Italianized form of the Irish name of the local townland which was called Imoe; there is no connection with Palladio's Villa Emo near Venice. The house was designed originally in about 1790 by James Gandon for the first Earl of Portarlington, who was one of those responsible for bringing Gandon to Ireland. Gandon also designed the nearby church at Coolbanagher. Dr Edward McParland has described

OPPOSITE Emo Court, was begun for the first Earl of Portarlington in 1790 by James Gandon, the architect of the Custom House and the Four Courts in Dublin.

The front hall has *trompe l'oeil* decoration in the two apsidal ends, echoing the original design by James Gandon, and a marble door-surround.

Emo as 'Gandon's anti-Wyatt manifesto, rising in defiance of Wyatt's greatest Irish house, Castlecoole'. An Ionic portico dominates the central part of the entrance front which is flanked by two projecting bays making it in all a nine-bay composition. Coadestone friezes representing the arts and a pastoral scene, dated 1794, crown their blind attics.

Emo Court was not completed when the first Earl died on campaign during the 1798 rebellion and the second Earl, who was very short of money, neglected it until 1834–6, when he employed the fashionable English architect, Lewis Vulliamy to make improvements. The latter completed the garden front, giving it its portico of four giant Ionic columns with a straight balustraded entablature, and also worked on the interior, assisted by two Dublin architects, A. and J. Williamson. The great rotunda, its copper dome rising from behind the garden front portico and also prominent on the entrance front, was completed in 1860 by William Caldbeck of Dublin.

In part of the grounds owned by the Forestry Commission stands an intriguing folly that is earlier than the present house. It consists of a triumphal arch surmounted by an octagon reminiscent of Wyatt's great Radcliffe Observatory at Oxford (1773). Although in a dangerous

condition most of the cut-stone ornamentation has survived and the room at the top which must have once enjoyed views of the park was probably used for dining. The monument is hidden now by fir trees.

The present owner, Mr Cholmeley-Harrison, undertook the monumental task of restoring this large house single-handedly. Siena marble was brought from Italy to restore the pilasters in the great round room whose bases had been removed when the room was combined into one with its neighbour to form the chapel. The single-storey apse-ended entrance hall has recently been painted in *trompe l'oeil* to represent the plaster decoration which Gandon intended for the room but which was never carried out. Mr Cholmeley-Harrison has also spent the last ten years in the creation of a picturesque garden extending to nearly fifty acres. This has improved the setting of the house immeasurably as it focuses attention on the lake below and gives the visitor a chance to enjoy the architecture of the house from different standpoints.

ABOVE The drawing room with its Connemara marble columns extends the entire way from front to back of the house; it is sometimes used for concerts.

OPPOSITE The gilt library ceiling dates from the 1830s when the white marble mantel with playful putti and grapes was probably installed. The marquetry floor has a geometrical design.

RIGHT The great rotunda with its coffered domed ceiling and giant Corinthian pilasters was completed in 1860 by William Caldbeck, a Dublin architect.

CASTLE COOLE
Enniskillen, Co. Fermanagh

Castle Coole stands in its beautiful park near Enniskillen, rising sheer out of the grassland, unencumbered by garden or yard to distract the eye from the purity of its lines. If Russborough is the most perfect Palladian house in Ireland, Castle Coole has to be without rival the finest neo-Classical country seat. The quality of the Portland stone masonry is excellent and all four fronts are equally perfect; this is unusual in Ireland where attention is so often concentrated on the main front alone.

A plantation castle was built here in about 1600 by Captain Atkinson, Provost Marshal of Lough Foyle and Derry, but was destroyed in the rebellion of 1641. Soon after, the estate was purchased by John Corry, a prosperous Belfast merchant, ancestor of the Earls of Belmore. His son, Colonel James Corry, built a modest 'Dutch' house, with a vast pediment, in 1709 to the designs of John Curle. This caught fire in 1797.

The present house was built for Armar Lowry-Corry. Born in 1740 he inherited the property through his mother in 1774. He married Lady Henrietta Hobart as his second wife in 1780. She was the daughter of the Viceroy, the Earl of Buckinghamshire; in the following year he was elevated to the peerage as Baron Belmore. In 1789 he became Viscount Belmore and in 1797, the year in which Castle Coole was completed, Earl of Belmore. As he advanced in the peerage he must have wanted to equal the much grander house of his brother-in-law and neighbour, the Earl of Enniskillen, at Florence Court. He determined to build a house that was not only greater in size but also more up-to-date in fashion. He succeeded admirably on both counts.

The earliest known designs for the house, dated 1789, are those of Richard Johnston, the Irish architect of Dublin's Gate Theatre, brother of the better known Francis Johnston. After the foundations were laid Lord Belmore must have decided to transfer his patronage to the more fashionable English architect, James Wyatt, who supplied his plans in 1790 using Johnston's basement layout. Wyatt's design was similar to the original but more skilled and powerful. Both Johnston's and Wyatt's drawings are on display in the house. Wyatt visited Ireland only once in 1785 so therefore can never have seen Castle Coole. Building commenced in 1790 under the supervision of Wyatt's assistant Alexander Stewart.

The interior is without doubt the finest of its date in Ireland. This was no mean achievement at the time, as Castle Coole is very remote from any fashionable centre; there is a harmonious unity and balance in the joinery and plasterwork which is of the highest quality. The inlaid mahogany doors made on a curve for the oval ballroom which is on axis to the front door provide one example of the incredible quality of the interior fittings here. The plasterer was Joseph Rose, who had worked for Robert Adam at Syon House and Harewood House in England. Rose's team demanded 'danger money' and were afraid of being press-ganged on the long journey. Richard Westmacott, the London statuary, supplied six marble mantels which were accompanied by two men competent to install them; these were in place by 1796. The legend that Lord Belmore, in true planter style, insisted on building his great house of materials brought from the land of his forebears is no doubt apocryphal.

Lord Belmore died in 1802, leaving debts amounting to £70,000.

Castle Coole was designed in 1790 for the first Earl of Belmore by the fashionable English architect, James Wyatt; it is the finest neo-Classical country house in Ireland.

His great house had cost nearly twice the estimated £30,000 to build and the restrained decoration of the interior may have been a measure of economy. The second Earl engaged the services of John Preston, a leading Dublin upholsterer, who furnished Castle Coole in the Regency style, bold and masculine by comparison with the delicate interior. There was a profusion of fringes, borders, rope and tassels, sumptuous wall hangings, pier glasses and suites of gilded furniture, much of it in the Grecian taste.

Each piece of furniture had either two or three protective covers especially made for it. The first set was of fine stamped cloth finished

with a gilt-leather border, the second of 'Superfine light Blue Cloth' with four 'Rich Gold Color Tassels' and the third made of 'Ell wide English Calico' lined with white calico. Preston also supplied 'soft Shamois for preserving covers of Gilt Furniture'. A magnificent State bed was made by Preston in anticipation of the visit of George IV to Ireland. It was hung with scarlet silk curtains which, together with those for the windows, cost over £1,000 for the material alone. The King, however, never came to Castle Coole.

Richard Morrison designed the newly restored farm and stable buildings out of sight of the house, joined to it by a long tunnel. The remains of a venerable oak avenue, that used to lead to the old house, and traces of the early formal garden can still be seen in the park. The lake is famous for having the oldest non-migratory flock of greylag geese breeding in the British Isles. These were introduced by Colonel James Corry in about 1700 – legend has it that if they leave Castle Coole, so will the Lowry-Corrys.

The National Trust was given the house and parkland in 1951 and has recently spent over three million pounds restoring Castle Coole and redecorating the interior.

ABOVE The family portraits in the dining room are older than the house, and the furniture is Regency; only the side table with its attendant urns is contemporary with the restrained decoration of the room.

RIGHT The bedroom landing, lit by an oval skylight, is two storeys high; the top floor windows are concealed by the balustrade that surrounds the central block.

OPPOSITE Corinthian pilasters of grey and black scagliola surround the oval ballroom at the back of the house. The furniture was especially made for the room in Dublin during the Regency period.

OPPOSITE The drawing room, in common with its neighbours, has Regency furniture. The cost of building work was so high that furnishing the interior had to wait for twenty years.

RIGHT The sumptuous State bedroom was prepared for a visit by George IV when he came to Ireland in 1821, but in the event he never visited Castle Coole.

BELOW The needlework room, above the ballroom, has spectacular views of the lake and park. The wallpaper was copied recently from a small scrap of the original.

DEERFIELD
Phoenix Park, Dublin

Colonel John Blaquiere came to Ireland as Chief Secretary to the Viceroy, Lord Harcourt, in 1772. Four years later he had just about completed the building of his residence in Phoenix Park, across the principal *allée* from his master. Like the former Viceregal Lodge opposite, the Chief Secretary's Lodge is surrounded by its own sixty-acre park with a belt of trees only broken to acknowledge the monumental view south towards the Dublin mountains. The site was evidently chosen on account of this ever-changing view across the 'Fifteen Acres', in fact an area of about 300 acres where, in the early morning mists, racehorses can be seen at exercise on the gallops.

The house, which cost £8,000 to build, is a two-storeyed structure with two projecting bowed ends facing south. An attractive row of eight round-headed windows link the two bows, giving light to the two principal reception rooms. A large staircase hall, bedecked with flags and presidential portraits is sometimes used for the receiving line. A large white ballroom has been added to one side, providing the space needed for receptions here. A generous *porte-cochère*, gleaming white, with a scarlet red front door, admits the guests under the watchful gaze of a larger-than-life bust of President Lincoln. The name of the architect has been lost in time, as has the identity of the person who laid out the extensive walled gardens, beautifully kept as is everything about this demesne. The gardens abound with fruit trees, glass houses and every kind of rose under the sun. Small wonder Ireland is such a coveted diplomatic post.

In 1784 the house was purchased by the government and made into an official residence for the Chief Secretary, the power behind the Viceroy. Successive Chief Secretaries have included Sir Arthur Wellesley (later the Duke of Wellington), Lord Castlereagh, Sir Robert Peel and Lord Randolph Churchill. When Sir Hamar Greenwood, the last of the line, departed in 1922 the house was deserted for some years. In 1927 the United States of America sent its first envoy, Fred A. Sterling, to the Irish Free State. Mrs Sterling discovered the empty house when out walking in the park one day and told her husband she had found the perfect place for the American Minister to live. Ever since it has been the residence of successive American envoys; the post was up-graded to an ambassadorship in 1950.

Paintings to ornament the main reception rooms are supplied by the 'Art in the Embassy' programme run by the National Gallery in Washington so that a personal choice is made with every new appointment and as a result the rooms are constantly changing. Each envoy has left something behind as a contribution to the beauty of the place. George Garrett presented a Steinway grand piano, Raymond

Deerfield was built for Colonel John Blaquiere, Chief Secretary to the Viceroy, in 1776. In 1927 it became the residence of the United States Minister to Ireland, a post that was up-graded to an ambassadorship in 1950.

LEFT The drawing room faces south across the 'Fifteen Acres' where Mass was celebrated by Pope John Paul II for a million people in 1979. A giant crucifix marks the spot.

BELOW The dining room contains a portrait by the distinguished American painter, Gilbert Stuart, who lived in Ireland from 1787 to 1793. It was presented to Deerfield by Raymond Guest, a former ambassador.

Guest a painting by the American artist Gilbert Stuart from his Irish period, and Walter Curley a set of cartoons from the old *Vanity Fair*. Mrs William Shannon commissioned a print room from Nicola Wingate-Saul that was executed in 1978, one of her finer creations. It was Mrs Shannon also who christened the house Deerfield and who wrote its history which now forms part of the Irish Heritage Series. In 1979, during the Shannons' reign, Pope John Paul celebrated Mass on the 'Fifteen Acres' for a million people.

A few examples still exist of a toile representing a military review in the Phoenix Park, which was advertised as follows:

> We have pleasure to inform the public, that Mr Harpur of Leixlip, linen printer, has now *nearly finished* on cotton from copper-plate, for Mr Clarke, proprietor of the Irish Furniture Cotton-Warehouse in Werburgh-street *a Volunteer Furniture*, in chintz colours, which is an exact representation of the last Provincial Review in the Phoenix Park ... (*Dublin Evening Post* 14.9.1782)

The design on the toile measures thirty-three inches square and shows 'a striking likeness of Lord Charlemont as reviewing General' according to Mr Clarke's sales talk. The first Earl of Charlemont is shown with hat in hand, riding past his troops as they present arms, with a mounted escort carrying bared sabres. Charlemont was the national head of the Volunteers, and the Earl of Moira was the head of those of the province of Leinster. Lord Moira's horse, with its dashing leopardskin saddle cloth, is listening intently to a drummer boy while on either hand spectators are kept at bay. Deer, still a familiar feature in the Phoenix Park, wander about among pretty Rococo trees. The Phoenix Column, erected by Lord Chesterfield in 1744, can be seen top right, and top left is the Chief Secretary's Lodge with its fish weathervane. At the base of the toile there is a picnic tent, with a bottle of wine and a ham awaiting two elegantly dressed couples with parasols. The striped carriages have 'C' for Charlemont and 'M' for Moira on their doors. Soldiers are removing a small boy who has climbed a tree to obtain a better view, and he is depicted in mid-air crashing headlong on to a lady who has set up shop to sell refreshments to the crowd from her basket.

The artist was, almost for certain, Gabriel Beranger (1729–1817), of a Huguenot family that had settled in Holland, who taught drawing, sold prints and attracted the attention and patronage of General Vallancey. The General sent him on expeditions to draw, measure and record Irish antiquities and there is an album of his discoveries in the Royal Irish Academy.

Samples of the Volunteer Furniture can be seen at Castletown in Co. Kildare (gift of Mr John S. Bereman), as well as at the Masonic hall, the National Museum and the Royal Society of Antiquaries, all in Dublin. A modern copy of it is obtainable from the Irish Georgian Society.

THE MUSSENDEN TEMPLE
Downhill, Co. Londonderry

The Earl Bishop of Derry, Frederick Augustus Hervey (1730–1803), was one of the great eccentrics of his age. Rich, profligate and extravagant, he enjoyed the company of women more than was appropriate for his position. He built three enormous houses, Downhill and Ballyscullion in Co. Derry and Ickworth in Suffolk, all three crowned with domes and crammed with paintings and statuary acquired on his travels.

The circular temple that stands precariously on a cliff top on axis to Downhill was named after Mrs Mussenden, a cousin of the Earl. She died in 1785 just before it was finished. The architect was Michael Shanahan, originally a master mason from Cork with whom the Earl Bishop had become acquainted while Bishop of Cloyne. In contrast to Shanahan's Downhill itself, a great house that was stylistically behind the times with its giant pilasters, the design of the Mussenden Temple was up to the minute. The architect wanted a golden roof to match the Latin inscription around the frieze, which originally was gilded, but the Earl Bishop determined on slates; these have since been replaced with lead. The inscription, from Lucretius, translates 'Tis pleasant to watch from land the great struggling of others when winds whip up the waves on a mighty sea'. The temple was originally used as a library; it had a coffered ceiling and scagliola columns. The Earl Bishop permitted the room below the library to be used for Mass by those who professed the Catholic faith, showing him to be well ahead of his time in matters of religious tolerance.

The Earl Bishop was already enjoying a large income as Bishop of Derry when his brother died in 1779 and he became the Earl of Bristol. The Bristol Hotels which are found in practically every capital city on the Continent were named after him because he travelled with such a large and extravagant retinue. He was taken ill on the road north from Rome and carried to a small farm house. However, when the Italians realized that the Earl Bishop was a heretic prelate they feared it would bring bad luck to the house if he was to die under their roof and accordingly met his end in the stable.

The Mussenden Temple is now in the care of the National Trust and open to the public.

The temple was designed by the Cork-born architect,
Michael Shanahan in 1785 for Frederick Hervey,
Earl of Bristol and Bishop of Derry. The Earl Bishop
named it after his cousin, Mrs Mussenden,
who died just before its completion.

THE ADVENT
OF THE
GOTHIC STYLE

When a castle stronghold was turned into a house in the seventeenth century, light was at last allowed to penetrate the ancient walls through casement windows with stone mullions. These were replaced by sash windows soon after 1700, with heavy glazing that became gradually more delicate as the eighteenth century progressed. After 1760 Gothic windows were introduced which were eminently suitable to the character of a castle. At this time, there was a significant development: Gothic-style houses began to be built, inspired by Horace Walpole's Strawberry Hill on the Thames near London. One of the earliest and grandest of these is Moore Abbey, Monasterevin in Co. Kildare, built for the Moores, Earls of Drogheda. The imposing fifteen-bay façade has Gothic windows but, like the Gothic front of Castle Ward, it has none of the asymmetry usually associated with Gothic design. Moore Abbey enjoyed a final flicker of fame in the 1920s when it was occupied by the great Irish tenor, Count John McCormack.

The taste for Gothic was to take so strong a hold that any architect with ambition had to become familiar with the pointed style, in which Irish imagination and inventiveness were soon to know no bounds. Several reasons account for the popularity of the Gothic castle-style of country houses in Ireland which could be (but is not) called Irish Baronial. Many of the box-like eighteenth-century Classical houses were so alike; they shared a common dullness and were lacking in either mystery or drama. Their owners yearned for the excitement of a turreted silhouette and it was not long before various factors helped to make their dreams come true. One of these was Napoleon's blockade of continental ports which brought prosperity to Irish agriculture, while another was that the Act of Union abolished the Dublin Parliament in 1801 which meant that there was less inducement to keep up an establishment in the Irish capital, and more time and money to spend on 'improvements' in the country once the town house was given up. When the pocket boroughs were abolished, also in 1801, £7,500 was paid to the owner in compensation by the Government for each Member of Parliament – the Earl of Longford had payment for two.

Modesty was not a besetting sin of the Anglo-Irish; it suited their pretensions to live in a castle even if it was not a real one, emblazoned with crumbling coats of arms, the hall adorned with a family tree tracing their roots to the Pharaohs, a knight in armour in every niche. A battery of rusty cannons, interspersed with pyramids of cannon balls, might be trained across the gravel towards the ha-ha and the gentle slope of the parkland beyond.

The castellated house was either built from scratch or was an existing house turned into a castle by some would-be Irish Arthurean. In some cases it was smothered in cement and looked as impermanent and unreal as a castle in Disneyland.

Battlements and turrets formed an outline of high drama and to this day arrow slits provide a perfect resting place for rooks and crows.

When a house was dressed up to look like a castle with the addition of decorative battlements, serious leaks would result. The more elaborate the alterations, the more difficult it became to keep the water out, a perennial problem at the best of times. Those that could not afford to gothicize the house might content themselves with a crenellated farmyard, or erect a gateway in the form of a portcullis, with accommodation in the flanking towers and above the arch, the whole surmounted by the inevitable family arms. One such grand gateway was designed by Francis Johnston for Bloody Bridge in Dublin. With the coming of the railway it had to be taken down stone by stone and was removed to its present position at the entrance of the Royal Hospital at Kilmainham. When it was moved, the architect's innocent ruse was laid bare – he had put his own coat of arms in a prominent position above the arch, concealed by a thin wooden board painted to match the stone. After a few years, when the board disintegrated, Johnston's arms would have been exposed to view in this exalted position.

Besides Francis Johnston, whose masterpiece in the Gothic style is Charleville Forest in Co. Offaly, there were many exponents of the Gothic in Ireland, for example the Morrisons, Richard (1767–1849) and William Vitruvius (c. 1794–1838), the Pains, James (c. 1779–1877) and George Richard (1793–1838) and James Shiel (fl. 1812–30). John Nash (1752–1835) designed at least two Irish castles; Shanbally in Co. Tipperary, now demolished, and Lough Cutra in Co. Galway, as well as a Gothic church in Cahir in Co. Tipperary. Richard Morrison designed Gothic gates for Lismore Cathedral as well as Castle Howard, a dower house for the Howards, Earls of Wicklow. Magnificently sited on an eminence above the Meeting of the Waters, it is a most successful composition. The principal seat of the Earls of Wicklow, Shelton Abbey, transformed into a Gothic Revival 'abbey' in about 1819 by Richard Morrison, lacks the drama of the dower house.

Just as farm buildings were incorporated into the overall design of a Classical house, to give an illusion of grandeur, so also with the Gothic. Tullynally Castle in Co. Westmeath has two utilitarian yards, housing the stables as well as the kitchen and laundry, both forming an essential part of the complex. On occasion cattle might be seen, chewing the cud and gazing lugubriously out of arrow slits from the comfort of their Gothic bower.

The change to Gothic was by no means universal and Classical houses continued to be built; moreover, the early years of the nineteenth century saw the advent of the Greek Revival. A love of Gothic did, however, take a lasting hold that continued right up to the reign of Queen Victoria and beyond.

CASTLE WARD
Strangford, Co. Down

In 1762, when the time had come for Mr Bernard and Lady Anne Ward to decide on the design of the new house they were to build, they were unable to agree with one another. It appears that Mr Ward wanted a plain, sober Classical house whereas his wife was more adventurous, and leaned towards the Gothic style just beginning to be fashionable after the lead given by Horace Walpole in 1748 at Strawberry Hill outside London. In the end the Wards reached a remarkable architectural and matrimonial compromise building a house of Bath stone which is Classical on the front and Gothic on the back. The rooms follow the two styles with the saloon, library and

OPPOSITE The Gothic side of Castle Ward faces east over Strangford Lough. The identity of the adaptable architect remains anonymous – surely he must someday be unmasked.

boudoir with its spectacular fan vaulting being Gothic, while the hall, dining room and staircase are in the Classical style. The name of the adaptable architect is not known, but the house survives to astonish its many visitors with the peculiar story of its conception.

In the front hall, now the music room, on the Classical side of the house the plasterwork is of two dates: that on the walls is quite naïve having been executed by plasterers from Dundrum, a neighbouring village, who worked here in 1828. The coat of arms above the pedimented doorcase opposite the entrance is that of the third Viscount Bangor who succeeded in 1827. The stucco wall panels and

ABOVE Castle Ward was built in 1762 for Bernard Ward, created first Viscount Bangor in 1781. This is the Classical façade, which was originally the entrance front.

OPPOSITE The Gothic saloon has an ogee Gothic mantel, a ceiling and cornice that are awash with Gothic ornament as well as sophisticated Gothic detail in the mahogany doors and dado.

LEFT The music room, originally the front hall; detail of the eccentric plasterwork added in 1828 by a team of stuccodores from the nearby village of Dundrum.

BELOW Arms of the third Viscount Bangor, who succeeded in 1827, done in plaster above the door leading from the music room to the Gothic saloon.

ceiling decoration are contemporary with the house (1762) and much more accomplished though less amusing. On the Gothic side the plasterwork in the boudoir was done in lath and plaster to imitate the stone fan-vaulting in the chapel of Henry VII at Westminster Abbey. In 1764 Lord William Gordon wrote to Mr Bernard Ward as follows: 'I left a Commission in England to send Lady Ann drawings of the Roof of Henry the eights [sic] Chapel, a Chineise Bed, & temple, which I hope her Ladyship has got and I shall not forget the Painted glass . . .'.

Sir James Caldwell, of Castle Caldwell in Co. Fermanagh, paid a visit to Castle Ward in 1772 and described it as not being finished by that date. He wrote 'During dinner two French horns of Lady Clanwilliam's played very fairly in the hall next to the parlour, which

had a good effect'. He went on to describe the beauty of the demesne, and had to admit 'This is the finest thing I have seen, though Fortescue and Sir Patrick say it is greatly inferior to Castle Caldwell'.

Castle Ward is particularly well sited, with the Gothic front facing across the beautiful Strangford Lough. A temple, based on Palladio's Redentore, stands beside the formal water or 'canall' that was created in the eighteenth century, some distance from the house. According to Mark Bence-Jones in *A Guide to Irish Country Houses* the Gothic fronts of Castle Ward and of Moore Abbey in Co. Kildare are the only examples of mid-eighteenth-century Gothic in major Irish country houses which are not old castles remodelled. The house now belongs to the National Trust but the Ward family still lives there from time to time.

LEFT The dining room is panelled in plaster which has been painted or 'grained' to resemble oak and picked out in gold. The far end of the room has a recess designed to hold a sideboard.

OPPOSITE The Gothic boudoir has an elaborate ceiling in lath and plaster inspired by the stone fan vaulting of Henry VII's Chapel in Westminster Abbey.

GLIN CASTLE
Glin, Co. Limerick

The family of the Knight of Glin is a branch of the Norman-Irish FitzGeralds who settled in Ireland in the 1170s. Thomas FitzGerald was granted lands in West Limerick and built his first Norman castle at Shanid, a few miles from Glin, of which the polygonal keep and motte still remain. *Shanid Abu* translated from the Irish means 'Shanid for ever' and was the battle cry of all the FitzGeralds of Desmond. The head of this family, the Earl of Desmond, revolted against Queen Elizabeth I and his vast estates were confiscated in the 1580s.

The fairytale title of the Knight of Glin dates back to the early thirteenth century; together with the White Knight and the Knight of Kerry, they form three branches of the FitzGerald House of Desmond.

These titles are anomalies, akin to Irish chieftainships, and illustrate the Gaelicization of a powerful Norman family. The present holder of the title, living on part of the lands held by his ancestors, is the twenty-ninth Knight of Glin in direct succession. One of their old castles is a shattered hulk in the village. In the seventeenth century they moved a mile westwards and built a relatively simple thatched house; at this stage they were still Catholics and the Penal Laws excluded them from the political activity of the new colonial Ireland. In the eighteenth century they changed their religion and married into the Ascendancy caste. By the 1780s Colonel John FitzGerald was determined to build a grander house, no doubt to upstage his settler neighbours.

The house was a plain many-windowed Georgian building attached

LEFT Glin Castle was built in the 1780s by Colonel John FitzGerald, Knight of Glin, and given battlements by his son in 1812. It faces across the Shannon Estuary to Co. Clare.

OPPOSITE The front hall has a delicately modelled plaster ceiling in the Adam style; a portrait of the builder of the original house in his Volunteer uniform hangs above the sandstone mantel.

ABOVE The drawing room; Selina Blennerhassett, whose portrait hangs above the mantel, was the only female member of the Limerick Hell-Fire Club.

OPPOSITE The Knight of Glin being handed a challenge to a duel; the painting by Highmore hangs above a grotesque blackened mahogany side-table with the family coat of arms.

RIGHT The flying staircase, in the centre of the garden front, is lit by a Palladian window surmounted by delicate plaster cornucopias.

to the walls of the old seventeenth-century thatched dwelling where the family had lived during the troubled years of the seventeenth and early eighteenth centuries. The important features of the new house were the splendidly decorated interiors. The front hall, with its screen of Corinthian columns and neo-Classical ceiling painted in delicate apple green and terracotta, leads to the great 'flying staircase' and a gracefully decorated Venetian window looking out on to the gardens. All the other reception rooms lead off this enfilade and the drawing room, with its bowed front window, has charmingly naive plaster decoration. In the library next door a broken pedimented mahogany bookcase artfully conceals a door leading back on to the staircase hall.

Colonel John was succeeded by his son John Fraunceis (born in 1791), and in the spirit of the Romantic Movement he felt that as the

holder of such an ancient and romantic title he should be living in a castle like his ancestors. He was married in 1812 and soon afterwards added the battlements and Gothic detailing to the plain exterior of his father's house which he rechristened Glin Castle. He built three sets of gingerbread lodges, one of which is modelled on the family crest of twin turrets, to 'defend' the demesne.

The interior of Glin has an interesting collection of family portraits including a magnificent full-length one of the duellist Knight, Richard FitzGerald, dating from the 1740s. Colonel John hangs over the mantelpiece in the hall wearing the uniform of the Royal Glin Artillery. This was a regiment of Volunteers raised by him not long before Grattan's Parliament – an exciting period of national Irish independence that sadly ended in the '98 rebellion and union with England in

1801. The building and decoration of Glin and the laying out of its park and woodlands was typical of the pride of Ireland's ruling classes in their newly won, if brief, autonomy. A portrait of Colonel John's son, known as the 'Knight of the Women', owing to his amorous exploits, hangs in the dining room. Other pictures tell something of the history of the family and demonstrate the varied quality of Irish eighteenth-century painting. There are landscapes, such as the view of Glin and the Shannon estuary in 1839 painted by a local Limerick master, J. H.

tions. The collection at Glin attempts to show the magnificent craftsmanship that was to be found in Ireland during the Georgian period. The fine plasterwork, joinery, carving, delft and brasswork serve as a vivid reminder of the considerable skills of Irish artisans. So much of their work has disappeared from the country through the dispersal of its great houses. Desmond FitzGerald, the present Knight of Glin, has made a conscious attempt at Glin to create a showcase of Ireland's art and craft of the eighteenth and early nineteenth centuries.

ABOVE The family kitchen filled with Irish country furniture and adorned with religious texts painted on tin.

OPPOSITE The mirror above the mantelpiece in the library was made in Dublin c. 1760 by Francis and John Booker. The library cabinet comes from Woodsgift, seat of the St George family.

RIGHT Portraits of the Knights of Glin surround the walls of the dining room, with its grand neo-Jacobean furniture.

Mulcahy, which is hanging on the stairs, and there are townscapes, of Ennis in Co. Clare and of the city of Limerick, by a travelling Englishman, William Turner de Lond, dating from 1820.

Perhaps the most important feature at Glin is the Irish furniture; some of this was always in the house but many pieces have been added to the collection over the last twenty years or so. Baroque mahogany side-tables with their fantastical animal masks jostle with early Georgian walnut chairs and tables. Gilt mirrors, labelled by their Dublin makers, and other documented examples of Irish craftsmanship decorate the rooms. One of the finest pieces is a mahogany bureau-bookcase which ingeniously pulls out and has a writing desk on a ratchet. It displays the typical characteristics of Irish eighteenth-century furniture, combining elaborate carving with noble propor-

The Knight is one of the foremost scholars in the field of Irish architecture and the decorative arts and has written extensively on the buildings, paintings, furniture and gardens of his country. An active conservationist, he is a director and past chairman of the Historic Irish Tourist Houses and Gardens Association (HITHA) which co-ordinates the various properties in Ireland that are open to the public. He is actively involved in the Irish Architectural Archive and is President and Chairman of the Irish Georgian Society and Foundation. He serves on the Castletown Foundation, represents Christie's in Ireland and also lectures frequently in the United States. His wife, Olda, is a prolific writer and takes an active role in the running of Glin. She welcomes many groups and guests to the house and is a pillar of strength in the preservation of Ireland's heritage.

LUGGALA
Roundwood, Co. Wicklow

The hills of Donegal, like the rocks of Connemara and the spectacular lakes of Killarney, are a long way from Dublin. It is not generally realized that dramatic wild landscape is also to be found on the very doorstep of the capital. A precipitous drive from Dublin goes over the Sally Gap and on down towards Lough Tay, at the end of which there is a white sandy beach sheltered on either side by tall mountains. Wild deer stand frozen at the approach of wheels. A small white Gothic shooting box comes into view – Luggala.

In 1753 David La Touche of the great Dublin Huguenot banking family bought an estate in Co. Wicklow overlooking the Glen of the Downs where he built Bellevue at the enormous cost of £30,000 and started to lay out an extensive landscape garden. His son Peter La Touche discovered Luggala and bought the enchanted valley in 1790 where he soon began to build his 'cottage mansion in the pointed style'

as a shooting box in which to entertain his friends. He had inherited Bellevue from his father where in 1793 he commissioned the Irish architect, Francis Sandys, to build a Turkish tent. His father, another Francis Sandys, who had died in 1785, had designed a Gothic dining room at Bellevue for Peter La Touche. The Knight of Glin has suggested that Francis Sandys Junior could have been the architect of

RIGHT Luggala is picturesquely sited at the head of Lough Tay, deep in the Wicklow mountains, about thirty miles from Dublin.

BELOW Luggala was built in 1790 for Peter La Touche, a Dublin banker, as a shooting box; the architect may have been Francis Sandys junior.

Luggala. He was later taken up by the eccentric Earl-Bishop of Derry for whom in 1796 he took charge of the construction of Ickworth in Suffolk.

The gleaming white façade of Luggala has six windows with Gothic hood mouldings. An early watercolour which is known to be accurate (thanks to a Victorian photograph) depicts it with Gothic windows which were subsequently squared off. The three central bays directly above the front door stand out above the rest, and small quatrefoil Gothic windows light the minute bedrooms. The house is built around a courtyard to which access is gained by an archway. The Knight of Glin has described the style of Luggala as 'the Gothic of pastrycooks and Rockingham china'.

The small black and white paved entrance hall, often used for dining, has a Gothic mantelpiece and a painting by Mainie Jellett. To the right, what used to be a dormitory is now a large dining room with a coved ceiling. To the left of the hall is the drawing room dominated by the de Laszlo portrait of Lady Oranmore and Browne against a mauve Gothic-style wallpaper with lilies designed by Pugin for the Houses of Parliament. Among the furniture can be seen an eighteenth-century Irish settee originally at Russborough in Co. Wicklow and other examples of 'Irish Chippendale'.

In the middle of the last century Luggala was purchased by Viscount Powerscourt whose descendant sold it to Mr Ernest Guinness, the father of Oonagh, Lady Oranmore and Browne, in 1937. Twenty years later, during her tenure, it suffered a disastrous fire but was rebuilt exactly as it had been. The decorator was John Hill of Green and Abbott, London; the architect was Alan Hope of Dublin.

In the fifties and sixties Luggala was a great centre of life. Lady Oranmore and Browne's friends were intellectuals such as Cyril Connolly and Robert Kee. She would enjoy mixing ambassadors and peers with the likes of the actor Micheál MacLiammóir and the author Brendan Behan. Oonagh was very beautiful and had many admirers, but there was no telephone at Luggala and one of her most ardent fans tried his best to keep in touch by wire. The post office was five gruelling miles away and a boy was given a shilling for delivering telegrams on his bicycle. One day the admirer sent no less than four – the last one simply read 'Goodnight darling'.

Once in the sixties a large party, which included the actress Siobhan McKenna, was snowbound at Luggala. What remained of the night was spent on sofas and the cars were pulled up the steep drive by a jeep in the morning. An old beggar came stumbling down the road covered in snow, with a sack on his head. Everyone yelled at him to get out of the way so that the jeep would keep going at all cost. The beggar turned out to be Lord Dunsany, who had been expected for dinner but was marooned on the mountain all night. He was not best pleased at his reception, having expected a hero's welcome after his freezing ordeal.

The house, and the valley, now belong to Garech Browne; it was he who helped the traditional Irish musicians The Chieftains on their road to fame and fortune. Promotion and recording of Irish poets and musicians have been his principal achievements.

A visit to Luggala is unforgettable and life here, in this century at all events, has never been dull. It is easy to imagine it as a setting for an Irish Mayerling.

OPPOSITE The front hall often serves as a dining room. The side table and the chair beside it, both ornamented with shells, are examples of eighteenth-century Irish furniture and the painting is by the Irish artist, Mainie Jellett.

ABOVE A harpsichord by Ferdinand Weber of Dublin, in the form of an obelisk. It appeared on the sleeve of a Claddagh record, made by the company founded by the owner of Luggala.

SLANE CASTLE
Slane, Co. Meath

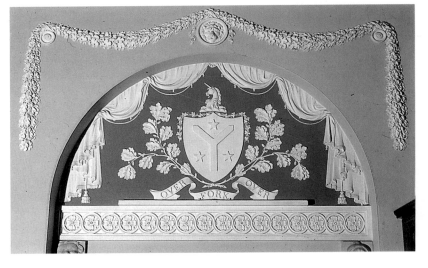

Slane Castle stands on a rock looking down across the River Boyne in one of the most picturesque situations imaginable. The Pale fortress of the Flemings, Lords of Slane since the coming of the Normans, had occupied the same site which is of strategic, as well as aesthetic, importance in its dominance of the valley. The Flemings were attainted after the rebellion of 1641 and all their lands and possessions were forfeited to the Crown. They were one of the leading Catholic families and one of the most militant. In 1687 the attainder was reversed by James II but two years later the Flemings took up arms once more and after the defeats at the Battle of the Boyne a couple of miles downstream and at Aughrim in Co. Galway, Slane was lost to them for ever.

The Conyngham family were established here by the end of the seventeenth century and in or around 1700 they built a grand house incorporating the foundations of the Fleming Castle. It was also a very peculiar house, in the Dutch 'Artisan Mannerist' style, with a pediment and a cupola, encircled by towers of different shapes and sizes. A drawing of it survives, though the whereabouts of a painting of it by Thomas Roberts in about 1773 is unknown. In accordance with the growth of their fortune, power and influence, by the 1780s the Conynghams wanted their dwelling-house more up-to-date and many

OPPOSITE LEFT The drawing room, tragically destroyed in a fire in 1991, had two landscape paintings by Thomas Roberts on either side of the mantel. That on the left was of Beauparc, the Palladian house on an eminence across the river from Slane, also the property of Lord Mount Charles.

OPPOSITE BELOW The decoration of the front hall was by Francis Johnston, who incorporated the family coat of arms in a stucco overdoor, with the motto 'Over fork over'.

ABOVE Slane Castle was rebuilt in 1785 by James Wyatt for the father of the first Marquess Conyngham. It is situated on a rock looking over the River Boyne.

an architect's heart must have beat fast at the prospect of being chosen to make the improvements. The quantity of drawings and projects and the famous names consulted indicate a deep interest in architecture on the part of the family. The unity of the building as it stands today is surprising considering that James Wyatt, Francis Johnston, 'Capability' Brown and Thomas Hopper all contributed to the castle and Brown designed the stable block. Wyatt produced drawings for the interior in 1773 and came to Ireland for the first time in 1785 when he appears to have remodelled the exterior of Slane, incorporating the towers that 'caged in' the original Conyngham house of 1700 and giving them battlements. He also raised the walls to conceal the roof and eliminated the pediment and cupola. The house had been turned back into a castle once more.

The front hall at Slane Castle is a huge and comfortable room, all but forty feet square, with an Irish elk facing the entrance and the Conyngham family arms in stucco above the mantels. The interior is by Francis Johnston, who completed the transformation of Slane into a castle for the first Marquess Conyngham whose uncle had initiated it. Johnston gave the hall a cornice of mutules and four freestanding Tuscan columns to take the weight of the ceiling. Like all the rooms here, except the Gothic ballroom, it is Classical in style.

ABOVE Elizabeth, Marchioness
Conyngham, was the mistress of
George IV and was already fifty-two
when they first met.

OPPOSITE The round ballroom,
designed by Thomas Hopper and
completed in 1812, was dominated
by a life-sized portrait of George IV
by Sir Thomas Lawrence. This
wonderful room has survived the fire
of 1991

RIGHT A corner of the drawing
room at Slane before the tragic fire of
1991; the satinwood writing desk
was the gift of George IV.

The round ballroom or library was completed in 1812 and is thought to have been designed by Thomas Hopper, the Prince of Wales's architect; the room takes up two storeys and has Gothic detailing of remarkable quality in the ceiling.

The village of Slane has four identical Classical houses facing each other diagonally at its crossroads, providing a most elegant square which is unique in Ireland. Three houses were at one time inhabited by female members of the Conyngham family who, it is said, could keep an eye on their sisters' comings and goings while never actually speaking to each other.

The famous Elizabeth, Lady Conyngham, the mistress of George IV, was the wife of the first Marquess, who was Steward of the Royal Household. It is said that when the King came to Dublin in 1821 he was in such a hurry to get to Slane that a special straight road was built to transport him thither. It cannot be denied that by Irish standards the road from Dublin to Slane is uncommonly straight, or that it seems to end at Slane and go no further.

In November 1991 the castle suffered a tragic and disastrous fire, causing extensive damage. A restoration programme is in progress that will take several years to complete.

LUTTRELLSTOWN CASTLE
Clonsilla, Co. Dublin

Luttrellstown is an old castle of the Pale cloaked in later additions, standing above the Liffey eight miles west of Dublin. It was originally the seat of the Irish branch of the Luttrells, Earls of Carhampton. The notorious Henry Luttrell was murdered in his sedan chair in a Dublin street in 1717; his sister Anne married the Duke of Cumberland, brother of George III. Another sister, Elizabeth, is said to have taken her own life in Augsburg having been sentenced to sweep the streets there, chained to a barrow, for being a pick-pocket.

Luke White MP purchased Luttrellstown from Colonel Henry Luttrell, second Earl of Carhampton, in 1800. In the absence of documentary evidence it is not certain whether the present aspect of the castle was given to it by Carhampton or White. The former was known to have been entertaining there lavishly in 1796 and the rebellion of 1798 was apparently one of the causes for his selling the property which had been in his family since the time of King John. It has been suggested that Richard Morrison designed the neo-Gothic façade with its Disney-like array of pepper-pots and turrets, possibly beginning the work for Carhampton and completing it for White.

The Knight of Glin has pointed out that in 1794 when alterations were made to the interior of the house, Michael Bryan, or O'Bryan, was working for Carhampton according to the surveyor Brian Bolger's list of decorative plasterers. Presumably this refers to the extremely interesting and unusual plasterwork in the splendid ballroom where a triple-vaulted ceiling is supported by clusters of spears and grimacing lion heads. The shields and sabres on the frieze may symbolize Carhampton's military career, as may the chained bow and arrow on the library ceiling. This room, at the centre of the garden front, was apparently the original entrance hall.

Luke White was an extraordinary man. He came to Dublin from the Isle of Man as a penniless boy and was soon selling newspapers on the streets. He eventually ran a bookshop on Essex Bridge, became a successful publisher and a partner in a lottery firm. To the astonish-

In 1800 Luttrellstown Castle was sold by Henry Luttrell, second Earl of Carhampton, in whose family it had been for generations. The purchaser was Luke White, MP, whose son was created Lord Annaly.

OPPOSITE The front hall leads to a Gothic octagon with four niches facing each other. The floor was paved in black and white in 1960.

ment of Dublin society he found himself in the extraordinary position of being able to offer the Government a loan of half a million pounds at five per cent interest. White's son was made Lord Annaly in 1863, and it was probably in his time that a Tudor banqueting hall was added, a gloomy room that was transformed in 1950 into the present dining room.

The prettiest approach to Luttrellstown Castle is the drive that winds its way up the glen, under the rustic arch with its wishing seat, until it reaches the lake where there is a little Doric temple. From here the garden front comes into view which is an excellent composition in paste-board Gothic, dating from the early years of the last century. Aileen Plunket, who lived here for over fifty years, created an interior of great wonder and elegance, in a variety of styles, with the help of Felix Harbord, the English interior decorator, a pupil of Sir Albert Richardson, the architect. The dining room was perhaps his most successful accomplishment, with its lively plaster birds and painted ceiling by de Wit. The Grisaille Room contains an important series of grey and white panels in oil by de Gree representing 'Mercury introducing the Arts and Industry to Hibernia'. These were originally executed in 1788 for John Foster, the last Speaker of the Irish House of Commons.

Mrs Plunket used to entertain in the grand manner at Luttrellstown, where two vast round tables could seat forty people with ease. It was a sad day for all her neighbours when she left Ireland and sold the house she loved so much. She used to explore the grounds here as a girl, as her father, Ernest Guinness, lived close by. Story has it that she sat on the wishing seat and wished for Luttrellstown to be hers one day, and eventually, when she married, her father made her a present of it.

The faintly Hollywood-style battlements of Luttrellstown Castle provided the ideal setting for filming *The Knights of the Round Table*, with Rex Taylor and Mel Ferrer, in 1955. Every horse in Ireland was caparisoned, and Rex Taylor sat, surrounded by his army, slumped in the back of a large black limousine, waiting for the sun to shine. It never did. Aileen Plunket threw a period banquet for the stars – dish after dish of Arthurean food was produced – but she got into trouble with the camera crew for trespassing in the park, as they thought she was the old lady who lived in the turret lodge. She loved that.

The castle, in its 600-acre park, now belongs to the Primwest Group and can be rented for grand house-parties, board meetings or simply as a luxurious place of escape from the world.

ABOVE LEFT The Grisaille Room contains a set of paintings by Peter de Gree representing 'Mercury introducing the Arts and Industry to Hibernia', signed and dated 1788.

LEFT The dining room was created in 1950 for Mrs Brinsley Plunket by Felix Harbord; a beamed ceiling was replaced with a painting by de Wit and the Mortlake tapestry was given an elaborate plaster frame.

OPPOSITE The ballroom mantelpiece was installed in 1950 and has been attributed to Sir Henry Cheere, the English sculptor. Paul Tilleman painted the series of hunting views and the chandeliers are from Czechoslovakia.

BIRR CASTLE
Birr, Co. Offaly

ormerly one of the many strongholds of the O'Carrolls, Birr Castle today is the creation of the Parsons family, Earls of Rosse. The castle is separated from its town by a gigantic battlemented curtain wall, creating a little secret garden in between. From the top floor the slate roofs of Birr, with its faded Georgian charm, once called Parsonstown after the family that built it, can be seen stretching away towards the gentle skyline. The Parsons family is renowned for its extraordinary scientific achievements. In 1842 the third Earl of Rosse, using a local workforce, constructed the largest telescope in the world; it was to remain so for almost seventy-five years. This was erected in the park, and the limestone structure that supported it stands to this day like a picturesque Gothic folly in front of the castle.

The fourth Earl followed in his father's footsteps and designed and made an instrument for measuring the heat of the moon. His younger brother, Sir Charles Parsons, invented the steam turbine which revolutionized naval transport throughout the world.

Birr Castle has the appearance of a Gothic Revival castle, and the main front was designed by John Johnston in 1804, apparently no relation of the well-known architect brothers Francis and Richard

OPPOSITE Once an O'Carroll stronghold, Birr Castle has been the seat of the Parsons family, Earls of Rosse, since 1620. The principal front was designed by John Johnston in 1804.

BELOW The front hall contains seventeenth-century furniture, tapestries, swords and cannon-balls; there is a handsome Gothic Revival ceiling.

LEFT The drawing room is hung with yellow damask and family portraits as well as a superb pair of Irish mirrors on either side of the mantel. The bowfronted brass grate is looped up like a stage curtain.

ABOVE Mary, Countess of Rosse, was a pioneer photographer in the nineteenth century, and the Mary Rosse medal, shown here, is awarded each year by the photographic school in Kevin Street Technical College, Dublin.

OPPOSITE By far the finest room at Birr Castle, the Gothic ballroom has a faded green demask wallpaper and dramatic views of the River Camcor, as it tumbles swiftly by.

Johnston. John Johnston also designed the Protestant church at Birr which stands opposite the Gothic entrance gates to the castle at the end of Oxmantown Mall. These forbidding gates were designed by Mary, Countess of Rosse, in the mid-nineteenth century and her model for them made out of visiting cards is preserved here to this day.

The castle is older than it appears to be; behind Johnston's delicate Gothic frontispiece there is a variety of features of much earlier date. A unique Jacobean frieze of about 1620, the date of the Parsons' arrival here, has recently been restored by the Irish Georgian Society. It features a crudely modelled human head with a moustache, possibly Apollo, surrounded by sunrays amidst the usual foliage decoration. The main staircase is of yew and also dates from the seventeenth century when all the furniture here was made of yew wood as mentioned in Thomas Dinely's *Tour of Ireland*, 1681. The chief jewel of the castle is the dramatic Gothic Revival ballroom, with tall windows that overlook the tumbling falls of the River Camcor.

The sixth Earl, who died recently, was active in the world of museums, gardens, the National Trust and the preservation of Georgian architecture both in England and Ireland. He lived part of the year in England, and served in the Irish Guards during the Second World War. He was appointed to the first Irish Arts Council by de Valera and was Vice Chancellor of Trinity College in Dublin. His talented widow, Anne, is the sister of the late Oliver Messel and the mother of Lord Snowdon. Brought up at Nymans in Sussex, she was instilled with a knowledge and love of gardening from an early age, and the gardens at Birr bear testimony to her genius.

Their elder son, the present Earl, was christened William Brendan, but prefers to use his second name; Brendan was the patron saint of Birr, not to be confused with the better-known St Brendan the Navigator. For eighteen years Lord Rosse worked with the United Nations Development Programme in the Third World. He was responsible for coordinating aid and disaster relief in deprived countries such as Bangladesh. Since the death of his father, he has taken on the responsibilities of the estate at Birr but he has been appointed more than once by the Irish Government to evaluate aid programmes in Africa. The reason these facts are of interest is that in this family the

The yew-wood staircase dates from the seventeenth century and has superb carving besides Gothic detailing added in the nineteenth century.

OPPOSITE The bow window in the dining room looks down across the secret garden to the battlemented wall that separates the castle from the town.

transition of allegiance from England to Ireland coincided with the inheritance of Birr by the present generation. One of the best-known clichés about the Anglo-Irish is that they were considered Irish in England and English in Ireland. Just as the old guard in America, after 1776, found it hard to adjust to the new 'patriot' regime, so it was in Ireland. At Birr the present Earl of Rosse has made a determined decision to be Irish.

The magnificent gardens and grounds at Birr are open to the public throughout the year and are famous for the thirty-foot-high box hedges, the variety of magnolias and the rare shrubs and trees from China and Tibet. A formal garden, surrounded by a tunnel of hornbeam creating the effect of a cloister, is the creation of Anne, Countess of Rosse. Each year a special exhibition is mounted for the summer season based on the collections that have accumulated over the years at Birr Castle. Since 1982 exhibitions have dealt with themes such as the *Scientific Achievements of Sir Charles Parsons* and *Impressions of an Irish Countess: Photographic heritage of Mary Rosse in the 1850s*.

Birr is one of the most attractive and best laid-out towns in Ireland and was recently designated the Georgian Theme Town by the Tourist Board. It is not on any major trunk road and visitors to Ireland tend to stay on the perimeter instead of exploring the heart of the country. Being in a backwater is part of the charm of Birr, but there is so much of interest in the demesne that it has become a mecca in its own right. The continuing presence of the Parsons family has ensured this. Without their guiding spirit the essence of Birr might soon evaporate. The survival of the original family in residence has become a rarity, and is especially valuable when it is a family with creative talent, energy and concern for the community.

KILLRUDDERY

Bray, Co. Wicklow

In 1618 the land where Killruddery stands was granted to Sir William Brabazon, created Earl of Meath in 1627. However, the original house was destroyed in 1645 and was rebuilt by the second Earl in 1651. An early eighteenth-century painting of Killruddery shows the seventeenth-century house, with its extensive formal gardens that have miraculously survived. There are avenues of lime, hornbeam and beech; statuary; a sylvan theatre and a round pond with a fountain and twin 'canals' which reflect the changing seasons.

In 1820 the tenth Earl of Meath made extensive alterations to the house, employing the then fashionable architects Richard Morrison and his son, William Vitruvius Morrison. They remodelled Killruddery creating a neo-Tudor edifice, an excellent example of its kind although immense in scale and impossible to heat. In 1953 the present Earl commissioned the architect Claud Phillimore to reduce the house to its present more manageable proportions.

OPPOSITE The house and garden from the air; Killruddery was greatly enlarged by Sir Richard Morrison in the Elizabethan style for the tenth Earl of Meath in 1820.

LEFT The Killruddery Hunt in full cry across the Sugarloaf Mountain in Co. Wicklow and a bird's-eye view of the seventeenth-century formal garden, one of the few to have survived in Ireland.

In the hall, the stained-glass window depicts William the Conqueror setting foot in Kent, with the cliffs of Dover in the background. The standard-bearer on his right is Jacques de Brabançon, whose name appears on the roll in Battle Abbey. The Brabazons settled in England until, in 1534, Sir William Brabazon was appointed Vice-Treasurer and General Receiver of Ireland. The Liberties in the heart of Dublin once belonged to the family which exercised quasi-feudal rights there.

The clock in the hall was made by the thirteenth Earl of Meath. The face is part of a dumb waiter, the pendulum is a copper bed-warmer and the weight on the bicycle chain is the lid of a cooking pot!

The drawing room was designed by the Morrisons and has plasterwork actually signed, by Simon Gilligan, and dated 1824, on the top of the cornice. The Axminster carpet was made for the room and has the arms of the Brabazons at the corners. The pier tables were made by James Delvecchio of Dublin in 1828 and have Connemara marble tops; the same firm also supplied the carved and gilded window pelmets. The tenth Earl imported the mantel for this room from Iacinto Macale of Italy in 1817. Gaspare Gabrielli, the Italian artist who worked at Lyons, was the agent. The gilt mirror decorated with grapes over the fireplace comes from Dunraven Castle in Wales, and belonged to the present Earl's mother who was a Wyndham-Quin, daughter of the fourth Earl of Dunraven.

The dining room, formerly the little drawing room, has a vaulted ceiling, the work of Henry Popje, incorporating musical instruments,

drapery and flowers in the decoration, and still retaining the original silk covering on the walls.

The conservatory was designed by William Burn in 1852. Originally it had a domed glass roof by Richard Turner, who also built the great glasshouse at the Botanical Gardens in Dublin. The marble statues were imported from Italy: of particular interest is Ganymede with the eagle of Jupiter, by the school of Thorvaldsen.

With great public spirit the present Earl and Countess have opened the house and extensive formal garden to the public which is a great boost for tourism in the area, especially since the burning of Powerscourt nearby.

ABOVE The design of the drawing room with its scagliola columns is typical of Sir Richard Morrison; the plasterwork is signed and dated Simon Gilligan, 1824, on the cornice.

OPPOSITE The conservatory was designed by William Burn in 1852 and contains some remarkable sculpture; concerts are held here in the summer.

LISMORE CASTLE
Lismore, Co. Waterford

The medieval castle of Lismore, built by the Bishops of Waterford, was in ruins when Richard Boyle, the Great Earl of Cork, bought the estate in 1602 from Sir Walter Raleigh. Lord Cork rebuilt the castle but it was sacked in 1645, and again made habitable by his son, the second Earl. The property came to the Dukes of Devonshire in 1748 when the fourth Duke married the Boyle heiress, Baroness Clifford. It was the sixth Duke of Devonshire, known as the Bachelor Duke, who gave the castle the aspect that is so admired today, standing high above the River Blackwater as it flows, stern and silent, beneath the massive stone battlements.

The first architect for this restoration work, which was a virtual rebuilding, was William Atkinson who worked here from 1812 to 1822. The interior, and in particular the Banqueting Hall, was remodelled and decorated by Crace and Pugin from 1850. The architect best known for having designed the Crystal Palace in London, Joseph Paxton, who had begun his career as a gardener at Chatsworth, the Devonshires' seat in Derbyshire, made extensive alterations and additions to Lismore between 1853 and 1858, also for the Bachelor Duke.

The garden has become one of the chief beauties of Lismore. One of its most attractive features stems from the fact that the garden walls, having been built to protect the castle, are wide enough to walk along. The yew walk must be one of the finest anywhere.

Lord Charles Cavendish, the uncle of the present Duke, made Lismore his home with his wife Adele Astaire, the dancer and actress. After his death in 1944 she paid annual visits with her second husband Kingman Douglass, and her brother Fred Astaire often stayed here with her.

Sir John Betjeman, later the Poet Laureate, stayed here and composed a poem titled 'Lament' for the sister of the present Duke, Lady Elizabeth Cavendish, while on a visit to Lismore. The following five verses are taken from it by kind permission of the Betjeman Estate:

LEFT The Banqueting Hall was designed by Crace and Pugin from 1850 and the Gothic mantel bears the inscription *Cead Mille Failte*.

OPPOSITE ABOVE Lismore Castle, which had become dilapidated, was virtually rebuilt for the sixth Duke of Devonshire, known as the Bachelor Duke, between 1812 and 1858; he employed several different architects.

OPPOSITE BELOW The drawing room with its Gothic ceiling is hung with tapestries and contains a magnificent mahogany Irish side-table.

A LAMENT FOR MOIRA McCAVENDISH

Through the midlands of Ireland I journeyed by diesel
And bright in the sun shone the emerald plain;
Though loud sang the birds on the thorn-bush and teasel
They could not be heard for the sound of the train.

The roll of the railway made musing creative:
I thought of the colleen I soon was to see
With her wiry black hair and grey eyes of the native,
Sweet Moira McCavendish, acushla machree.

At Castletownroche, as the prospect grew hillier,
I saw the far mountains to Moira long-known
Till I came to the valley and townland familiar
With the Protestant church standing locked and alone.

O vein of my heart! upon Tallow Road Station
No face was to greet me, so freckled and white;
As the diesel slid out, leaving still desolation,
The McCavendish ass-cart was nowhere in sight.

Flow on, you remorseless and salmon-full waters!
What care I for prospects so silvery fair?
The heart in me's dead, like your sweetest of daughters
And I would that my spirit were lost on the air.

177

TULLYNALLY CASTLE
Castlepollard, Co. Westmeath

OPPOSITE The front hall, with the Pakenham arms in stucco, is used for concerts by the Derravaragh Musical Society.

The castellated gateway that leads across the park to Tullynally Castle stands about a mile from the town of Castlepollard. Not until the visitor has entered the porch, which resembles a portcullis, and penetrated to the drawing room, however, does he have any idea of the magnificent sweep of the landscape that drops away so dramatically from its windows. The house was known as Pakenham Hall from the late seventeenth century until 1961. In that year the present owner, Thomas Pakenham, restored the Irish name, Tully-nally, as the estate was known before it was granted to the Pakenhams in the 1650s.

After the Act of Union with Great Britain in 1801, which abolished the Dublin Parliament, the great Irish landowners who had controlled most of the seats in Parliament, were compensated by the Government at the rate of £7,500 a seat. The Earl of Longford, head of the Pakenham family, had controlled two seats in the borough of Longford; no doubt he spent part of his £15,000 compensation 'in improving' his country seat. The original house was apparently built at some date in the seventeenth century, for it was described as an 'old

LEFT Tullynally Castle, formerly known as Pakenham Hall, is the seat of the Pakenhams, Earls of Longford. Several architects effected the transformation of the Classical house into a Gothic castle from 1803 onwards.

house' in 1737. It was enlarged and altered several times in the eighteenth century, and Graham Myers, the architect to Trinity College, gave it a five-bay Classical façade in the 1770s. In 1803, the second Earl of Longford began to throw a mantle of Gothic architecture over it. The house was converted into a castle, with all the battlements and turrets that the architects could invent, so as to conjure up 'visions of the true rust of the Barons' wars'. Four architects were involved in these alterations: Francis Johnston, Richard Morrison, James Shiel and J. Rawson Carroll.

Francis Johnston worked here from 1803 to 1806 for the second Earl of Longford and was responsible for the battlemented parapet and corner towers. In 1820 James Shiel added the bow to the east front and redesigned the entrance hall. In 1839 Richard Morrison enlarged the house still further providing unusual self-contained apartments for the family to the left of the entrance. In 1860 J. Rawson Carroll added a tower to the northeast corner of the stable yard; his best-known work was Classiebawn in Co. Sligo, for Lord Palmerston, the statesman.

The castle style suited the picturesque Westmeath landscape and was also appropriate for a family of military tendencies. The second Earl of Longford, who began these alterations, had two brothers, Sir Hercules and Sir Edward, both generals in the Peninsular War, and a sister, Catherine, married to the Duke of Wellington. One of these brothers, General Sir Edward Pakenham, was later Commander in Chief of the British army in North America during the war of 1812. He was killed leading his men at the Battle of New Orleans in 1815. His body was shipped back, preserved in a barrel of rum, to be buried in Co. Westmeath. Thomas Pakenham will tell you that there are thirty

bedrooms, each named after a defeat suffered by one member of the family or another.

The life of Edward, sixth Earl of Longford, who died in 1961, was centred around the Gate Theatre in Dublin where from time to time his own translations of the classics were performed. Seats in the last two rows were to be had for a shilling – not much to pay for an excellent performance of a play by Wilde or Shaw. Edward Longford used to stand on Grafton Street shaking a collecting box, as the theatre was always in need of money. His wife Christine was, like him, an intellectual. She wrote a brilliant book on Dublin, and her novel

Country Places describes the first years of her marriage, her Westmeath neighbours all too thinly disguised for comfort.

Edward's brother Frank, now seventh Earl of Longford, is a Socialist politician, well-known for taking up good causes, including lost ones. He has written at least twenty books, including lives of Richard Nixon, President de Valera and Jesus Christ, and is a convert to Catholicism. His book on the Anglo-Irish Treaty of 1921, *Peace by Ordeal*, published in 1935, remains the standard work on the subject.

ton and Queen Victoria. His sister, Lady Antonia Fraser, has been acclaimed for her biographies of *Mary, Queen of Scots* and *Cromwell*. The Pakenhams have made the wise decision in this century to lay down the sword and take up the pen, and it would be hard to find a more gifted or prolific family of writers.

A legend associated with Tullynally and Lough Derravaragh, the lake beside which it stands, is the story of the Children of Lir. Lir, the chieftain of a strange tribe near Ulster, married Eve, the daughter of

RIGHT The library is dominated by a portrait of General Edward Michael Pakenham who lost his life at the battle of New Orleans in the war of 1812.

OPPOSITE The Gothic dining room has a wallpaper designed by Pugin for the Houses of Parliament, hung with family portraits.

In September 1930 the names in the visitors' book include Lord David Cecil, Maurice Bowra, John Betjeman and Evelyn Waugh, all Frank's contemporaries at Oxford. His sisters, Pansy and Violet, were also staying; one went on to marry Henry Lamb, the painter, and the other the novelist Anthony Powell.

Thomas Pakenham continues the literary tradition – his wife, his parents and his brothers and sisters are all authors. Amongst other books he has written a brilliant account of the 1798 rebellion in Ireland, *The Year of Liberty*. His mother, Elizabeth Longford, has written several important biographies including lives of the Duke of Welling-

Bov the Red. They had a daughter and three sons. On Eve's death Lir married her sister, Aoife, who became jealous of Lir's love for his children. Her evil spell turned them into swans and they were condemned to spend 300 years on tranquil Lough Derravaragh, 300 on the stormy sea of Moyle and 300 on Inis Glora on the wild Atlantic. The sound of a Christian bell called them to Kemoc, one of St Patrick's followers. His blessing broke the heathen spell and the feathers fell away as they prayed, leaving a very old woman and three withered, feeble old men. When they were buried a holy man at their grave saw four beautiful swans winging their way into the heavens.

DROMOLAND CASTLE
Newmarket-on-Fergus, Co. Clare

The O'Briens of Dromoland descend from the great warrior, Brian Boru, High King of Ireland, who died in 1014. The present Dromoland Castle was built in about 1826 by Sir Edward O'Brien, fourth Baronet, to the design of James and George Richard Pain. They were pupils of John Nash; he sent them over to Ireland to execute his commissions and they worked on Lough Cutra Castle in Co. Galway from 1811. Once in Ireland they set up in practice on their own account designing churches, country houses and civic buildings, besides Gothic Revival castles which were their speciality.

The castle consists of three principal towers, one octagonal, one square and one circular. The outline is enhanced by the variety of heights; the one, two and three storeys of the linking buildings. The entire complex is battlemented and the Gothic entrance resembles a portcullis. The square front hall opens into a long gallery as at Michelstown in Co. Cork (since demolished) which was also designed by the Pain brothers. The dining room has Gothic panelling up to the chair rail, and a Gothic cornice and mantel; the staircase has Gothic banisters.

When Sir Edward demolished the early eighteenth-century house of John Aheron (the first Irish architect to publish his designs in a book), he fortunately preserved many of the original features such as caryatids and overmantels. Even earlier than these is the seventeenth-century gateway, now in the walled garden, brought here by Sir Donough O'Brien from Lemaneagh when Dromoland became his principal seat. Sir Edward O'Brien's son succeeded his kinsman as thirteenth Lord Inchiquin and his descendants remained at Dromoland Castle until 1962 when it was sold by the sixteenth Lord Inchiquin. His daughter, Grania, has chronicled the absorbing history of her family in *These My Friends and Forebears* (Ballinakella Press, 1991).

Still displayed at Dromoland Castle, which is today a hotel, are the portraits of the O'Briens, mostly by Irish artists, on loan from the family.

Dromoland Castle was built *c.* 1826
to the designs of James and George Richard Pain,
for Sir Edward O'Brien, fourth Baronet.

THE DROMANA GATEWAY
Cappoquin, Co. Waterford

Dromana, near Cappoquin in Co. Waterford, stands on a rocky promontory high above one of the most picturesque stretches of the Blackwater estuary. The Dromana Gateway, reflected in the waters of the River Finisk, a tributary of the Blackwater, is a strange reminder of the Orient to come upon in a sleepy Irish valley. This Hindu-Gothic gate-lodge is based on the freestanding gateway in front of the Brighton Pavilion in Sussex. It was designed by Martin Day in 1849 who produced an alternative in the form of a Moorish arch; both sets of drawings are in the possession of Mr James Villiers-Stuart. The Duke of Devonshire had been instrumental in establishing a rail link between Mallow and Lismore. In 1846 the Great Southern Railway floated shares to have the line extended to Waterford; Dromana was only three miles from Cappoquin, where there was a station. This called for a different approach to the estate; until then the main gates to Dromana had been from the east at Moneyvroe but to reach Cappoquin by this route would have doubled the distance.

There is a delightful story that the gateway was erected in 1826, made of lath and plaster, to welcome home Henry Villiers-Stuart and his Austrian bride, Theresia Pauline Ott, when they returned from their honeymoon. They are supposed to have liked it so much that it was rebuilt in stone with a copper dome and cast-iron minarets, but the dates do not fit and the tale must be apocryphal. Until recent years the gateway and bridge had been left to deteriorate but they have now been sensitively restored with the help of the Irish Georgian Society, Waterford County Council and the National Heritage Council.

The Hindu-Gothic gate-lodge at
Dromana in Co. Waterford was designed
by Martin Day in 1849 for Henry
Villiers-Stuart; it overlooks the River
Finisk, a tributary of the Blackwater.

REGENCY ARCHITECTURE AND A RETURN TO MASCULINE TASTE

The last great flowering of Irish architecture came not long before the famine of 1845–9 during the years that roughly correspond to the Regency period (1810–20). George III had become insane and his son, later George IV, ruled until succeeding to the throne. The Prince Regent was a large man and the architecture, as well as the furniture designed during the Regency period, in a sense, reflected the scale of his person. The delicate, sometimes decadent interiors fashionable during the reign of George III were forgotten. This was the beginning of male supremacy, of the billiard room, the smoking room and a separation of the sexes that created a new order in the house.

Francis Johnston (1760–1829), a native of Armagh, dominated the architectural scene in the first years of the nineteenth century. His houses in the Classical style were austere and devoid of exterior ornament. Townley Hall in Co. Louth was his masterpiece in this style and contains a wonderful circular hall and staircase with a domed ceiling and skylight. Outside, however, Townley is plain to the point of dullness. Johnston invented a new vocabulary for his Classical interiors infinitely stronger and more masculine than the style associated with the name of Robert Adam. His chief rival was another native Irishman, Richard, later Sir Richard Morrison (1767–1849) from Cork and his son William Vitruvius Morrison (1794–1838). Although Johnston and the Morrisons excelled in the Gothic style, they were much in demand as Classical architects and the Morrisons also designed country houses that were modest in scale like Bear Forest in Co. Cork, which is more like a villa than a country house.

After the Act of Union of 1801 when Dublin was reduced to the level of a provincial city, architectural activity continued more in the public than in the private sphere. Johnston and the Morrisons met the demand for banks, court houses, asylums, post offices and villas in the suburbs. At the same time some architectural commissions of an enormous size were executed, such as Ballyfin in Co. Laois (1821) for Sir Charles Coote, of the Cromwellian family, and Borris House in Co. Carlow, restored in 1820 for The Kavanagh of the ancient Irish dynasty. Both Ballyfin and Borris were given their present aspect by the Morrisons, father and son; both have superb Regency interiors with heavy plasterwork and lavish use of scagliola columns according to the fashion of the times.

The Morrisons were partners and enjoyed a thriving practice that died out with the Famine. It did not follow with them, however, that behind a neo-Tudor exterior there would be rooms to match. Their ponderous Classical interiors have something of the Grand Hotel about them: lofty, opulent and imposing. For all that, their houses were often badly built, and it is said that they patronized a timber-yard which supplied wood that was not properly seasoned, and as a result hastened the spread of dry-rot.

John Nash (1752–1835), the Prince Regent's architect, is remembered for the gleaming white terraces in Regent's Park, London:

Augustus at Rome was for building renown'd
And of marble he left what of brick he had found;
But is not our Nash, too, a very great master?-
He finds us all brick and he leaves us all plaster.

Quarterly Review, 1826

Nash also enjoyed a country-house practice in Ireland. He designed Shanbally Castle in Co. Tipperary (now demolished), Lough Cutra Castle in Co. Galway and Killymoon Castle in Co. Tyrone. He added a domed hall and colonnade to Caledon in Co. Tyrone; his most ambitious Classical house in Ireland was Rockingham in Co. Roscommon. The Pains, James (1779–1877) and George Richard (1793–1838), who had been apprentices in Nash's office, were sent to Ireland to execute his commissions and stayed on, establishing their own successful practice here, their best-known creation being Dromoland Castle in Co. Clare.

Single-storey Regency terraces were built in Dublin with generous steps going up to the main floor allowing plenty of light for the bedrooms in the basement below, creating a house that, in a sense, was upside down. Country houses in this manner are quite common and an excellent example is Killoughter in Co. Wicklow which has the entrance doorway at the head of a long flight of steps surmounted by a shallow segmental fanlight. The fashion for this topsy-turvy arrangement gave rise to the theory that such houses were built by members of the Catholic faith who were taxed if they had more than one storey. In fact, no such restriction ever existed. A similar apocryphal legend has it that 'Speaker' Conolly, because he was an 'upstart', was restricted to two chimneys on his great house at Castletown by the older gentry who were resentful of his fortune.

William Tinsley (1804–85) lived in Clonmel and practised architecture in Co. Tipperary and Waterford, prosperous parts of Ireland until the famine. In 1851 he was forced to emigrate and settled in Cincinnati where he built several Gothic colleges in the Midwest. Lakefield in Co. Tipperary, which Tinsley designed in 1831, has a five-bay façade and an Italianate overhanging roof. The flying staircase is the best feature of the house and resembles that at Glin Castle in Co. Limerick. It is of wood with delicate banisters that curve in a most elegant manner. He remodelled Grove in Co. Tipperary using to advantage the spectacular views along the river towards Slievenamon and the distant towers of Kiltinan Castle. He gave the house a long staircase hall lit by a little rotunda of wooden Doric columns. It would be fascinating to know what sort of interior he designed for his ambitious Gothic house, Tullamaine Castle in Co. Tipperary, built 1835–8, which was burnt during the troubles around 1920 and rebuilt in about 1925. Mark Bence-Jones has described Tinsley as 'The last of the Georgians'.

LYONS
Newcastle, Co. Dublin

Lyons was built in 1797 for Nicholas Lawless, first Lord Cloncurry, the son of a prosperous blanket manufacturer who had purchased the estate from the Aylmer family which had owned it since the Norman invasion. The house was designed by Oliver Grace who had supervised the completion of Cashel Cathedral in 1783 for Archbishop Charles Agar (the tower and spire were added by Richard Morrison in 1791). The original house was built of granite and curved colonnades linked the central block, with its double-bowed front, to the two-storeyed wings. Lyons is the only major country house of this date to feature bow windows on the main façade.

Only five years after Grace's house was completed the second Lord Cloncurry employed Richard Morrison to replace the curved sweeps with straight colonnades as he was later to do at Carton in Co. Kildare, for the Duke of Leinster. Morrison faced the ground floor of both central block and wings with rusticated granite; on the insides of the wings facing across the forecourt he designed blank arches flanked by recessed columns, creating architectural features necessary after the removal of Grace's curved colonnades.

Lord Cloncurry, who had spent two years in the Tower of London on account of his involvement with the United Irishmen, travelled to Rome while the work proceeded at Lyons, and while there he married Eliza Morgan and they rented the Palazzo Accaioli which they shared with his sister Charlotte and her husband, Edward Plunkett, later Lord Dunsany.

While in Rome in 1804 Lord Cloncurry purchased four granite columns twelve feet in height, three of these came from the golden house of Nero and the fourth from the Baths of Titus. Morrison used the four columns to create an entrance portico surmounted by the family coat of arms with a bull and a ram as supporters. Although absent while the building was going on Cloncurry took a great interest in the work and Morrison had to incorporate his Italian purchases in his alterations to the building.

Cloncurry formed a valuable collection of antique sculpture while he was in Italy. This was displayed at Lyons in the colonnades and the front hall, where there was a frieze of ox skulls and tripods borrowed from the Temple of Fortuna Virilis in Rome. Sculpture was also used to ornament the vast Classical garden that stretched from the back of the house to the manmade lake, beyond which rises the Hill of Lyons, visible for miles around. A boat-load of more sculpture, on its way here from Italy, went down off the Wicklow coast in 1804. Some was later salvaged.

Lyons remained in the hands of the Cloncurrys until the death in 1958 of the Hon. Kathleen Lawless who was the last of the line. She bequeathed the property to a cousin, Mark Winn, who sold it four years later to University College, Dublin. Lyons was used by the School of Agriculture which erected the handsome entrance gates removed from Browne's Hill in Co. Carlow. In 1990 the property was acquired by Dr Michael Smurfit.

LEFT Lyons was built to the designs of Oliver Grace in 1797 for Nicholas Lawless, first Lord Cloncurry, whose son employed Richard Morrison to built the straight colonnades to either side and to add the porch.

OPPOSITE The drawing room at Lyons was decorated in a series of wall paintings in panels, depicting the times of day, by an Italian artist, Gaspare Gabrielli, in 1805.

MOUNT STEWART
Newtownards, Co. Down

Alexander Stewart purchased the land here in 1744 but no trace of his original house survives. The western end of the present house was built in 1804 for his son Robert, later first Marquess of Londonderry. It was designed by the celebrated London architect George Dance (1741–1825), remembered above all for being the master of Sir John Soane. It was in this house of modest scale, but with an interior of elegant refinement, that the sons of the first Marquess, Robert and his half-brother Charles, grew up. Robert was to become the great politician and statesman, Viscount Castlereagh, the arbiter of Napoleon's downfall.

In 1819 untold riches came to the family when, as his second wife, Charles married Frances Anne, the heiress of Sir Henry Vane-Tempest on whose estates in Co. Durham there was an endless supply of coal. In 1822 Charles became third Marquess of Londonderry and it was he who, with his wife's money, commissioned William Vitruvius Morrison to enlarge Mount Stewart out of all recognition. Morrison died in 1838, but his designs were executed by a local architect, Charles

Campbell. Most of the work of George Dance remains intact at the west end of the present house, the whole being unified by a handsome stone balustrade.

The main feature of the Morrison extension is a vast central hall, with an octagonal gallery, lit from above. During the reign of the fourth Marquess, who incidentally created the lake, this hall was replete with stuffed animal heads, heraldic banners and upwards of 3,000 antlers. The floor was flagged in a pale stone and the walls were white. There were suits of armour in the niches, and coloured glass in the skylight; the fourth Marquess was a romantic, a man after the heart of Sir Walter Scott.

The original Morrison balustrade of the central octagonal gallery was replaced with ironwork by Edith, Marchioness of Londonderry, the well-known political and literary hostess who presided with such brilliance over Londonderry House in Park Lane.

Double doors beyond the central hall opened at one time into another galleried hall, supported on four columns and lit from above.

LEFT The staircase in the 'black and white hall' which takes its name from the grey stone floor with intersecting octagons in black slate. Sir Henry Vane-Tempest's horse, Hambletonian, painted by Stubbs, is shown being rubbed down after winning a race at Newmarket in 1799.

OPPOSITE Mount Stewart was designed in 1825 by William Vitruvius Morrison, incorporating an earlier house of 1804 designed by George Dance. Its garden is reputed to be one of the most outstanding in the British Isles.

This was changed by Edith Londonderry between the wars to make a bedroom above and a smoking room on the ground floor, looking out across the garden. Wicker furniture, with which it had been filled as befitted a 'villa by the sea', was replaced with continental pieces, English Queen Anne walnut and black chinoiserie lacquer. The fine collection of *famille rose* has found ideal display cabinets in the central octagon. Brighter colours than might have been chosen were used in the belief that they would soon fade, which modern paint cannot be relied upon to do. The house has been kept very much as she left it. The friendly 1920s atmosphere, with comfortable clutter and parchment lampshades, pervades.

Among the most important furnishings in the house are the twenty-two chairs used at the Congress of Vienna brought here by Lord Castlereagh. Each chair has been embroidered with the coat of arms of one of the delegates and the country he represented, among them Talleyrand, Metternich and Wellington. A vast painting of Hamble-tonian, a gleaming stallion being rubbed down by an apprehensive groom, hangs on the staircase. It was the star of the recent Stubbs exhibition at the Tate Gallery in London and must be the most important sporting picture in Ireland. Hambletonian belonged to Sir

ABOVE The dining room with the Congress of Vienna chairs ranged beneath life-sized portraits, by Sir Godfrey Kneller, of the first Earl and Countess of Albemarle, forebears of Lady Mairi Bury's late husband.

OPPOSITE The music room in the centre of the west front, which was designed by George Dance in 1803. The ceiling echoes the design of the delicate inlaid floor.

Henry Vane-Tempest and had just beaten Mr Joseph Cookson's Diamond at Newmarket in 1799, when he was painted.

In 1782 the first Marquess commissioned James 'Athenian' Stuart to build a little banqueting house inspired by the Temple of the Winds in Athens on a high point looking down over Strangford Lough. No visitor should go to Mount Stewart without seeing it. The inlaid wooden floor, made by John Ferguson, and the delicate plasterwork by William FitzGerald are exquisite examples of craftsmanship – the Temple of the Winds and the Mussenden Temple in Co. Londonderry are Northern Ireland's answer to the Marino Casino near Dublin.

The gardens at Mount Stewart encompass an area of eighty acres and are the creation of Edith Londonderry. The house had been dark inside as enormous trees shaded the south or garden front and so Lady Londonderry pushed the trees back, creating imaginative Italianate gardens with the Red Hand of Ulster planted up as a flower bed. The lie of the land is sheltered from the sea winds, and warmed by the gulf stream so that an abundance of azaleas and rhododendrons flourish here, at their best in late May and June.

Lady Mairi Bury, the daughter of the seventh Marquess, gave the property to the National Trust which maintains the house and enormous garden impeccably. She farms the rest of the land and has the right to live at Mount Stewart thanks to the National Trust which recognises that without a family a house becomes a museum, and that people prefer to visit places that are still lived in.

FOTA ISLAND
Carrigtwohill, Co. Cork

Just outside the limits of the city of Cork, on the road towards Cobh, lies the island of Fota. It belonged to the Barrys, Earls of Barrymore, who were descended from David de Barry, a Norman adventurer. Their main castle was at Buttevant in Co. Cork, and the family motto is the ancient war-cry *Boutez en Avant* which has been variously translated as 'hit out' or 'spit forward'. John Smith-Barry was a member of the Carlton House set and a boon companion of the Prince Regent. In 1825 he decided to make his principal residence here and called on Richard Morrison and his son, William Vitruvius, to improve the small house that already existed, giving it a solid Regency flavour. The Morrisons also built the gates, which carry the family motto, the lodges and the demesne wall, as well as helping to lay out the park, plantations and pleasure grounds. They designed all the ancillary buildings including the kennels and a house for the huntsman which is a reduced version of the main house itself. William Morrison also submitted a very grand Elizabethan-style design which was published in *The Builder*, 21 September 1850, and must have been rejected.

The exterior of the house is plain and the splendours that lie indoors come as a surprise therefore. A Grecian front porch leads into the long hall which extends to either side like a wide corridor, lit by all the ground floor windows of the main block and terminating in niches adorned with urns. Ornate plasterwork, typically Morrisonian, decorates the ceiling and wreaths alternate with the Barry crest in the frieze.

Richard Morrison and his son, William Vitruvius Morrison, enlarged an existing house to create Fota Island for John Smith-Barry, whose grandson became Lord Barrymore in 1902.

Pairs of Ionic columns in deep yellow scagliola support the walls above. The staircase, which has brass banisters, is cantilevered and has an oval domed ceiling. The interior detailing has fortunately survived intact, apart from the ceiling of the drawing room, painted and stencilled by the Dublin firm of Sibthorpe about a hundred years ago, which has recently suffered a partial collapse.

Famous for his open-handed hospitality, John Smith-Barry was known as 'John the Magnificent'. Lady Charlotte Smith-Barry writing later in 1933 tells of 'the great quantity of wine that was consumed there, the big decanter which holds nine bottles, and is still at Foaty, being re-filled many times, the door having been previously locked and the key thrown out of the window'.

In the 1840s John Smith-Barry's son, James Hugh, reclaimed the swampy land and created the famous arboretum, as well as water gardens and a semi-tropical jungle. The arboretum at Fota is a mecca for those in search of rare specimen trees, which flourish in ideal conditions here because of the mild climate. James Hugh Smith-Barry did not spend much time in Ireland, however, choosing to avoid the damp climate and the tribulations of the Famine.

It was his son, Arthur Hugh, who, with the help of William Osborne, the gardener, developed the great garden which became so renowned. He married Lady Mary Wyndham-Quin, sister of the fourth Earl of Dunraven. After the birth of their son a curse was put on the family. An English wet-nurse had been employed, but the baby arrived prematurely so a local girl took her place. She was dismissed when the English nurse arrived and, in a fury, swore that no male heir would ever again inherit. The baby died within a year and the house has never since passed from father to son.

Arthur Hugh Smith-Barry was created Lord Barrymore in 1902 at the coronation of King Edward VII, reviving the old family title of his forebears. His daughter, Dorothy Bell, maintained the house and grounds until her death after which, in 1975, the estate became the property of University College, Cork.

ABOVE The drawing room, which contains part of the fine collection of Irish pictures and furniture on loan to Fota Island by Richard Wood, has an unusual painted ceiling.

OPPOSITE The front hall is punctuated with pairs of Ionic columns in yellow scagliola and takes up the entire seven bays of the central block.

LISSADELL
Sligo, Co. Sligo

In Memory of Eva Gore-Booth and Con Markievicz
The light of evening, Lissadell
Great windows open to the south,
Two girls in silk kimonos, both
Beautiful, one a gazelle,
But a raving autumn shears
Blossom from the summer's wreath;
The older is condemned to death,
Pardoned, drags out lonely years
Conspiring among the ignorant,
I know not what the younger dreams –
Some vague Utopia – and she seems,
When withered old and skeleton-gaunt,
An image of such politics,
Many a time I think to seek
One or the other out and speak
Of that old Georgian mansion, mix
Pictures of the mind, recall
That table and the talk of youth,
Two girls in silk kimonos, both
Beautiful, one a gazelle.

                    W. B. YEATS

The Gore-Booth family of Lissadell stems from an Elizabethan soldier-settler, Sir Paul Gore, whose descendant Nathaniel Gore of Ardtermon married Letitia Booth in 1711. In 1830 Sir Robert Gore-Booth, fourth Baronet, commissioned Francis Goodwin, a distinguished English architect, to build a house overlooking Sligo Bay in the Greek Revival style.

At first glance Lissadell appears rather barrack-like but on closer acquaintance the sophistication and subtlety of the design become apparent. The cut grey limestone blocks, quarried at Ballysodare in Co. Sligo, have been delicately chiselled; each is framed by a plain band measuring half an inch. The somewhat austere treatment of the exterior, with its plain window surrounds and strong horizontal friezes, closely resembles Goodwin's work at Macclesfield Town Hall, Cheshire (1826). Lissadell has eighteen blank windows, the backgrounds painted white to match the blinds that were drawn by day.

Broad steps, framed by curved screen walls, lead from the grandiloquent entrance porch up to the front hall. An enfilade of 120 feet stretches from the top step to the very back of the house, straight across the gallery to the 'great windows' of the library immortalized by Yeats's poem. The gallery or music room with its apsidal ends is top lit and measures sixty-five feet in length. It has freestanding columns to one side and pilasters opposite giving the effect of an Egyptian Hall.

Lissadell was designed by the English architect, Francis Goodwin, for Sir Robert Gore-Booth whose descendants still inhabit the great house by the shores of Sligo Bay.

The drawing room with its compartmented ceiling and unusual mantelpiece is, like most of the rooms on the ground floor, in the part of the house that is open to the public.

The Gothic chamber organ, by Hull of Dublin (1812), is pumped by bellows in the basement and appears in Goodwin's engraving of the room dated 1833. The three library windows, in the bow of the garden front, perpetuate the curved theme to the end of the house. Two lesser axes comprise the drawing room/ante room/dining room and the Kilkenny marble double staircase/hall/billiard room.

Sir Robert's son Sir Henry Gore-Booth was an explorer of note, principally remembered for having sailed on his yacht *Kara* to the rescue of the arctic explorer Leigh Smith, whose ship had foundered on ice. Sir Henry was the father of Constance and Eva Gore-Booth, whose portrait by Sarah Purser hangs in the dining room. The pilasters of this room were each adorned with life-sized portraits by Count Casimir Markievicz, Constance's husband, representing the butler, the gamekeeper, Mordaunt Gore-Booth who is to the left of the mantel, the artist himself, who is to the right, and the forester wearing a cap. The head housekeeper was too shy to pose and so her column is blank.

W. B. Yeats was staying in the house and one night crept out to the top of the stairs and woke the entire household with shouts that he had seen the long-dormant ghost of Lissadell. His host, who was a hard-working man, did not take kindly to being woken with such news. 'Would you ever go to Hell' he advised the pyjama-clad poet.

Eva Gore-Booth was a distinguished poetess and her sister Constance Markievicz had an extraordinary life. She became involved in the Dublin Lockout of 1913 and befriended James Larkin, the great orator and labour leader. She took part in the Easter Rising in 1916, for which she was imprisoned, and was elected to the House of Commons in the General Election of 1918 as a candidate for Sinn Fein, making her the first woman ever to gain a seat in the Westminster parliament. All the successful Sinn Fein candidates refused to take their seats and met instead at the Mansion House in Dublin to form the first *Dáil*; she was made Minister for Labour in the provisional government.

When the house was built there was no back door; a long tunnel provided service access to a sunken courtyard. Here the pond where a pet seal was kept can still be seen. Buckets of coal could be winched up from the basement where the kitchen and other offices were situated. A beam in the old servants' hall is ornamented with the arms of the various countries belonging to the Empire and the account books for the famine years are still preserved. The house was mortgaged at the time of the famine and no rents were accepted by the estate.

The present owner of Lissadell is Josslyn Gore-Booth, nephew of Aideen Gore-Booth, who with her late sister Gabrielle has devoted much of her life to the house. It is now open to the public.

OPPOSITE The dining room must be unique in having portraits of the family, as well as the gamekeeper, forester and butler, painted on the pilasters by Count Casimir Markievicz who had married Constance Gore-Booth.

RIGHT The main staircase is made of solid blocks of black Kilkenny limestone polished to resemble marble, flecked with white fossil shells.

RIGHT The music room or gallery, which is lit by a clerestory and skylights, is sixty-five feet in length and curved at either end.

SWISS COTTAGE
Cahir, Co. Tipperary

The Swiss Cottage stands on a hillock above the River Suir at one end of the long, narrow demesne of Cahir Park which stretches upstream towards the castle and the town. The mid-eighteenth-century Butler family-house, now a hotel, stands in the main square of Cahir.

It is believed that the little thatched folly, known as the Swiss Cottage, was designed by the Prince Regent's architect, John Nash, in 1810 for Richard Butler, the twelfth Lord Cahir. Nash also designed the Protestant church in Cahir among other Irish commissions. During his stay in Ireland he sent back to England designs for an entire village made up of *cottages ornés* near Bristol called Blaise Hamlet, much visited and admired today. The Swiss Cottage was not built for taking tea, like Lady Louisa Conolly's cottage by the Liffey at Castletown 'lined in Tonbridge ware'. Nor was it built for shooting-lunches, a use that was found in later years for her sister Emily's Shell Cottage at Carton nearby which was originally thatched and also has a verandah, supported on rustic columns of iron. The Swiss Cottage was actually built for Richard and Emily, Lord and Lady Cahir, to live in. They spent little time in Ireland, or else they would have built themselves a more substantial house – perhaps they did intend to do so later on.

The Cahirs were a fashionable young couple in London and Paris where they must have found the French scenic wallpapers for the Swiss Cottage that have now been so carefully restored. Rustic timbers were used for the support of the verandah; they give life to the building, which has been described by Dr Mark Girouard as 'the finest surviving *cottage orné* in the world'.

The cottage was looked after by a caretaker until his death in 1980, after which its condition began to give cause for alarm. Being in an isolated spot it was prey to vandalism. In 1985 a group of people bought the cottage for £35,000 of which the Irish Georgian Society paid £10,000. Mrs Christian Aall, whose Port Royal Foundation has helped restore many unusual buildings such as the Desert de Retz near Paris, adopted the Swiss Cottage. She wanted it all to be on view so she built a new house for the caretaker nearby and paid for the substantial repairs and redecoration. The well-known Dublin fashion designer Sybil Connolly carried out the decoration; among her many achievements here she commissioned some ideally suitable rustic chairs which are very much at home.

The Office of Public Works helped with the restoration; it has accepted the building from the owners and most generously agreed to maintain it and open it to the public. This will ensure that the future of the Swiss Cottage is safeguarded and that this unique creation can be seen and enjoyed by everyone.

RIGHT The fabric on the walls of the bedroom is a copy of the Irish 'toile' manufactured by Robinson of Ballsbridge in the 1770s and copied recently by Brunschwig & Fils of New York.

OPPOSITE The Swiss Cottage was designed in 1810 by John Nash, architect of the Brighton Pavilion, for the twelfth Lord Cahir. It was restored by the Port Royal Foundation of New York and opened to the public in 1989.

LEFT The Swiss Cottage has one of the few coloured scenic wallpapers in an Irish house that is open to visitors. Made by Zuber in 1816, it represents the Banks of the Bosphorus.

BARONS COURT
Newtownstewart, Co. Tyrone

The parkland that provides such a dramatic setting for the great house of the Hamiltons, Dukes of Abercorn, rises up at the most improbable angle, studded with venerable oak trees; a series of three lakes completes the picture. George Steuart was the first of several architects involved. He was a Gaelic speaker from the north of Scotland who was best known for having designed Attingham Hall in Shropshire in 1783 for the first Lord Berwick. Steuart's work in Ireland began in earnest in 1779 when he came over with a team of seventeen masons, six carpenters and two plasterers from London. Estate workers made up the balance of the building team.

The bachelor eighth Earl of Abercorn, who had commissioned Steuart, died in 1789 and his nephew John James Hamilton inherited; he was to be created first Marquess of Abercorn and is still known in the family as the 'Old Marquess'. He had already employed Sir John

garden. Soane proposed replacing Steuart's central staircase by an oblong billiard room with an oval domed ceiling, in a similar design to his proposed dining room for the Earl Bishop of Derry at Downhill. Unfortunately a fire in 1796 destroyed Soane's improvements. It was not until 1835 that the second Marquess paid ten guineas 'to Mr Morrison inspecting the house'. This could refer either to Richard or to his son, William Vitruvius Morrison, as Richard was not knighted until 1841. Gervase Jackson-Stops believes it refers to the son, whose health was soon to deteriorate and who died in 1838. If so, his work would have been completed by the father, as father and son were partners. In 1946 the late Duke commissioned Sir Albert Richardson to draw plans for the north side of the house, which resulted in the demolition of two substantial wings. In 1973, Raymond Erith was employed to draw plans to demolish the service wing to the east. As a

LEFT Barons Court, the garden front, formerly the entrance front; the original seven-bay house with a pediment containing the Hamilton arms is in the centre.

OPPOSITE The rotunda at the heart of the house, once used for billiards, is now a dining room. It is lit from above, the domed and coffered ceiling supported by a ring of Ionic columns.

Soane to enlarge Bentley Priory outside London the year before he inherited and Soane was dispatched to Ireland in 1791 to make recommendations for 'improving' Barons Court. Although he was a consummate architectural draftsman, when he drew the elevation and plan of the existing house for his client to consider, Soane deliberately made Steuart's elevation appear awkward and amateurish. This elevation and plan, in the collection at the Soane Museum in London, are the only record of the original Barons Court.

Soane proposed radical alterations; the principal one involved turning the house back to front, replacing internal partition walls with Corinthian columns to make one long room facing south across the

result, the portico stands out even taller and more overpowering than ever. The family arms in the pediment were carved by Terence Farrell.

The front hall has a coffered ceiling with stars set into squares and a handsome pedimented mantel with a frieze of oak leaves. The Hamilton crest (as has been shown at Stackallan in Co. Meath, where the same device is incorporated in the plasterwork on the staircase ceiling) consists of an oak tree with its trunk being traversed by a saw bearing the word *Through*. Three miniature green Hamilton oaks with golden acorns crown the hall mantel.

Directly on axis to the hall and leading straight into the gallery beyond is the rotunda, now used as a formal dining room. It is lit from

above; this was eminently fitting when it was a billiard room, besides, being buried in the heart of the house it is without windows. Green scagliola columns with Ionic capitals support a frieze of panthers and female masks which in turn carries the blue and white coffered dome.

The gallery is light, comfortable and elegant, eighty-eight feet in length (therefore longer than that at Castletown in Co. Kildare) and lit by ten tall windows with delicate glazing. David Hicks, a family friend, re-ordered the interior for the present generation in the 1970s. The gallery had been divided into three rooms by Sir Albert Richardson for the late Duke. Now it is whole again and probably the finest Morrison room anywhere, providing a handsome backdrop for the paintings, books and furniture that it houses. It is perhaps invidious to single out any particular object, but there is a fascinating pair of inlaid marble-topped side tables with the Hamilton crest on a black background that are close to the work of Belloni and must have been ordered from Italy.

The staircase has been painted a deep red lacquer, against which the

ABOVE The old dining room, now the family room, contains the famous painting by Lawrence of Frances Hawkins, mistress of the first Marquess of Abercorn, with their son, Arthur Fitz-James.

OPPOSITE The library, with its typically Morrisonian ceiling; the carpet was designed for the room by David Hicks who recently redecorated the house.

Classical columnar screen stands out a stark white. Near the foot there hangs a large Landseer; the artist was a frequent visitor and it is said that he was in love with the first Duchess. The library, never a light room, has been made darker still by Mr Hicks who conceived the idea of using the old purple velvet curtains from the large dining room to line the walls. He also designed the carpet which was made for the room.

The old dining room has a life-size portrait by Sir Thomas Lawrence of John James, first Marquess of Abercorn, and over the mantel a famous Lawrence of his mistress, Frances Hawkins, with their son, Arthur Fitz-James (b. 1799). Paintings of the Marquess's legitimate children, also by Lawrence, in 'sunburst' frames, surround the portrait. The mantel was brought here from Duddingston near Edinburgh, which was built for the eighth Earl in 1763 and is now a hotel. Sir William Chambers was the architect and the design of this mantelpiece has also been ascribed to him.

The second Marquess of Abercorn served twice as Lord Lieutenant of Ireland, 1866–8 and 1874–6. He was created a Duke in 1868 after his first term of office. When his widow, a daughter of the sixth Duke of Bedford, died in 1905 she had 162 descendants.

The present Duke and Duchess maintain the house to perfection and are in the process of restoring the wing where the Duke's parents lived. An extensive horticultural enterprise, employing some twenty-four staff, combined with commercial forestry, helps with the upkeep of this gigantic house which is very much a family home rather than a museum. In 1987 the Duchess, who descends from the Russian poet Alexander Pushkin, inaugurated a creative writing competition for Irish school children from both sides of the border aged eleven to twelve who compete for the annual 'Pushkin Prize'. This involves her visiting each school and discussing their entries with the contestants, a praiseworthy venture indeed.

OPPOSITE The staircase is hung with family portraits and at its foot there is a large sporting picture by Sir Edwin Landseer, a frequent visitor to the house.

RIGHT The gallery, eighty-eight feet in length, takes up the entire garden front of the original house, a most impressive yet comfortable room.

THE GRAND
VICTORIAN
HOUSES

Queen Victoria came to the throne in 1837 and ruled for sixty-four years, a period that saw her country become the richest and most powerful in the world, at the hub of a vast empire. The situation in Ireland during this time was very different. The potato famine of the 1840s decimated the population and the starving people had little choice but to emigrate in search of food and work. The climate was hardly conducive to country-house building or 'improvement', except in parts of Ulster where Belfast was the most significant Irish industrial city with its linen and shipbuilding industries. In England a great many wonderful houses, such as the Elizabethan Longleat in Wiltshire, were radically altered in the prosperous Victorian era. The great Georgian houses in Ireland, generally speaking, remained untouched through lack of funds.

Until the end of the Regency period there were essentially only two choices when it came to the design of a country house, namely Classical or Gothic. During the Victorian era discretion was thrown to the winds, and every shape and style of building came into its own. Elizabethan and Jacobean from England, the *palazzo* style from Italy, and that of the French *château* were added to the staple diet, jostled together in a self-confident *mélange* that seems to caricature rather than to copy. The Victorian period saw a great religious revival which fostered high-mindedness and charitable works. The eighteenth century was now regarded as decadent and its art and artefacts went out of fashion.

Interiors became very crowded, and windows were swathed in layers of tasselled curtains and lace. Gas lamps, buttoned furniture, mother-of-pearl and bric-a-brac of all kinds filled the rooms. Georgian mantels were bedecked with red velvet and the household clock demanded the place of honour on them, necessitating a wide shelf for its support. Cast iron in all sorts of disguises was widely used. At Carton in Co. Kildare the overhanging tiled roof of the Victorian museum attached to the eighteenth-century Shell Cottage is supported by purple cast-iron tree trunks. Whereas in the eighteenth century the decorative potential of natural objects such as shells and fircones was appreciated, now there was a preference for anything manmade.

After the Famine the Victorian style was ushered in with a vengeance; there was no longer any architectural time lag between England and Ireland. The smaller, conservative Irish gentry, hard hit by the Famine, could not afford the pleasant late Georgian houses which they doubtless would have built themselves well into the middle of Victoria's reign. The railways opened up areas of great scenic beauty such as Kerry, Galway and Donegal and in these mountainous regions the castle style seems particularly at home. Mitchell Henry, a Liverpool industrialist, spent one and a half million pounds on Kylemore Castle (now Kylemore Abbey) in Co. Galway because he and his wife had fallen in love with this romantic spot on their honeymoon. Sir Benjamin Guinness, sometime Lord Mayor of Dublin, restorer of St Patrick's Cathedral and sole owner of the brewery that bears his name, bought Ashford Castle in Co. Mayo in 1855 and transformed the modest shooting box into a French *château*. These picturesque beauty spots could never have brought in an income, the land being of the poorest kind. They were an indulgence for those with time and money to spare who could afford fashionable architects with up to the minute ideas.

Most of the great Victorian houses in Ireland were paid for, not from land rents, but with foreign money brought in. In 1837 the Duke of Manchester built a neo-Tudor manor house in Co. Armagh called Tanderagee Castle, where his son entertained the Prince of Wales at a shoot to satisfy the social ambitions of his American heiress wife. In order to impress his exalted guest he placed a large order for pheasant with an English game farm but when the birds arrived their wings had been clipped as it was assumed they were for breeding purposes. With great presence of mind the Duke turned to the Prince of Wales, as the birds trotted out of the wood, saying 'In Ireland the pheasants do not fly', and they shot them quite happily on the ground. Tanderagee is now a potato crisp factory.

There are some magnificent Victorian public buildings. Irish railway stations deserve a book of their own; the rival railway companies vied with one another in the splendour of their architecture. They come in all shapes and sizes – Gothic, Tudor, Classical and Italianate. The Egyptian-style Broadstone Station on the north side of Dublin, now a furniture store, is railway architecture at its greatest. Dun Laoghaire is the most intact Victorian town in Ireland, with reticent terraced houses of great charm and character and its four splendid nineteenth-century yacht clubs beside the sea.

In around 1850 a new generation of architects emerged to take the place of the Regency group who had died or retired. With improved communications it became easier for fashionable English architects to extend their practice to Ireland to the disadvantage of local talent. Among the Irish practitioners were Sir Thomas Deane (1792–1871) and Benjamin Woodward (1816–61) who together designed the Kildare Street Club and the Museum Building at Trinity College in Dublin. William Barre (*c.* 1830–67), who designed Clanwilliam House in the suburbs of Belfast, and James Joseph McCarthy (1817–82), the disciple of A. W. N. Pugin (1812–52), were also native Irishmen. Charles Lanyon (1813–89) was born in England but established the successful practice of Lanyon and Lynn, which dominated the architectural scene in Belfast for a generation. They built the magnificent Dunderave in Co. Antrim in the Italian style as well as major public buildings in the city. English architects of the period include William White (1825–1900), responsible for Humewood in Co. Wicklow, and E. W. Godwin (1833–86), who designed Dromore in Co. Limerick, incorporating a round tower to give it an Irish flavour, its silhouette resembling the Rock of Cashel.

In the Victorian period the garden returned to the house from its lonely exile, walled up and out of sight. From 1850 it once more became fashionable to have a formal garden outside the windows, and sheep and cattle were banished to their rightful place beyond the ha-ha. Gravel paths and yew hedges framed the colourful borders tended by an army of gardeners. The practical side of the Victorian character resented having to employ so many gardeners without being able to see the flowers that they tended from the house. Carton in Co. Kildare and Lyons in Co. Dublin illustrate this change of heart. Foreign travel had become much easier and people vied with each other in introducing rare species of flowers and trees from far away places. The average Irish park was surrounded by a belt of trees, generally beech, often pierced by a ride; lakes were dug especially during the famine years and demesne walls were built or added on to. Trees were planted on the parkland to add to its beauty, and at Lyons in Co. Dublin it was said that they were planted in the battle formation of the troops at Waterloo.

For sheer variety and inventiveness the Victorians were unsurpassed, however much their excess of ornament might overwhelm those who appreciate simple lines and enduring proportions.

CARRIGGLAS MANOR
Longford, Co. Longford

A short distance from the county town of Longford stands Carrigglas Manor, one of the only two country seats in that county to remain in the hands of the family for which it was originally built, the other being Castle Forbes. Carrigglas was designed in 1837 for Thomas Langlois Lefroy, Lord Chief Justice of Ireland, 1852–66. Lefroy is remembered for his adolescent intimacy with Jane Austen which he later described as 'a boyish love'. 'He is a very gentlemanlike, good-looking pleasant young man', Jane wrote to her sister Cassandra. He was the inspiration for Mr Darcy in *Pride and Prejudice*.

Carrigglas was designed by Daniel Robertson of Scotland in the Tudor-Gothic Revival style, replacing a decrepit seventeenth-century house. It was finished in 1840 and has remained substantially unaltered since then.

In the words of Mark Bence-Jones 'The Robertson Tudor-Gothic houses stand at the watershed between Georgian and Victorian; with a Victorian seriousness that is lacking in those of the same style by the Morrisons. They are more solid, with steeper gables, smaller windows and greater expanses of rather hard stonework. Yet they still have the picturesque charm of the earlier Gothic Revival, with a Georgian symmetry'.

The front of Carrigglas is symmetrical and two slender turreted watch towers stand like sentries on either side of the gabled porch. The front hall leads into the staircase hall with its Georgian-Gothic mantelpiece. The staircase balustrade is cast-iron. The three main

Carrigglas Manor, the garden front. Designed in 1837 by Daniel Robertson of Scotland, the year Queen Victoria ascended the throne.

BELOW The farmyard at Carrigglas, designed by Ireland's foremost neo-Classical architect, James Gandon, and completed before 1790. It is now being restored.

reception rooms, drawing room, library and dining room, take up the entire garden front and open into one another in a most welcoming manner.

From 1984, as funds have become available, the house has been restored and sympathetically modernized. It contains attractive neo-Tudor plasterwork ceilings and most of the furniture originally installed that was brought from earlier Lefroy houses. Robertson's plans for Carrigglas are still in the house and there are copies at the Irish Architectural Archive in Dublin.

The Lefroys are a Huguenot family like the Trenches (La Tranche), La Touches and Le Fanus; they can trace their origins to Cambrai. Thomas Lefroy acquired the property from the established Co. Longford family of Newcomen whose heiress had married Sir William Gleadowe, a banker in Dublin who assumed his wife's name. For this reason the Newcomens came to be considered *nouveaux* – their very name sounded it, giving rise to the following couplet:

Though many years I've lived in Town

As New-Come-In I'm only known.

Nevertheless they were people of taste who were not afraid to employ the best talent when it came to designing both their bank and their country seat. Their former bank, on Castle Street beside Dublin Castle, still stands and retains its magnificent interior. It was designed in 1781 by Thomas Ivory, the Cork-born architect chiefly remembered for having built the Blue Coat School in Dublin. Unfortunately the bank never recovered from inflation in the Napoleonic War period, exacerbated by family quarrels; it finally failed in 1825 causing the second Viscount Newcomen to shoot himself.

It was no less a personage than James Gandon, the architect of the Custom House and the Four Courts in Dublin and the foremost neo-Classical architect in Ireland at that time, who was chosen to design the Newcomen country seat. Alas, the design remained on paper; Gandon's drawings for it are in the National Library in Dublin. They show a handsome house with a portico, pediment and dome. Fortunately a magnificent double courtyard stable and farm complex was built here before 1790 to Gandon's designs, and although in a parlous state in recent times, it is gradually being brought back as the present generation of Lefroys breathes new life into the place. Gandon's country commissions are few and far between, he was so heavily engaged in the capital; the survival of the stables with their original partitions, and the dairy with its fittings, is indeed fortunate. In 1988 the Irish Georgian Society gave a grant towards roof repairs in the twin yards. There is a good case here for putting the yards back as they were, provided arrangements can be made to satisfy the demands of modern agriculture, particularly as the house and grounds are now open to the public.

The entrance gates, little used today, were also designed by James Gandon in the form of a triumphal arch. As Dr McParland, Gandon's biographer, has pointed out, this arch is a near relative to those at the Four Courts in Dublin. The cut-limestone skin is very thin and water has penetrated at the back causing some of it to move. Gandon must also have designed the symmetrical flanking lodges. The Irish Georgian Society is hoping to help restore this beautiful monument in the near future.

TOP The dining room, with a portrait of Chief Justice Lefroy, the builder of the house, above the mantel, and a Chinese painted leather screen.

ABOVE The library, with its Tudor-Gothic doors and ceiling, is lit by the bow window at the centre of the garden front.

OPPOSITE The drawing room. Most of the house is open to the public on a regular basis and is much enjoyed by visitors on account of its untouched charm.

ADARE MANOR
Adare, Co. Limerick

The great Victorian seat of the Earls of Dunraven has recently been turned into a hotel and fortunately the interesting interior has been kept intact. Empty since the contents were sold in 1982, the Manor has become once again a centre of life and a source of employment in the locality.

Adare Manor was built in the Tudor style by the second Earl of Dunraven from 1832 and completed by his son the third Earl in 1862. According to his own account, the second Earl acted largely as his own architect, being 'prevented by gout from shooting and fishing'. 'This goodly house was erected by Windham Henry, Earl of Dunraven and Caroline his Countess without borrowing, selling or leaving a debt AD 1850'. These words are inscribed on a stone tablet on the south front of the Manor, at the western end. Giant stone letters on the parapet read *Except the Lord build the house, their labour is but lost that build it.*

In fact several people besides the Lord were employed in the massive undertaking and unravelling the threads involved has been complicated by the exceedingly long time the Manor took to build, and Lord Dunraven's wish to be thought of as the designer. The original house was built by Valentine Richard Quin in about 1730, an astute lawyer who conformed to the Protestant faith in 1739. It was of two storeys, with seven windows across, and a pediment. Quin's grandson was made Lord Adare in 1800 and Earl of Dunraven in 1822, taking this title from the immense Welsh estates of his daughter-in-law. In 1828, the architect James Pain, who had already built a family mausoleum here after the death of the first Earl in 1824, produced designs for a new house. Taught by John Nash, James and his brother George Richard Pain were based in Cork and were the foremost architects of the time in the southwest of Ireland. The work began under the supervision of James Connolly, master-mason. Connolly and his team of craftsmen married their carved woodwork to Flemish work purchased by the Dunravens on the Continent between 1834 and 1836. In 1840 James Pain was replaced by Lewis Nockalls Cottingham who acted as the

ghost for his master the Earl. Lord Dunraven wrote to Pain: 'Building is my amusement and I am a dabbler in architecture and I have now for some years been carrying on the new work entirely from my own designs and without any assistance whotsoever.' Cottingham designed the openwork parapet and doubtless much besides although his drawings do not survive; perhaps his master wished them not to.

The most impressive chamber at Adare Manor is the Great Gallery, 132 feet in length, twenty-six feet high and twenty-one feet in breadth; its timbered roof and stained glass windows give it a monastic air. Lady Dunraven, the wife of the builder, was a Wyndham heiress from Dunraven Castle, Glamorgan; she wrote: 'The stained glass of these windows, illustrating the pedigree of the ancient and noble family of Wyndham, was designed and executed by Thomas Willement of London FSA in the year of our Lord 1838, and erected by Windham Henry, second Earl of Dunraven in love and honour of Caroline Wyndham, his Countess'. Her husband wrote to her 'The gallery almost looks like a Cathedral, I do not know how we shall ever fill it'.

The future third Earl, a convert to Catholicism, employed A. W. N. Pugin to design interior details and furniture for Adare Manor shortly before the death of the second Earl in 1850. These included the hall ceiling, the staircase and plans for the dining room, library and terrace. Pugin died in 1852 and P. C. Hardwick completed the house in the Pugin manner in 1862, which year saw the coming of age of Lord Adare, the future fourth Earl. The original designs are in the possession of the Earl of Dunraven.

The beauty of the demesne is enhanced by the River Maigue, a tributary of the Shannon, which flows past the Franciscan Friary (1464) and the Augustinian Abbey (1313). The village of Adare, situated at the gates of the Manor, has two rows of delightful thatched cottages designed by Detmar Blow, chiefly known for his work on the Grosvenor Estate in London at the end of the nineteenth century. Adare is one of the most picturesque villages in Ireland.

LEFT Adare Manor was built by the second and third Earls of Dunraven between 1832 and 1862; several architects were involved in its design, including the patrons themselves.

OPPOSITE The great gallery is one of the longest in Ireland, 132 feet in length, and can be compared to the Victorian picture gallery at Kilkenny Castle.

KYLEMORE ABBEY
Letterfrack, Co. Galway

Kylemore is dramatically situated at the foot of a hill overlooking Kylemore Lough in the wilds of Connemara. It was built in the 1860s by James F. Fuller and Ussher Roberts, brother of the Field-Marshal, for Mitchell Henry, MP, a rich Liverpool merchant. He and his bride, Margaret Vaughan from Co. Down, had stopped in the Pass of Kylemore on their honeymoon for a picnic. The emptiness all around and the beauty of the landscape moved them and they caught sight of a shooting box in the hill-side opposite. Mitchell Henry found out who owned the property – nine thousand acres of mountain, bog and lakes, and bought it in order to build their dream house.

Mitchell Henry had built a drawing room, dining room, breakfast room, morning room, library, study, billiard room, ballroom with sprung floor, thirty-three bedrooms and staff quarters. It was one of the few houses in Ireland equipped with a Turkish bath, which partly made up for the fact that when built, Kylemore had only two bathrooms – one for the Henrys and the other to be shared between their guests. Henry also commissioned a model farm, laundry, saw-mill and an ornate chapel. There were to be all kinds of gardens and glass-houses as well as a Gothic church which was in part a replica of Norwich Cathedral, originally built by the English Benedictines.

The fine stonework, the grouping of turrets and battlements, the mullioned windows and oriels create a lasting impression of fairytale beauty. As a result Kylemore has become one of the most photographed and admired buildings in the West of Ireland. The labour for building this elaborate house was found locally with a few Dublin artisans and some Italians for the intricate ceiling detail. The bill for the work came to one and a half million pounds.

The Henrys had nine children but when Margaret died, soon to be followed by the death of one of their daughters in a driving accident, Henry returned sadly to England and sold Kylemore. In 1900 Eugene Zimmerman of Cincinnati bought the property for his daughter, Helena, on her marriage to the ninth Duke of Manchester.

In 1665, Dame Lucy Knatchbull had established an Abbey for the Irish nuns in Ypres which was destroyed amid the fighting during the First World War. In 1920 they bought Kylemore where they established a well-known girls' school and a variety of shops selling every kind of souvenir.

Kylemore Abbey, with its myriad
battlements and turrets, nestles comfortably
at the foot of a barren mountain,
overlooking a lake of the same name. It was
built in the 1860s for Mitchell Henry, of
Liverpool, and designed by James F. Fuller.
and Ussher Roberts

ASHFORD CASTLE
Cong, Co. Mayo

The first sight of the demesne is the imposing wall that surrounds it and the turreted gate-lodge where uniformed attendants stand on guard. Although the park is now a golf course, the natural beauty of the layout and the glistening waters of Lough Corrib create a breathtaking first impression. At the heart of the great Victorian castle with its stepped battlements is the modest five-bay Georgian shooting box built by the Browne family, from whom Lord Oranmore and Browne descends.

Benjamin Guinness, sole owner of the Dublin brewery, had a keen interest in architecture, and restored the decaying St Patrick's Cathedral in Dublin at his own expense. He bought Ashford Castle in Co. Mayo in 1855 and created a French *château* beside the existing house. Benjamin's son, Arthur Guinness, first Lord Ardilaun, added the castle to the French *château* and the Georgian shooting box in 1870, employing James F. Fuller and George Ashlin to design this addition. They also built the great castellated six-arch bridge across the river with its embattled gateway surmounted by a gigantic 'A' and a Baron's coronet. When he was elevated to the peerage in 1880 Lord Ardilaun took his title from a small island on the lake, a neighbouring island called Cleenilaun being unaccountably ignored. He and his wife employed 300 people to beautify the demesne and planted nearly one million trees and flowering shrubs. He developed the 35,000-acre shoot at Ashford so that it broke the European record for woodcock.

An Austrian-oak front door, nine feet high, leads into the hall which has a floor, walls and ceiling with finely carved detailing, all in oak, like the rest of the principal reception rooms. Dances, concerts and receptions were part of life at Ashford in Lord Ardilaun's day. In 1908 the Prince of Wales, later King George V, stayed here for a month.

Lord Ardilaun is best remembered for buying out the key-holders around St Stephen's Green which he presented to the people of Dublin as a public park; a statue of him on the green faces the College of Surgeons. He married Lady Olive White, daughter of the Earl of Bantry, but they had no children and when he died in 1915 the title died with him. The castle and surrounding estate passed to the Iveagh Trust representing the Guinness family until 1939, when Noel Huggard converted it into a hotel which has since had many distinguished visitors, including Prince Rainier and Princess Grace of Monaco and President Reagan.

Ashford Castle stands at the head of Lough Corrib; it was mainly built in 1870 by Sir Arthur Guinness, first Lord Ardilaun to the designs of J. F. Fuller and George Ashlin.

HUMEWOOD
Kiltegan, Co. Wicklow

Humewood is a very large Victorian house in Co. Wicklow that has not changed hands outside the family since it was built in 1867. A series of pointed granite towers ascend gradually to an oblong crenellated tower over one hundred feet in height; the massive blocks of local granite are irregular in size and the mouldings around the windows simple. The whole effect is a rich extravagant mixture of line and form designed with inspiration and vigour; chimney stacks, buttresses with batters, gables and soaring spires produce an elaborate and bold composition silhouetted against the Wicklow mountains – a joy to behold. The house appears much larger than it really is and blends perfectly with its mountain backdrop.

Humewood was designed by the English architect William White for W. W. F. Hume Dick and was intended to be 'an occasional resort in the summer recess or the shooting season'. William White was a brilliant eccentric with a great understanding of building materials; the architect of many churches, schools and some country houses; an individualist, inventor, mountaineer, writer and lecturer who spent most of his retirement trying to prove that Shakespeare was Bacon!

An English contractor named Albert Kimberley from Banbury was employed to build the house. White undertook not to exceed an expenditure of £15,000 but, in the event, over-ran his estimate by £10,000. As a result, Kimberley took his client and the architect to court because they refused to pay the excess, and after five years won his suit, leaving White's career in ruins.

In spite of the enormous scale of Humewood the reception rooms, apart from the billiard room, are intimate in size and being on an upper floor they enjoy views across the park to a lake. They are approached by a dramatic stone staircase lit by a stained-glass window depicting the

arms of the Hume family. The window must be one of the finest of its kind in Ireland. The perfection with which the house and grounds are maintained combined with the continuity of ownership and family mementoes show how attractive and comfortable a Victorian house can be.

The venerable oak avenues bear testimony to the former existence here of a much earlier house. The late owner, who inherited the property, was Madame Jacques Hume-Weygand. She was brought up in France spending holidays at Humewood, and married the son of Marshal Weygand. She could remember her coming-out dance in the vast billiard room, also used as a banqueting hall, surrounded by statues of white marble goddesses. These alluring ladies were mounted on ball-bearings so that the billiard players could choose which aspect to admire while awaiting their turn. As a girl, Madame Hume-Weygand loved to play the violin standing on the gallery that overlooks the billiard room, the music flowing past the white marble statues to the cold grey mist of the Wicklow hills beyond.

ABOVE Two tall windows, with Hume family coats of arms in stained glass, cast light on to a massive stone staircase that leads to the reception rooms.

OPPOSITE Humewood, an incredible apparition, was designed by the English architect, William White for W. W. F. Hume Dick in 1867, and has remained in the Hume family ever since. The round tower was an afterthought, not designed by White, who by then was on bad terms with his client.

RIGHT The drawing room, cluttered with comfortable furniture, as such rooms were in Victorian times, and lit by plate glass windows, has a painted ceiling and a round turret room beside it.

GLENVEAGH CASTLE
Churchill, Co. Donegal

Glenveagh Castle was built in 1870 by Mr John Adair and his wife, the American heiress Cornelia Wadsworth, as a remote and romantic shooting box in the wilds of Co. Donegal. Mrs Adair was a great hostess in her day, and entertained Queen Victoria's son, HRH the Duke of Connaught and his Duchess here. Edward VII sent over a stag from Windsor to help start the herd of deer. The architect was Adair's cousin, Mr J. T. Trench.

A four-mile drive from the Eagle Gates winds its way across the moon-like landscape in a gentle descent towards Lough Veagh. At the last bend in the road the forbidding towers and battlements of the Victorian castle come into view, the severity of the granite walls greatly softened in spring and summer by banks of pink hydrangeas. Three sides of the forecourt are taken up by the castle with the entrance on the right. The narrow barrel-vaulted vestibule with black and white Victorian tiled floor is decorated with a naïve arrangement of sea-shells all painted white. This leads to the main drawing room with Irish Chippendale furniture covered in flowered cretonne whose design is echoed in the Donegal carpets. The round tower beyond contains the music room lined in green tartan and festooned with antlers which are the keynote not only of the castle but of the outbuildings and gardens as well.

In 1929 Glenveagh was purchased by Professor Arthur Kingsley Porter, a distinguished archaeologist and Professor of Fine Arts at Harvard. In 1933 he went off alone for a walk from his cottage on the island of Inishbofin and disappeared, never to be seen again. His widow sold the property in 1938 to the late Mr Henry McIlhenny whose grandfather had emigrated to the United States from Co. Donegal.

Henry McIlhenny, President of the Philadelphia Museum of Art, connoisseur, collector, wit and scholar, transformed his castle on Lough Veagh into a marvellous hub of life. He created a remarkable garden at Glenveagh first with the help of Jim Russell and then Lanning Roper. The *potager* was carefully laid out so that the rows of vegetables interspersed with cutting flowers, bordered with wild strawberries and box, were shown off to the best possible decorative effect. At the foot stands the Gothic Revival conservatory designed by Philippe Jullian. By contrast the informal garden surrounds a well-tended flat green lawn, with palms, tree ferns and rhododendrons clustered around it. Plants usually associated with a conservatory or cold house flourish here thanks to the shelter provided by the trees and warmth from the Gulf Stream. Various 'rooms' with statuary and formal planting complete this remarkable creation beautifully tended today by the State to Mr McIlhenny's original conception. Twenty-five thousand acres of wild mountainous landscape provide a damp and sombre backdrop for the luxurious castle, until recently lit up by laughter and clever talk.

It was interesting for the neighbours to have a chance to meet the endless stream of exotic pilgrims that visited Glenveagh to worship at Henry's shrine. Every sort and kind of museum curator and art expert seemed to find his or her way there. A stream of regular Irish friends came year after year providing a continuo, such as Lord and Lady Dunsany, or Commander Bill King and his brilliant wife, the writer Anita Leslie. Although children were not usually invited, the poet

Glenveagh Castle was designed by J. T. Trench for Mr and Mrs Adair in 1870. It is now in State ownership and open to the public.

OPPOSITE The drawing room looks over Lough Veagh; the carpets were made in the Donegal carpet factory in the 1950s, the floral design copied from the cretonne on the seat furniture.

LEFT The floor of the entrance hall is tiled in black and white and the walls have been adorned with shells and whitened; antlers abound.

LEFT At the foot of the round tower is the music room, lined in tartan, with tables, a mirror and a chandelier made of antlers.

Stephen Spender did manage to bring his daughter Lizzie at a very early age. Another regular pilgrim was the great historian of the Crusades, Professor Sir Steven Runciman. Edward James, Charles de Beistegui, Sarah Churchill, Aileen Plunket, Yehudi Menuhin – actors, decorators, social butterflies and garden lovers all made the tedious journey here and nobody ever regretted having gone to the trouble. A tour of the immense garden with Henry, accompanied by a pack of golden retrievers, was an education in itself. 'I can't stand earth', he would say, and any bald patch he chanced to notice would be quickly planted up. 'Anne Leitrim gave me this'; the plants would be introduced one after the other like friends at a party – his knowledge was prodigious.

There was stalking on the mountain and fishing in the lake, accompanied by an army of keepers and ghillies clad in a uniform of specially woven Donegal tweed. The butler and footmen wore green Austrian jackets with bone buttons, and the maids were dressed in dirndls to match. Antlers abounded, disguised as chairs, firescreens and inkwells, or merely hung about on the tartan walls. Victorian paintings of sporting scenes by Landseer and Ansdell were completely at home in

The design for the conservatory in the walled garden was taken from a sketch by Philippe Jullian to blend in with the stone battlements which surround it.

these surroundings. When the season was right a generous haunch of venison would be pressed on the departing guest.

Staying in this castellated Gothic outpost was rather like being marooned in a comfortable Victorian railway carriage abandoned by its engine. Time stood still. The curtain of mist was seldom raised whatever the time of year. People came for the brilliance of their host and the enjoyment of his company; Glenveagh was an oasis of laughter in the middle of nowhere. Everything about the place was run like clockwork in spite of the avenue being four precipitous miles long and, until the 1960s, the absence of both electricity and telephone.

The Irish Government purchased the 10,000 hectares of the Glenveagh Estate in 1975 for £400,000. In 1983 Henry McIlhenny gave the castle and gardens to the Irish State. The whole property is now managed as a National Park, in which nature is conserved, and is visited by some 90,000 people each year.

BALLYWALTER PARK
Ballywalter, Co. Down

Ballywalter was aptly described by Professor Alistair Rowan as 'a building with a metropolitan air and all the architectural trappings of a London club' (*Country Life*, 2 March, 1967). It was built for Andrew Mulholland soon after 1846 when he acquired the house and lands of the Matthews family, then known as Springvale, which dated from 1810. This house is incorporated within the present structure, designed by the distinguished Belfast architect, Sir Charles Lanyon. Among his other well-known commissions were Queen's University and the Custom House in Belfast, besides Scrabo Tower in Co. Down for the Marquess of Londonderry. The Antrim coast road was one of Lanyon's first commissions after he was appointed Surveyor to the County.

Mulholland became Mayor of Belfast in 1845, and was the father of the first Lord Dunleath. The family business was originally in cotton spinning, but subsequent to the complete destruction by fire of their mill on York Street in Belfast in 1828 they decided to switch to linen, as cotton was on the decline due to competition from England. The fire proved providential, and the family business prospered after the change was made, largely because the Mulhollands were the first to realize the advantage of steam power in mechanizing the process of flax spinning.

Andrew Mulholland would have moved in the same circles as his architect, and was chairman of the committee for building the Ulster

Ballywalter Park was built in 1847 by Sir Charles Lanyon for Andrew Mulholland, whose son became the first Lord Dunleath; their fortune was built on the manufacture of cotton and linen in Belfast.

OPPOSITE In 1863, shortly before he died, Andrew Mulholland once again commissioned Lanyon, this time for the building of a vast conservatory at right angles to the house.

ABOVE The free-standing columns at the top of the staircase are carried on as a screen around the well of the stairs, lit by a domed skylight.

OPPOSITE The library has the original Victorian mahogany bookcases and overmantel; fortunately very little in the house has been changed making it such an excellent example of its period.

RIGHT The music room, with some of the collection of keyboard instruments amassed over the years. On the left is an eighteenth-century Broadwood piano, formerly at Castletown in Co. Kildare.

Institute for the Deaf, the Dumb and the Blind. This was one of Lanyon's earliest commissions, begun in 1843, and was a long gabled building in the Tudor style that was a much-loved landmark in Belfast until its demolition in 1964, against the wishes of conservationists. Lanyon was born in England in 1813 and worked as a civil engineer in Dublin. He was appointed county surveyor for Co. Kildare but moved to Co. Antrim, at his own request, where he designed roads, bridges and railways. Lanyon was knighted in 1869; when he died in 1889 he was the head of the firm of Lanyon, Lynn and Lanyon, the foremost architectural firm in Belfast.

Ballywalter is the most complete example of a nineteenth-century Italianate *palazzo* in Ireland. The front lodge, in the same style, gives advance notice of the pleasures to come. There is a handsome *porte-cochère* with coupled Doric columns and the area which gives light to the basement is protected by an unusual latticed balustrade. The hall is panelled in mahogany and leads to the domed staircase hall which is the most memorable feature of the house. The staircase is of white marble, lit by a stained-glass dome, with a colonnade of Corinthian columns forming a loggia or landing at the top. Mulholland's porcelain and alabaster urns, collected by him on the Continent, are housed here. The detailing throughout the house is carefully thought out and impeccably executed. The organ on the staircase, made by Mander in 1966, is part of the remarkable collection of musical instruments at Ballywalter assembled by the present owners. It is a reminder that in 1863 Lanyon was one of three trustees involved in a deed of gift of a grand organ, made by Hill, presented to the people of Belfast by Andrew Mulholland 'for the improvement of their minds and taste'.

Three years before Andrew Mulholland died, in 1863, he added on a vast cut-stone conservatory with a domed roof at right angles to the house, also designed by Sir Charles Lanyon. Miraculously nothing has changed, and the character of the place, softened somewhat by the passage of time, has been faithfully preserved to the present day.

STRAFFAN HOUSE
Straffan, Co. Kildare

The chequered history of Straffan House seems set fair at last for the happy ending it deserves. The house looks down towards an island on the River Liffey, across formal gardens; it has been beautifully restored and filled with superb Irish works of art. Replete with lovely old marble mantels and brand new 'Adam' ceilings, it makes an appropriate final entry for a book on Irish country houses, being almost entirely a new creation itself.

Hugh Henry, a Dublin banker, purchased the land here on both sides of the Liffey and built the original house in around 1720. It resembled Oakley Park, near Celbridge, which has been attributed to Thomas Burgh both on stylistic and geographical grounds. A project for adding on to the house, which shows how the pre-Palladian building looked, is in the collection of architectural drawings at the National Library in Dublin. This is signed and dated 1808, by the Dublin architect, Benjamin Hallam, who also designed Rockcorry in Co. Monaghan.

Hugh Henry married Anne Leeson, sister of the first Earl of Milltown, the creator of Russborough in Co. Wicklow. Their second son Hugh married his first cousin, Lady Anne Leeson, and they built

Lodge Park, Straffan, about a mile from Straffan House, in 1775. Lodge Park consists of a central block, curved sweeps and two pairs of wings, to remind Lady Anne of Russborough where she had grown up. The Knight of Glin has attributed the design of Lodge Park to the amateur architect, Nathaniel Clements, who built a house for himself in Phoenix Park that is today the residence of the President of Ireland. The Earl of Milltown, Hugh Henry's brother-in-law, was one of the most refined and cultivated Irishmen of the day and it seems that the Leeson-Henry circle was devoted to art and architecture. Joseph Henry, Hugh's elder brother who also lived at Straffan House, was mentioned by Robert

OPPOSITE The plasterwork in the former front hall of the house is less than twenty years old, but even the keenest eye might be excused for believing it to be of the period.

BELOW The garden front of Straffan House, with its Italianate campanile, looks down across formal gardens to a little island on the River Liffey.

OPPOSITE A portrait of Mrs St
George by William Orpen hangs in
the reception hall, one of the Irish
works of art that have recently come
to Straffan in its new guise as a
country club.

RIGHT One of the reception rooms is
hung with paintings by Jack B.
Yeats, brother of the poet. A bust of
the artist can be seen on the left.

Adam in Italy in 1757 as being 'an Irish gentleman of great estate and esteemed the traveller of most taste that has been abroad these many years' (John Fleming, *Robert Adam and his Circle*, London, 1962).

Straffan House was then bought by Hugh Barton (1766–1854), grandson of Thomas Barton who had established a flourishing wine business in Bordeaux in 1725. The branch of the Bartons that live in Glendalough is descended from the same Hugh Barton; they are related by marriage to the Childers family who produced a Protestant president for Ireland. Robert Barton of Glendalough belonged to Sinn Fein, represented his county in Parliament, was a signatory of the Treaty with the United Kingdom in 1921 and became a minister in the Dáil when it was formed.

Hugh Barton demolished the burnt-out house of the Henrys and built a new house beside the eighteenth-century carriage yard in 1832. It was subsequently given an Italianate campanile, descendant of the

tower built for Queen Victoria at Osborne on the Isle of Wight. The house proved too large and impracticable to live in, so Captain F. B. Barton pulled down half in 1937 as a measure of economy, and sold the house twelve years later. Mr and Mrs John Ellis from Yorkshire were the purchasers; their son Patrick, Master of the North Kildare Harriers, kennelled the hounds here; Patrick Desmond, the huntsman, lived in the front lodge. Mr Stephen O'Flaherty was the next owner, followed by Mr Kevin McClory, a film producer. He and his wife Elizabeth, the daughter of Dr Vincent O'Brien, sold Straffan to a Persian general, and, after two more changes of hands, the present owner is Dr Michael Smurfit. He has in effect doubled the size of the original house using a granite porch from Ballynegall in Co. Westmeath (1808) to tie the two sides together. He has not only created a hotel here but also furnished it with important Irish works of art, an enterprising venture that deserves every success.

THE
DECORATIVE
ARTS

The decorative arts in Ireland did not begin to flourish in earnest until the late seventeenth century when the upheavals of the earlier decades subsided and political stability was established. There are few remaining examples of artefacts from Medieval times, but there are tantalising pieces of evidence to suggest that there were at least some areas of great domestic luxury in this earlier period. At Dunluce Castle an inventory of about 1630 describes sixty-six pairs of curtains of the finest materials, mostly for beds, together with three-quarters of a mile of tapestries including a set that had belonged to Cardinal Wolsey. Also mentioned are mirrors, paintings and inlaid cabinets. While many of these may have been brought from Europe, there is evidence that decorative pieces, such as silver and furniture, were produced in Dublin and provincial centres throughout the seventeenth century. Little has survived apart from some ecclesiastical plate.

In the realm of public buildings the seventeenth century closes with the spectacular carving and plasterwork at the Royal Hospital, Kilmainham. Some of this was the work of Huguenots, such as the Tabary family, who came to Ireland from France after the revocation of the Edict of Nantes in 1685. The significance of Kilmainham is that it acted almost as a school for generations of plasterworkers, joiners, carvers and wrought-iron workers, who endeavoured to imitate its superb quality.

During the course of the eighteenth century Dublin rose to become one of the major cities of Europe. This brought full awareness of artistic developments abroad. Native workmanship was given a cosmopolitan flavour by the presence in Ireland of British and foreign artists and craftsmen, such as the Van Nosts, Bartholomew Cramillion, the Lafranchini, Willem van der Hagen, Simon Vierpyl, James Gandon and Richard Castle. Rosemary ffolliott writes of the eighteenth century: 'Socially and artistically, Ireland took its place again in the mainstream of European culture, a place which it had not occupied for nearly 1,000 years' – that is, not since the time of monastic learning when Ireland was known as the 'Island of Saints and Scholars' and Irish wisdom spread throughout Europe. The period 1740–1800 saw the apogee of design and manufacture in the decorative arts. After 1740 the Rococo influence from France, its exuberant designs full of life and movement, replaced the plainer restrained style which had been in fashion up until then. This was, in turn, followed by the sober neo-Classical trend with its traditional motifs inspired by Greek and Roman art.

The records surviving from the eighteenth century show a fully organized resident tradition in the crafts of plastering, stone and woodcarving, wrought-ironwork and silver as well as in the finer arts of painting and design. There is a widespread belief that the artists and craftsmen responsible for the decorative arts in Ireland were mostly foreigners. In fact, the names of members of the various guilds from the sixteenth century onwards are on record and they show that an amount of native talent existed. In 1731 a further impetus was added with the founding of the Dublin Society by an enlightened group of Irish intellectuals and connoisseurs. The Dublin Society Schools were established to teach architecture, painting and sculpture and in connection with the existing apprenticeship system, they helped to foster the various trades and skills. John Hickey, the designer of the La Touche monument in Delgany, Co. Wicklow, studied there. As he was a pupil of John Van Nost he is also a prime example of the Continental influence on native Irish craftsmen. The Society was actively supported by the Irish Parliament and became the Royal Dublin Society in 1820. It continued to teach painters and watercolourists well into the nineteenth century.

The loss of the Irish Parliament after the Act of Union in 1801 dealt a severe blow to the fabric of Anglo-Irish society. Dublin lost its importance as a capital and the arts suffered from lack of patronage. The Anglo-Irish landowning class could no longer exercise financial and political control and many chose to live in the country, abandoning their town houses in Dublin. Fortunately, Dublin has managed to retain row upon row of terraced Georgian houses, some with magnificent plasterwork but none with the original contents. It is a sobering thought to consider the wealth of beautiful things that once adorned these houses; the silver, the books, the chandeliers, furniture and pictures – all now dispersed.

The depressed economic conditions after the Union led to a dependence on potatoes as the staple diet of the rural population. The failure of the potato crop resulted in the Great Famine of 1845–9, a disaster of massive proportion resulting in the death of a million people and the emigration of even more. There was an increased swell of Nationalist agitation throughout the population that remained, inspired by high-minded reformists including such eminent Protestants as Robert Emmet, and later Charles Stewart Parnell. With the Anglo-Irish influence now on the wane, and encouraged by the newly released patriotic sentiment, the native Irish craftsmen began to turn away from European design and a Celtic Revival movement developed. It looked for inspiration to the superb craftmanship of the early Celts before the coming of Christianity; to the famous illuminated manuscripts, such as the Book of Kells and the Book of Durrow, which were priceless examples of early Christian art. This Celtic Revival was expressed in literature by W. B. Yeats, in the theatre by John Synge and Lady Gregory. In the visual arts harps, shamrocks, Hibernias, round towers, Irish wolfhounds, stylized animals, and Celtic designs appeared. The archaeological discoveries of ancient Irish buried treasures such as the Tara Brooch in 1850, and the Ardagh Chalice in 1868, encouraged this interest.

The English Arts and Craft movement of the late nineteenth century was created as a protest against the ugliness and confusion of style that some felt had developed during the Victorian period. William Morris was one of the leaders of this movement, founding his wallpaper, chinz and tapestry firm in 1862 which advocated clarity, simplicity and a return to naturalistic flower- or bird-motifs. Cottage industries in Ireland adopted this new concept, also embracing Celtic designs, particularly in ceramics, silver and textiles. Craftsmen relied on local materials: furniture was often made of bog oak and decorated with Irish symbols. Needlewomen were encouraged to use Irish fabrics and designs, and Irish pottery was made at Belleek from the 1860s where suitable porcelain clay was available. Today Belleek china, with its borders of shamrocks and harps, is greatly prized.

From the wealth of examples available, the following selection of Irish decorative arts demonstrates some of the main trends, focussing, in particular, on the golden age of the eighteenth century. Although there has been no mention of jewellery, metalwork, tapestry, lace, musical instruments, estate maps, engravings, aquatints or portrait medallions, these and much more were produced in Ireland at the time and are part of its splendid heritage.

PAINTING

There is virtually no evidence of painting in Ireland before 1650 due to the domestic turmoil prevalent in the preceding centuries, and also perhaps to lack of interest; tapestry seems to have been preferred in the more important castles. Charles II granted a Charter to the Guild of Dublin Cutlers, Painter-Steyners and Stationers in 1670 and this was a great encouragement to the art of painting. The early artists were influenced by the Low Countries, their principal output consisting of portraiture with or without a landscaped background. The principal centre of training was the excellent Dublin Society Schools set up in the 1740s under Robert West and James Mannin who had studied in France. Landscape painting at this time reached a very high standard; paintings of country houses became fashionable and many of the finest landscape artists of the eighteenth century such as Thomas Roberts found this a helpful source of income.

There was a dearth of sporting pictures, surprising in Ireland where outdoor pursuits have always been so popular, and also a lack of painting with any political flavour though the heady days of Grattan's Parliament in the 1780s did produce the occasional exception, such as Francis Wheatley's *Volunteers on College Green* in the National Gallery of Ireland. The history of painting in Ireland through the eighteenth and nineteenth centuries shows that many artists left to achieve fame abroad but that painting was enriched by some foreigners such as Willem van der Hagen who came and stayed.

The first portrait illustrated here is of *Maire Rua*, 'Red Mary' O'Brien, a fearsome-looking lady, proud of her lace finery and her

elaborate Renaissance pendant, by an unknown artist. She was born in 1615, the daughter of Torlach Rua McMahon, hereditary Gaelic lord of Clonderlaw on the Shannon Estuary. 'Red Mary' married three times; her second husband Conor O'Brien of Lemaneagh Castle was killed in a fracas with Cromwell's General Ludlow in 1651. To save her son's lands she marched to Limerick to marry one of Cromwell's men, a soldier called Cooper. It is said that soon after he fell to his death, pushed (so the story goes) by his loving bride. She was the mother of Sir Donough O'Brien whose monument at Kilnasoolagh in Co. Clare, is also illustrated, page 242.

By contrast, the portrait illustrated opposite is highly accomplished, painted by the most fashionable painter in Dublin of his day, Stephen Slaughter (1697–1765). The subject is Mrs Windham Quin of Adare in Co. Limerick, 'the dame of the slender wattle', from whom are descended the Earls of Dunraven. She is painted with her favourite hound by her side, about to go riding, slightly over-dressed, with all her elaborate lace frogging. In *The Querist* (1735) Bishop Berkeley wonders 'What would be the consequence if our gentry affected to distinguish themselves by fine houses rather than fine clothes?'

The portrait illustrated of Sophia Baddeley (1745–86), wife of the well-known actor Robert Baddeley, is in pastel. She was described as a 'very beautiful woman but a bad actress' and died in poverty. The artist, Hugh Douglas Hamilton (*c.* 1739–1808), was the best known of the large school of Irish pastellists; his little oval family portraits in chalk are still to be seen in many an old Irish house. These were often

LEFT *Maire Rua* ('Red Mary') O'Brien, of Lemaneagh Castle in Co. Clare, painted in 1654 by an unknown artist. A recent biography suggests that her character was less outrageous than local lore would have it.

ABOVE The Black Dog at Adare, Co. Limerick, painted *c.* 1750 by an unknown artist, probably more at home decorating carriages or shop signs. The ruins of Quin Abbey are in the background.

duplicated by the artist; he drew the same person a number of times if
there were several relations in need of a set of family likenesses. He
worked so fast at his profession and was kept so busy 'that he had to put
off to the evening the picking out and gathering up of the guineas
among the bran and broken crayons in his crayon boxes, where in the
hurry of the day he had thrown them'.

Together with William Ashford and George Barret, Thomas
Roberts (1749–78) was one of the foremost landscape painters of his
day. Two years before Roberts died he painted four of the six views of
the park at Carton which hung originally in the Duke of Leinster's
library, the other two being by Ashford. He is, understandably,
sometimes confused with Thomas Sautelle Roberts (1760–1826), his
younger brother. The park at Carton is of great natural beauty, and the
small river, the Rye Water, that flows through it was ingeniously
dammed and widened to add to its delights. In the painting, the house
can just be seen to the left of the large tree; on the skyline stands the
Prospect Tower which is sited at a point close to the centre of the 1,000-
acre demesne. The bridge was designed in 1763 by Thomas Ivory, the
Cork-born architect who also designed the bridge that spans the
Blackwater at Lismore, Co. Waterford. On the right can be seen a herd
of deer.

The final painting illustrated is *Market Day in Ennis* in Co. Clare with
the stage coach arriving and the old Court House in the background. It
was painted by William Turner de Lond, signed and dated 1820.

The nineteenth century was a difficult time for artists and those that

remained did not portray the great political and social changes that
took place. Many left to study abroad such as Nathaniel Hone and
Roderic O'Conor. Walter Osborne, John Lavery and William Orpen
adhered to a traditional approach to portraiture and subject work. The
most popular and lasting painter of the first half of this century is
undoubtedly Jack B. Yeats, who developed his own unique individual
style, capturing the essence of Ireland – its myths and its people.

SCULPTURE

The first fully developed Baroque monument in Ireland is in the remote Protestant church of Kilnasoolagh in Co. Clare. It was erected soon after 1717 as a memorial to Sir Donough O'Brien, first Baronet, who died in that year. Sir Donough was the son of Conor O'Brien of Lemaneagh and his wife 'Red' Mary. The monument is signed *Kidwell fecit* on the base of the columns. The sculptor William Kidwell was born in England, and was apprenticed to Edward Pierce whose bust of Sir Christopher Wren, 1673, was considered 'probably the best piece of sculpture made by an Englishman in the century' (Whinney and Millar, *English Art 1625–1714*, Oxford, 1957). By 1690 Kidwell was established in Westminster with a yard and workshop, and it is not known why he moved to Ireland in 1711. His fame preceded him, and he was made a Freeman of the City of Dublin at Christmas the year he arrived. He died in Dublin in 1736.

Homan Potterton (*Irish Georgian Society Bulletin*, July–December 1972) has made out a good case for attributing to Kidwell the architectural framework of 'Speaker' Conolly's monument in Celbridge. This well-hidden work of art, only twelve miles from Dublin, is locked up in total darkness in part of an old church in Celbridge, most of which was destroyed by fire in 1798.

The Conolly Monument is a vast architectural work framed by four columns that support a massive triangular pediment. The figure of William Conolly is semi-recumbent; his eyes are closed to indicate that he had died. His widow Katherine survived him by twenty-three years; she gazes down at him, holding a prayerbook in her left hand. Their monograms are worked into the iron railing in front. Both statues are signed by the English sculptor Thomas Carter the Elder. They were shipped in August 1736, as was reported in *The Dublin Gazette* (No. 959):

> On Friday last two curious fine Monuments, lately finished by Mr Carter near Hyde Park Corner, was put on board a Ship in the River in order to be carried to Ireland, to be erected in the Church of Castletown near Dublin, to the Memory of the Right Hon. William Conolly Esq. late Speaker of the House of Commons, and his Lady.

As Potterton has pointed out, this report mentions 'two curious fine Monuments', that is, the two figures, Mr and Mrs Conolly, but there is

no mention of the architectural surround. The similarity of the frieze decoration in between the triglyphs on a known monument by Kidwell, that to Viscount Duncannon at Fiddown in Co. Kilkenny, who died in 1724, points to Kidwell as the author of the Celbridge memorial surround. In the metopes of the Conolly Monument are scallop shells from the Conolly coat of arms, mullets from the arms of the Conynghams, and in the centre the crests of the Conynghams and the Conollys.

John Hickey (1751–95), a Dublin born statuary, entered the Dublin Society Schools in 1764 and carved one of the most splendid memorials in Ireland. It stands in Delgany Church and was erected in 1789 to the memory of David La Touche who had died four years previously. The La Touche Monument is twenty-five feet high and incorporates five life-sized statues of the La Touches, a family of Huguenot bankers. Edmund Burke secured for Hickey the commission for the monument to David Garrick in Westminster Abbey, but the sculptor was already in poor health, due to his intemperate habits, and did not live to execute it.

The best-known Irish sculptor of the late Georgian period was Edward Smyth (1749–1812), because most of the statues, bas-reliefs and coats of arms on the public buildings in Dublin are by him, notably the Riverine Heads on the Custom House. He was born in 1749, possibly at Navan in Co. Meath, and died in 1812 in Dublin. He studied at the Dublin Society Schools and was apprenticed to Simon Vierpyl, the protégé of Lord Charlemont. While still Vierpyl's apprentice, Smyth (when only twenty-three) modelled a figure of Dr Charles Lucas, MP, which he exhibited in 1772 in the competition for a statue of Lucas to be erected in Dublin. Smyth won the competition and the statue can be seen in the City Hall. His talents soon came to the attention of James Gandon who employed him at the Custom House, Four Courts, Parliament House and King's Inns in Dublin.

A wooden statue of Christ on the cross in Navan Catholic church is signed by Smyth and dated 1792; this has given rise to the theory that Navan was his birthplace. This crucifix has been described by Anne Crookshank as 'the only such work known to have been carved by an Irish artist in the eighteenth century'.

OPPOSITE LEFT Monument to Sir Donough O'Brien, Baronet, who died in 1717, signed by William Kidwell; Kilnasoolagh Church, Co. Clare. Sir Donough is depicted with his eyes open, gazing heavenwards.

OPPOSITE RIGHT Monument to 'Speaker' William Conolly of Castletown, who died in 1729; Celbridge, Co. Kildare. The figures are by Thomas Carter the Elder, and the grandiose architectural framework has been attributed to William Kidwell.

LEFT Monument to David La Touche, who died in 1785, by John Hickey; Delgany Church, Co. Wicklow. The marble sarcophagus rests on La Touche's three sons.

ABOVE Crucifix, Navan Catholic church, Co. Meath, carved in wood by Edward Smyth; signed and dated 1792. Smyth is best known for his sculpture on Dublin's public buildings, notably the Riverine Heads on the Custom House.

The amassing of silver served two purposes. It paraded the wealth of the owner and provided him with a readily convertible source of cash. Side tables were equipped with grooves and rails for the display of family plate. However, no manifestation of wealth would be worthwhile unless it accorded with fashion – only an eccentric would hoard his plate as a curiosity of the past, unless it had some royal or otherwise memorable connection. By comparison, therefore, pieces of silver with a history attached have survived proportionately more than mundane objects such as cups and spoons. Just as the jewels of the very rich are reset from time to time to reflect changes in taste, so silver would be melted down and refashioned to bring it up to date. It is sad to think of the amount of silver pieces that have disappeared because they had become outmoded. Church plate has survived in great quantities because there was never any excuse for modernizing it, and church silver is often inscribed and dedicated to the memory of a particular parishioner.

Trinity College, Dublin has an excellent collection of silver. Parents of students would present plate to the college when they graduated, as a memento of their attendance. There is the Trinity Mace, for ceremonial processions, a derivative of the battleaxe that in the Middle Ages would be carried in front of dignitaries to represent a bodyguard. Sometimes when funds were needed the silver would be sold. In the college records for 3 October, 1645 there appears the following: 'Received for a piece of plate which was broken up and coined to supply the college with provisions against the approaching siege ...

RIGHT Limerick Freedom Box presented by John Craven, Mayor, to Lt William Brown in 1693, depicting the arms of the city. Attributed to Jonathan Buck.

LEFT Flagon for holding wine before consecration; the earliest known Irish hallmarked piece of silver; James Vanderbeck, Dublin, 1638.

ABOVE Porringer, made in Dublin c. 1680 by Timothy Blackwood. The side handles are each capped with a dolphin and the lid handle is a bacchanal with bunches of grapes.

BELOW Two dish rings with farmyard scenes made in Dublin in c. 1765. These rings were used to keep china bowls off the polished surface of the dining table.

'£30. 19. 8d.' This expropriation of college silver was compulsory because the army was starving. Douglas Bennett's great work, *Irish Georgian Silver*, has unfortunately for long been out of print. He has, however, recently published an account of the silver collection at Trinity College as part of the celebrations for the four hundredth anniversary of the founding of the College in 1592.

It is the dish ring, sometimes erroneously referred to as 'potato ring', and the extraordinary variety of designs that evolved from this one small object with which the Irish silversmiths are particularly identified. Dish rings were made to support hot dishes and keep them off the polished surface of the dining table. The earliest Irish dish rings date from 1740 and at first the pattern was repeated all around the ring. From 1760 'farmyard' decoration appears which is unique to Ireland. Milkmen, cows, pigs and dogs proliferate and thatched cottages complete the picture which continues freely around the ring. A sportsman might be seen stalking through the Rococo foliage with his gun at the ready, lifelike in the extreme. As with the plasterwork, by 1770 this Rococo exuberance was frozen in the icy grip of the neo-Classical Revival. From then on the design became repetitive once more – elegant swags perhaps – and the excitement of Rococo freedom and imagination is lost.

Under the Charter of 1637 granted by Charles I to the Company of

Goldsmiths of Dublin, it was decreed that two marks should be struck on all articles of gold and silver. First, the 'Maker's Mark' was stamped in the silversmith's workshop. Second, the 'Harp Crowned' was stamped in the Goldsmiths' Hall to indicate that the piece contained the right amount of precious metal, 925 parts of silver and seventy-five of copper out of 1,000. If the piece failed the test it would be broken up and the fragments returned to the maker. The all-important 'Date Letter' is not mentioned in the Charter of 1637. However, the Company of Goldsmiths took it upon themselves to supply a date letter from 1638, as was done in London, and the custom became official in 1729 under an Act of Parliament in the reign of George II. These marks became known as hall marks because they were struck in the Assay Office at the Goldsmiths' Hall, as they are to the present day.

In 1730 a fourth mark, in the form of Hibernia, was introduced to denote the payment in tax of sixpence an ounce. At this time the date letter was omitted on most items of holloware, not to be reintroduced until 1772. Fortunately the date letter continued to be struck on flatware, which includes such mundane objects as spoons and forks. It follows that throughout the great Rococo period there was rarely a date letter on the more interesting and important pieces of Irish silver. However, as the punches wore out and were replaced they tended to display certain variants which, when compared with spoons and forks that *were* still dated, has made it possible to establish a dating pattern for more interesting pieces. Ida Delamer, Kurt Ticher and Liam O'Sullivan have published a booklet on the subject, representing the fruits of many years' research. This was a worthy undertaking, throwing valuable light on one of the most innovative periods of Irish craftsmanship.

A great deal of plate was made in Cork, Limerick and Kilkenny; to a lesser extent it was also produced in Galway, Kinsale and other country towns. This provincial silver was supposed to be brought to Dublin for marking but, on account of the risks involved in the journey, a local mark was often used instead. From the early eighteenth century the word *Sterling* is often found on provincial silver instead of the crowned harp.

In 1820 there was a clumsy return to Rococo which in turn was drowned in the heavy seas of Victoriana. In 1850 an old lady collecting driftwood on the beach in Co. Meath found the Tara Brooch, one of the most important examples of Celtic Irish metalwork, now in the National Museum in Dublin. She sold it for seven pence to a blacksmith in Drogheda who in turn obtained £7 from Waterhouse, the watchmaker, of Dame Street in Dublin. Waterhouse sold it to the Royal Irish Academy for £200 having made two copies of the brooch which were exhibited at the Great Exhibition in London, 1851. Queen Victoria bought both of the copies and the Celtic Revival was born. When the Arts and Crafts Movement reached Ireland it was for the most part from Celtic design that it derived its inspiration.

LEFT Standing cups or goblets presented to Trinity College, Dublin, as a memento of their son's attendance by two grateful fathers. On the right the Palliser cup bears the arms of Trinity College and those of Sir William Palliser; on the left the Duncombe cup by Thomas Bolton, Dublin, 1696.

PLASTERWORK

A map of Dublin dated 1728 and illustrating the arms of the Dublin guilds shows that those of the plasterers are quartered with the bricklayers as it was a combined guild from 1670. The craft was practised long before this, though the portrait of Queen Elizabeth I at Carrick-on-Suir Castle is probably the first example of figurative plasterwork in Ireland.

During the seventeenth century plaster ceilings, when decorated, were divided into compartments to create a geometrical pattern which was derived, it is thought, from the early decoration of beams with plaster fretwork. The chapel of the Royal Hospital, Kilmainham (1680), contained by far the most important seventeenth-century ceiling in the country. It is coved and divided into compartments with broad bands of flowers and foliage but there is no decoration on the flat panels within. Unfortunately, about one hundred years ago the plaster ornament, much of which was freestanding, started to fall on the heads of those at worship, who found themselves rewarded unexpectedly from on high. It seems that the plaster flowers were made on a bench and were suspended using green oak branches or twigs so that the fresh plaster would not crack as it dried out. With the passage of time, however, the oak became rotten and in 1902 the ceiling had to be taken down; it was replaced with a *papier mâché* replica to save the weight on the beams.

During the early years of the eighteenth century the compartmented ceiling continued to be used, forming an extension of the restrained panelled walls then in fashion. An excellent example can be seen at Bellamont Forest in Co. Cavan (*c.* 1730), a house designed by Sir Edward Lovett Pearce where the ceilings are elaborately coffered and compartmented.

Paul and Philip Lafranchini, who were born in the Italian part of Switzerland, first came to Ireland in 1739 and their arrival is of outstanding importance as they are generally credited for introducing

ABOVE The dining room of Riverstown House, Glanmire, Co. Cork was decorated with Classical and allegorical figures in 1745 for Dr Jemmett Browne, Bishop of Cork, by Paul and Philip Lafranchini.

LEFT The chapel of the Royal Hospital, Kilmainham (1680), on the outskirts of Dublin, contains a replica of the most elaborate seventeenth-century ceiling in Ireland.

LEFT Juno (Air) with her attendant peacock; detail of an allegorical ceiling moved from Mespil House, Dublin to Áras an Uachtaráin, a building of the same date (1751).

RIGHT Bartholomew Cramillion, the Italian stuccodore, decorated the Rotunda Hospital Chapel, Dublin, with almost freestanding allegorical figures in 1755. Allegory of Faith blindfold with cross, bible and plummet of righteousness.

Baroque decoration with figures to plasterwork. They executed the magnificent ceiling of the 'Eating Parlour' at Carton in Co. Kildare, for the nineteenth Earl of Kildare, whose son James was created Duke of Leinster in 1766. Carton was much frequented and this commission, secured through Richard Castle, the architect, led to many others in Ireland, among them Kildare (later Leinster) House, Tyrone House and Nos. 9 and 85 St Stephen's Green in Dublin as well as at Castletown in Co. Kildare; Riverstown and Kilshannig, both in Co. Cork and Russborough in Co. Wicklow.

Despite the widespread belief that decorative plasterwork in Ireland was of foreign authorship, the fact is that, so far as is known, only one other foreigner ever came to Ireland to work in this medium. His name was Bartholomew Cramillion and he is described in Strickland's *Dictionary of Irish Artists* as a 'French statuary'. He came to decorate the ceiling of the Rotunda Hospital Chapel between 1755 and 1758, a maternity hospital run for the poor of Dublin that was financed by public subscription and with the help of Parliament. The £585 9s. 9d. that it cost might have been considered a frivolous expense for a charity such as the Rotunda to put up such an elaborate ceiling in the chapel, but in fact it was a sensible investment. A good tear-jerking charity sermon could raise as much as £1,000, but however good the sermon it could not reap the necessary reward unless people with long purses were there to hear it. The elaborate decoration would have helped to attract the affluent here of a Sunday morning.

Robert West (*fl.* 1752–65), an Irish architect and stuccodore, had the contract for the rest of the plastering in the hospital, and it is tempting to imagine him watching Cramillion at work in the chapel. West's plaster birds in his own house, No. 20 Lower Dominick Street, are almost freestanding, as are some of the figures in the chapel. His decoration on the staircase of No. 86 St Stephen's Green shows how skilful he was at modelling birds; he may have drawn his inspiration from the seagulls on the Liffey as his builder's yard was beside the banks of the river.

Bartholomew Cramillion, during his six to seven years in Ireland, is thought to have worked at Belvedere in Co. Westmeath and Mespil House in Dublin some years later. No account of Irish plasterwork would be complete without reference to the sensuous modelling and playful Rococo mood of the work in these two houses. Fortunately, when Mespil House was pulled down the ceilings were saved; that

ABOVE Staircase decoration by Robert West at No. 20 Lower Dominick Street, Dublin (1755), his own house, a stone's throw from the Rotunda Hospital.

LEFT No. 20 Lower Dominick Street, detail of a plaster bird, mounted on wire and almost freestanding, by Robert West.

ABOVE The saloon, Headfort, Co. Meath; the interior of Headfort was designed by Robert Adam in 1771 for Sir Thomas Taylour. Headfort School uses this great room for assembly and prayer.

RIGHT Staircase, Belvedere House, Great Denmark Street, Dublin. One of the most distinguished neo-Classical houses in Dublin, it was completed in 1786 for the second Earl of Belvedere by Michael Stapleton who was both architect and stuccodore.

representing 'The Elements' is now in the house of the President of Ireland in the Phoenix Park and two others have been installed in Dublin Castle. Also in the President's house is an *Aesop's Fables* ceiling which was commissioned by Nathaniel Clements and is attributed to Cramillion.

Headfort, near Kells in Co. Meath, has the only surviving neo-Classical interior in Ireland by the great Scottish architect, Robert Adam. The house was designed by George Semple and built from 1760 onwards for Sir Thomas Taylour, first Lord Headfort; Adam's interiors are dated 1771 and his drawings for them are at the Yale Center for British Art in America. Part of Headfort is now a preparatory school.

The finest neo-Classical plasterwork interior in Dublin is at Belvedere House which was built by the second Earl of Belvedere and completed in 1786. Belvedere College is the present occupant, whose most famous past pupil was James Joyce. Michael Stapleton was both architect and stuccodore for the house and the work on the stairs and in the principal reception rooms is of superb quality, bearing witness to his consummate talent as an artist. Often described as an Irish Adam, he was a pupil of Robert West and took over his practice. Stapleton was original and imaginative, and much of his work was freehand. Adam had other followers in Ireland but none with as much talent as Stapleton.

Sadly, the use of the repetitive mould eventually sounded the death-knell to the exuberant plasterwork of the 1740s and fifties and concomitantly put an end to one of Ireland's most striking contributions to the decorative arts.

RIGHT The Diana room, Belvedere House, Dublin with the hunting goddess driving her chariot in the central plaque; the decoration throughout is equally sensitive and imaginative.

FURNITURE

The decorative arts in Ireland have a distinctly Irish character and nowhere is this more marked than in furniture. However, neither the extraordinary inventiveness of the Irish cabinet-makers of the Georgian period, nor the exceptional quality of their work, has so far attracted much attention. Although the furniture that they made is now eagerly sought by collectors, the literature on the subject consists only of one small booklet and a number of articles written by the Knight of Glin; a book on Irish furniture is eagerly awaited.

Hardly a piece of furniture exists prior to 1700 and the only information available before this date is found in the inventories of the great houses. Most of the furniture would have been made of walnut, oak, bog oak, and yew as well as pine. The Earls of Kildare had very elaborate furnishings in their castles as did Richard Boyle, the first Earl of Cork, who imported 'plancks of walnut tree' from France in 1613 and who mentions the Dublin 'Joyner' who will supply his 'Rownd table'.

Furniture making made great strides during the eighteenth century. By 1786 there were twenty-eight cabinet-makers, twelve carvers and gilders, three joiners and upholsterers and six harpsichord and musical instrument makers at work in Dublin. Mahogany was introduced in about 1725, and was used so extravagantly it must have been available without duty. The early furniture was in many cases over-elaborate and burdened with ornament; massive side tables were often carved with festoons, foliage and masks. Other carved features were grotesque masks of human heads, satyrs, serpents, birds, and imaginary beasts intertwined with one another with humour and vitality which are reminiscent of the decoration seen in The Book of Kells or on early Irish jewellery. Many other characteristics deviate from the trends in England at that time. A form of apron decoration of baskets of flowers or urns was used on tables, more usually found in French carved gilt furniture. Solid background punching, such as is usually seen in gessowork, is often found on these carved pieces. This could be in the form of a lightly carved trellis pattern often punched in the centre of each diamond. Tables also occasionally had an additional protrusion like a hock, often decorated with leaves, and claw-and-ball feet could be webbed, and are found on all four legs of a chair instead of the two front legs only. Mahogany plate-buckets, to remove plates from the table, were popular and large turf barrels, often hooped, were made to hold fuel. Aside from mahogany, Japanned and lacquered furniture was produced in the first half of the eighteenth century, as an inventory of Killeen Castle, Co. Meath, dated 1736 shows.

Besides the heavily carved and grotesque furniture, unmistakably Irish, elegant and sophisticated plain furniture was also made, with graceful lines and little or no carved ornament. A great deal of this furniture was exported to America when colonial furniture began to be taken seriously there in the 1920s and thirties. When the pieces came on the market their Irish origins were forgotten. Scientific research into the identity of the secondary woods can sometimes establish whether a piece was in fact made in Ireland or America.

In the eighteenth century, both Irish and American furniture were provincial expressions of that made in England. Moreover, Irish and American cabinet-makers share common characteristics, such as the trifid foot, that are not found elsewhere. This is not surprising as craftsmen travelled from Ireland to America bringing these ideas with them; when they set up shop they would announce in the local papers 'Recently arrived from Dublin' preceding a catalogue of their talents.

LEFT Blackened mahogany ceremonial chair, mid-eighteenth century; Friendly Brothers of St Patrick, Dublin, formerly from the Kinsale Knot of that Order.

RIGHT Blackened mahogany mid-eighteenth-century stool with bulging hocks, square hairy-paw feet and the background to the apron carving tooled, all Irish characteristics.

ABOVE Eighteenth-century mahogany plate bucket with brass carrying handle and a side opening to allow for the collection of plates.

LEFT Blackened mahogany side table with grotesque masks. Note how top-heavy it is; the legs appear too flimsy for the load which they have to bear.

BELOW Wine cooler, 1810, at Áras an Uachtaráin bearing the emblems of the Knights of St Patrick. Francis Johnston's drawing for it is in the Irish Architectural Archive, Dublin.

Irish furniture was often blackened, either to resemble bog oak, or, in the nineteenth century, to simulate a Jacobean look making it appear older than it was. It seems strange to blacken mahogany, such a beautiful wood in its own right, but the custom was widespread. When an Irish sideboard was bequeathed to the museum in St Louis in Missouri that was smothered in blacking when it arrived, the curator said with pride – 'Of course we've stripped it all off'. Surprisingly enough there was a continuing demand in the nineteenth century for the grotesque furniture which was made, and often still blackened, until well into the twentieth century.

As the eighteenth century drew to a close, Irish furniture lost much of its individuality as it conformed to the Sheraton and Hepplewhite styles. Regency furniture was heavier, sometimes decorated with lyres and Classical figures and often made of exotic wood, while Victorian furniture was extremely eclectic, reviving the Renaissance, Gothic and Rococo styles.

LEFT Mid-eighteenth century mahogany card table with trifid feet, very different in its simple lines to the grotesque blackened furniture.

GLASS

It is curious that in the early eighteenth century when Ireland's political subordination to Great Britain was especially marked, a national style in the decorative arts should be more prominent than during the time of Grattan's Parliament in the 1780s. The exception to this rule is to be found in Irish glass, for here it seems that national symbols such as the harp and the shamrock became exceedingly popular at this time. Furthermore, the Irish glass industry was inadvertently encouraged when England imposed taxes on its own industry which gave Ireland, a free-trading country at that time, the opportunity to expand its markets to the Continent, North America, Africa and even India. Factories were established in Dublin, Belfast, Cork and Waterford and skilled craftsmen came from England such as John Hill and his workers from Stourbridge who helped the Penrose brothers start the famous Waterford factory.

Ireland is particularly known for its richly cut glass, sometimes of a heaviness in keeping with the heavy drinking that was not only customary but obligatory in male society. Lady Anne Conolly, later the mistress of Castletown and mother of Tom 'Squire' Conolly, wrote in 1733 of her husband William: 'His head has not been enough settled to do anything; for drinking, you know, does not agree with him, tho' he must practice it a little at his first coming into the country, or he would not please'. After Lord Longford had paid a visit to Inveraray Castle in Scotland, he wrote in his diary that he was happy to be without the delicate furnishings that he had seen there, as if he had them in his house in Ireland they would be smashed to bits within a week. So it is with the glass, or at any rate, with much of the glass that has survived, which may be the very reason that it has.

Boat-shaped dishes with a turned-over rim, sometimes mounted on a stem, are characteristic of Irish glass, as are bowls with scallop rims like the silver Monteith bowls with their waved edges. Cut glass was produced in great quantities in Dublin, Cork and Waterford and much of the best glass was produced in the twenty years following the Union. Contrary to a widespread misapprehension Waterford glass was not tinted and is famous for its clarity and whiteness. Dudley Westropp, past Curator of the National Museum in Dublin has written; 'As far as I can judge from examining many authentic pieces, the metal of Waterford glass is much whiter than that of other of the old Irish glasshouses.'

It is no coincidence that all the Irish glass-makers were established on the coast – this was because the sand used had to be imported by ship. Their proximity to the sea made it easy for them to export their glassware. In 1825 a duty of £12.10s on 1,000 lb weight of lead glass made in Ireland was imposed causing the trade to decline and the factories to close – Cork went out of business in 1835, Waterford in 1851, Belfast in 1868 and Dublin in 1893.

Two glass-makers of note were Thomas and Richard Pugh who made glass from about 1855 and used the decorative Irish symbols of the Celtic Revival movement such as the shamrock and harp but eventually were ousted by competition from England.

The Waterford factory was reopened in 1951 and has a world-wide reputation for cut crystal, concentrating in particular on reviving the old patterns from the eighteenth century.

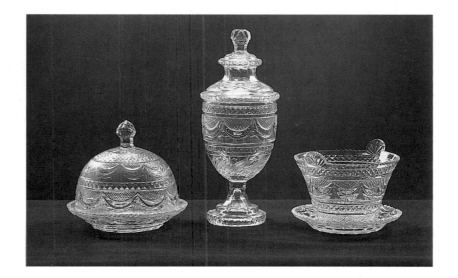

ABOVE Decanters, wine glasses and a wine-glass cooler made for the Principal Kinsale Knot of the Friendly Brothers of St Patrick in about 1840. The date 1754 refers to the founding of the Knot.

RIGHT Waterford celery vase with prismatic cutting above the stem and a sugar bowl, both with diamond-cutting and fan or scallop rim and solid feet.

ABOVE Covered bowl, covered urn and ice-pail, part of a fifty-piece dinner service, displayed in the Council Chamber of the City Hall, Waterford. Presented to the Corporation by Senator E. A. McGuire in 1964.

LEFT Waterford sugar bowl, c. 1820 with handles derived from a silver piggin, strawberry diamond-cutting and moulded foot.

POTTERY AND PORCELAIN

It is not easy to distinguish Irish Delft, or 'tin-glazed earthenware', from that made in Liverpool and elsewhere, as clay from Carrickfergus in Co. Antrim was universally used and the markings were erratic, if indeed there were any at all. That there were factories in several different parts of Ireland – Youghal in Co. Cork, Rostrevor in Co. Down, Belfast, Waterford, Wexford and Limerick, as well as Dublin – all comparatively short-lived – shows how precarious the business was.

Fully documented pieces of Irish Delft were gathered at Castletown in Co. Kildare in December 1971 for the first and only exhibition devoted to the subject. By far the most interesting of all the ware on display was that produced in Dublin by Henry Delamain from 1752 to 1757. Delamain made armorial plates, apothecary jars, wine barrels, wall cisterns, jugs, bowls, sweetmeat dishes with interlaced sides, and all the usual table ware. His delft was usually white with the design coloured in manganese or blue, and the idea of using landscapes to decorate his pieces was original to him. The artist chiefly responsible was Peter Shee, employed by Delamain as 'painter and clerk'. Sometimes there are ruins or a folly in these landscapes, sometimes a coach and horses, or a pair of figures, usually drawn from behind as if admiring the view. On plates the pattern often flows across the rim, unless the rim has a decorative border. Shee's work is highly individual and very different from anything being done elsewhere at the time.

LEFT Wall cistern made by Henry Delamain in the 1750s at his Dublin manufactory and decorated in blue by Peter Shee.

BELOW Chinese Export armorial plate possibly made for the eighth Earl of Abercorn (d. 1789), decorated with the Hamilton arms.

ABOVE Chinese Export jug made for the Irish market, early nineteenth century, with the chain of the Knights of St Patrick around the rim.

Clay from Carrickfergus was not the only Irish clay that was exported for making delft, as is shown by the following excerpt from the *Dublin Evening Post* for 22 November, 1785:

> The English take away our clay from Carrickfergus, for the Liverpool earthenware manufacture, and *the Dutch procure it from Waterford, for the manufacture of their Delft and Rouen ware.* So valuable is this article to them, which is brought on horses from the Devil's-bit mountain in Co. Tipperary, to Clonmel and from thence transported in small boats to Waterford, that our correspondent has known a Dutch vessel of 200 tons burden, remain nine months in the river waiting for a cargo.

David Howard, author of *Chinese Armorial Porcelain* (London, 1974), estimates that in the Georgian period upwards of one hundred dinner and tea services are likely to have been ordered for Irish families, that were made in central China and at Canton, with coats of arms. The crest was generally copied from a bookplate, not always with accuracy, as in the case of the dinner service ordered for a family with the motto 'Unite' which, when it arrived, read 'Untie'. This is not to be wondered at considering the Chinese were unfamiliar with either the lettering or the language that they were attempting to copy.

ABOVE LEFT Spirit barrel and plate, made by Henry Delamain in the 1750s and decorated in manganese with landscapes by Peter Shee.

ABOVE Octagonal dish, thought to be of provincial Irish manufacture thanks to the lack of sophistication in its design and its clumsy potting.

ABOVE Spirit barrel with naïve scrollwork decoration in blue.

ABOVE A nest of sweetmeat dishes; the five small dishes are made so as to fit exactly in the mother dish.

LEFT Highly characteristic Irish delftware octagonal plate made in the eighteenth century as part of a dinner service.

The jug illustrated bears the inscription *Longford Hunt* and a picture of a rambling country house that could represent Pakenham Hall, seat of the Earls of Longford (recently renamed Tullynally Castle). Around the rim of both the jug and its lid is the ceremonial chain or 'collar' worn by the Knights of St Patrick, an order, now extinct, that was founded in 1783 as an Irish equivalent of the Garter. The second Earl of Longford (1774–1835) was a member of that Order. The actual collar consisted of twenty-seven pieces in all, seven roses and six harps placed alternately and joined together with fourteen golden knots symbolically tying England and Ireland together. The central portion of the collar, from which the badge was suspended, consisted of an Imperial crown above a harp, emphasizing the central role of the Crown in Ireland. The heads of the female Hibernias have a distinctly Eastern cast.

The motto of the Order, *Quis Separabit*, was borrowed from the Friendly Brothers of St Patrick. This motto and a chain linking roses to harps with knots, but without the central crown, can also be seen on a Chinese export dish made for the Connaught Rangers, the 88th Regiment, in about 1795.

BOOKBINDING

In some cases, the craft of bookbinding rose in eighteenth-century Ireland to the status of fine art. An English expert on the subject, H. M. Nixon, wrote 'Dublin vied with Paris for the leadership of the art'.

As with Irish furniture, silver and plasterwork, the highpoint of Irish bookbinding had already been reached by 1760. After that date there is less freedom of expression, even though perfectly correct and elegant neo-Classical bindings were produced, sometimes closely echoing the design of Adamesque ceilings.

All kinds of decorative motifs were used by the Irish binders. As with Irish plasterwork, birds are often found, sometimes with a spray in their beaks, or peacocks with long golden tails. Urns, two-handled jugs, waves, harps, crowns, foxes, dogs, human figures, acorns, leaves, roses, tulips and flames can all be found decorating bookbindings. Sometimes parallel curved lines would be cut with gouges to catch the light in a most attractive way. The tools used were made of brass, with wooden handles. The brass was heated and then pressed down on the gold leaf, the leather surface having first of all been painted with egg white. If there was a fault it was a tendency to overload the decoration. This can surely be excused considering the youthful spirit of experiment and enthusiasm that prevailed in Ireland from 1730 to 1770.

'Morocco' was the most expensive leather, goatskin imported from Turkey and North Africa, and the best bindings were made of it. 'Calf' or cowskin was available locally and therefore cost less. Once a book was stitched it would be sold ready for binding, rather like a paperback today. It might be sent over from England to Ireland to be bound at the time when an Irish binding was sought after by those who loved their books. The bindings themselves were seldom dated or signed, and the date of the binding could be years later than that of the printing. When the binding was dated it was usually at the top of the spine with *Dublin* at the base, or sometimes a name. Unfortunately this was generally the name of the firm that employed the binder rather than his own name, and it is believed that the craftsmen themselves moved freely from shop to shop according to demand.

'Probably the most majestic series of bound volumes in the world' wrote G. D. Hobson, an authority of international eminence, of the Journals of the Irish Parliament which went up in smoke in 1922 during the siege of the Four Courts. These 149 volumes, standing twenty-one inches high and bound in red morocco, were in pristine condition and (except when more than one volume was necessary to cover the proceedings of a particular year) all different. For sheer quality, imagination and magnificence they stood on their own; fortunately several of them were photographed and rubbings were taken of others. Their loss was a great tragedy.

The next most important customer for bindings in Georgian Dublin after the Irish Parliament was Trinity College. The first major publication of the Irish Georgian Society is entitled *Gold-Tooled Bookbindings Commissioned by Trinity College, Dublin in the Eighteenth Century* by Joseph McDonnell and Patrick Healy, which was published through the generosity of J. Paul Getty, Jr in 1987. It is the only book in print on Irish bindings, Dr Craig's pioneering *Irish Bookbindings 1600–1800* (1954) having for long been unobtainable.

The best collection of Irish bindings on view to the public can be seen at Castletown in Co. Kildare. It was given to the Irish Georgian Society by J. Paul Getty, Jr and one of the volumes is illustrated here, *Irish Statutes*, bound in Dublin by Boulter Grierson, 1765. It is of red morocco, gilt, with an inlay of white leather opened to reveal an underlay of royal blue.

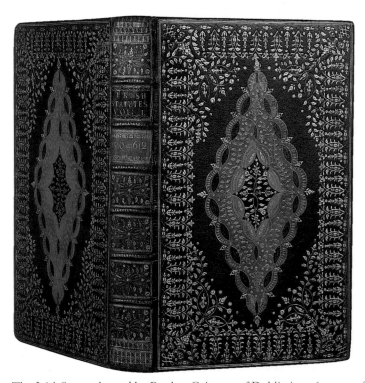

The *Irish Statues*, bound by Boulter Grierson of Dublin in 1765; part of a set presented to the Irish Georgian Society by J. Paul Getty Jr, on display at Castletown, Co. Kildare.

PAPER ART

During the second half of the eighteenth century there was a vogue for paper cut-outs and paper crafts generally which spread through Europe and America. Cut coats of arms and other heraldic devices were particularly fashionable and the art was perfected by Nathaniel Bermingham who promoted his talent as '. . . an improver of the curious art of cutting . . . with the points of a pen knife' (Hodges, *Period Pastimes*, 1989). The coat of arms illustrated here is by

Cut paper arms made *c.* 1740 by Nathaniel Bermingham.

him and represents the Arms of John, fifth Earl of Cork and Orrery, who married Margaret, daughter and heiress of John Hamilton of Caledon, Co. Tyrone, in 1738. This exquisite piece was probably commissioned to commemorate their union.

Two artists in particular who are heralded as raising the status of paper crafts to the heights of a sophisticated art form are Samuel Dixon and Mary Delany.

Samuel Dixon's embossed *papier-mâché* pictures of birds, flowers, shells, butterflies and fruit, with their black and gold 'japanned' frames, have become greatly sought after and extremely valuable. The National Museum in Dublin does not as yet possess an example of Dixon's work but it can be admired in the National Gallery and at Malahide Castle.

Dixon issued three sets of *basso-relievo* pictures from his warehouse and showroom in Capel Street in Dublin. In 1748 he sold his first set of twelve flower pictures: 'These Flower Pieces which are a new invention, are not only ornamental to Lady's Chambers, but useful to paint and draw after, or imitate in Shell or Needle Work . . . '. Each 'Piece' shows a bunch of flowers in low relief tied with a ribbon, measuring about ten by eight inches depending on the width of the

frame. Auriculas, anemones, bluebells, carnations, columbines, convolvuli, lilies, sweet peas, peonies, poppies, ranunculi, roses and tulips were depicted, all of which are still popular favourites. Samuel Dixon 'takes this opportunity to acquaint such of the Nobility and Gentry as have not yet subscribed . . . to favour him with their Directions . . .'.

It is impossible to ascertain how many sets were manufactured, but judging by the fact that at one stage he is known to have employed three young art students to do the hand colouring, the quantity must have been considerable. The outline of the design was impressed on coarse grey paper, dampened, using copper plates from the back with a screw press, giving a three-dimensional effect.

Dixon's second set came on the market in 1750 and consisted of twelve pictures of 'Foreign Birds'. These were borrowed from the first four volumes of George Edwards's *Natural History of Uncommon Birds*, published in 1743–51. They were larger than the flower pictures, measuring approximately twelve by ten inches, again depending on the width of the black and gold frames.

Dixon did not stop at borrowing from Edwards both the birds and the descriptive text: he also made use of Edwards's arrangement of branches, rocks and bushes. When Dixon in turn was imitated, however, his righteous indignation knew no bounds. In Faulkner's *Dublin Journal*, 27 October, 1750, Dixon complained about 'a base imitation of my foreign Bird Pieces in *Basso Relievo*, hawked about this City by a Woman, likewise put into Auctions, in order to deceive the unwary'. He pointed out that his pictures 'are sold at no Shop, or anywhere, but at my Picture Ware-Room in Caple-street, and at Mrs Elizabeth Breton's in Cork'. Dixon's 'Foreign Birds' were all numbered and carried a description of the bird on the back. Mary Taverner was his imitator, and to add insult to injury, when her inferior colours faded, her copies of his pictures would be brought to him to revive. He understandably refused such requests, determined to have nothing to do with 'the Spurious and unnatural Productions of others'.

Dixon's third and largest set was issued to subscribers in 1755 and measures fourteen by eighteen inches or thereabouts. It was entitled 'Foreign and Domestick Birds'. Whereas only No. 1 of the 'Foreign Birds' carried a dedication – to the Earl of Meath – this latest set had a separate dedication label on the back of all twelve, together with the description of the birds and Dixon's signature. He dedicated the pictures to eleven great Irish ladies; the Duchess of Dorset, whose husband was the Viceroy at the time, was the twelfth. He chose the Duchess of Hamilton because she was a popular Irish beauty, one of the Gunning sisters from Co. Roscommon, who had captured her Scottish duke in 1752. These dedications were partly to enhance what would now be called the 'image' of his *oeuvre* and partly to make life yet more difficult for his imitators.

Dixon's 'Foreign and Domestick Birds' set, also borrowed from Edwards, was his last. He moved to Leixlip in Co. Kildare where he started a factory for the printing of linens, cambrics and cottons from metal plates. He evolved a method of fixing the colours so as not to fade in bleaching and washing, and produced 'hangings of rooms, beds and window curtains, which for design, drawing and engraving, exceeds anything as yet done in that way'.

Dean Delany was a friend of Jonathan Swift and shared his passion for planting and 'improving'; he created an elaborate garden for Delville, at Glasnevin near Dublin, where he lived. His wife meanwhile was busy ornamenting their private chapel 'done with cards and shells in imitation of stucco. In the chancel are four Gothic arches . . . made also of shells in imitation of stucco . . . The wreath round the window is composed of oak-branches and vines made of cards, the grapes, nuts, and large periwinkles, the corn real wheat painted, all to look like stucco'.

It was Mary Delany's work making silhouettes that gave her the necessary training with scissors that was to stand her in such good stead when she came to make flower pictures out of cut paper. In 1772, when she was seventy-two years old, the notion first came to her. To quote Ruth Hayden (*Irish Georgian Society Bulletin*, 1983):

> With the plant specimen set before her she cut minute particles of coloured paper to represent the petals, stamens, calyx, leaves, veins, stalk and other parts of the plant, and, using lighter and darker paper to form

the shading, she stuck them on to a black background. By placing one piece upon another she sometimes built up several layers to complete a flower head with perhaps hundreds of petals. Over and again we see her interest in botany, for she might include a bunch of berries beside the main plant which she had depicted in blossom; sometimes she would include the roots and bulbs.

Most of the paper she used came from China but was supplemented by paper-stainers (wall-paper manufacturers) – if their colours had run they were happy to sell it to her, sometimes she dyed the paper herself to get the exact botanical shade . . .

Her 'paper mosaicks', as Mrs Delany called her collection, occupied her till October 1782, when failing sight constrained her to stop, but she had completed nearly one thousand. She placed her pictures in ten volumes, each volume has its own index of botanical and English names written in her clear hand; they are now in the Prints and Drawings Department of the British Museum, London.

Mary Delany paper mosaics; ABOVE LEFT '*Alcea Rosea*' *Chinese Hollyhock,* ABOVE RIGHT '*Rosa Spinosissima*', *Burnet Rose* FAR LEFT '*Helianthus Annuus*', *Great Sunflower.* LEFT '*Spiraea*', *Red Meadow-sweet.*

RIGHT Reverse side of *Black-billed whistling duck, purple waterhen and corals.* FAR RIGHT Example of a Dixon dedication label.

Samuel Dixon *papier mâché* pictures. ABOVE LEFT *Summer duck, red-billed whistling duck and shells.* ABOVE RIGHT *Goldfinch, honeysuckle, ranunculus and other flowers.* CENTRE LEFT *Cock butcher bird, roses and other flowers.* CENTRE RIGHT *Bullfinch, blue titmouse and fruit.*

LIST OF ARCHITECTS AND CRAFTSMEN

ADAM, ROBERT (1728–92). Born in Fife, Scotland, Robert Adam made the Grand Tour and on his return set up practice in London, joined by his brothers James and William. A brilliant decorator, he was made Architect of the King's Works and became the most fashionable architect in England from 1760 to 1780. He was one of the main protagonists of neo-Classicism which, from the mid-eighteenth century, supplanted the neo-Palladianism of Lord Burlington, William Kent and others. His designs for the interiors at Headfort were his most elaborate Irish project.

AHERON, JOHN (?–*c*.1761). Worked at Dromoland for the O'Briens, building the rotunda and gazebo as well as the house. He wrote the first Irish architectural book, *A General Treatise on Architecture*, Dublin, 1754. His other works include the eighteenth-century Stradbally House, Co. Laois, and Rockforest, Co. Cork, both demolished.

ASHLIN, GEORGE (1837–1921). A prolific architect of churches in Ireland. Among his best works are Thurles Cathedral, Co. Tipperary, Armagh Cathedral, and Cobh Cathedral, Co. Cork. The most important castle he built was Tulira Castle, Co. Galway. He collaborated with James F. Fuller in rebuilding Ashford Castle for Lord Ardilaun where he designed the north gates.

ATKINSON, WILLIAM (*c*.1773–1839). Born in Durham he was originally a carpenter. He was a pupil of Wyatt and succeeded him as architect to the Board of Ordnance. He was best known as an architect of Gothic country houses and carried out alterations and repairs to Lismore Castle from 1811 for the sixth Duke of Devonshire, his only recorded work in Ireland.

BARRE, WILLIAM J. (1830–67). As a young architect from Newry, Co. Down, he won a competition for one of the largest music halls in the British Isles – Ulster Hall. The exterior is Italianate, while the impressive interior has, according to C. E. B. Brett, 'a fine alderman-bellied balcony on pineapple-pie pillars'. It was built 1859–62 and given a magnificent organ by Andrew Mulholland in 1862. In 1864 Barre designed Danesfort, Belfast, according to Larmour 'One of the finest High Victorian mansions in Ireland'.

BERANGER, GABRIEL (1729–1817). Born in Rotterdam of a family of French Huguenots who came to Ireland when he was 21. An artist by profession, he was commissioned by the Irish Antiquarian Society to draw ancient monuments throughout the country. Strickland describes him as 'a painstaking draughtsman and an accurate delineator of ancient buildings'. He is thought to have designed the Volunteer Fabric.

BLOW, DETMAR (1867–1939). Born in London, he trained as an architect and toured Italy with John Ruskin. He was joined in partnership by Fernand Billerey from the *École des Beaux-Arts*, Paris. They developed a practice for alterations and additions to important country and town houses of the eighteenth century, especially in Mayfair in London. He worked also in churches: the Kitchener Memorial in St Paul's Cathedral, the south aisle altar in Westminster Abbey and work in King's College, Cambridge. He designed Adare Village which remains one of the most attractive in Ireland.

BROWN, LANCELOT 'CAPABILITY' (1716–83). Born in Northumberland he worked as a gardener from the age of 16. When he was 25, as head gardener to Lord Cobham at Stowe, he was given responsibility for building as well as gardening. He became the greatest landscape gardener in England and after Lord Cobham's death, he set up a practice in both gardening and architecture. The stables at Slane Castle are his only known work in Ireland.

BURGH, THOMAS (1670–1730). After a career as a military engineer, he was appointed Surveyor General in 1700. He was responsible for the rebuilding of Dublin Castle and for many beautiful buildings in the city, including the old Custom House, the library at Trinity College and Dr Steevens's Hospital. Stackallan is attributed to him.

BURN, WILLIAM (1789–1870). A Scottish architect patronized by the Dukes of Hamilton and Buccleuch. In Ireland he built Helen's Tower for the first Earl of Dufferin at Clandeboye, Co. Down, besides alterations and additions at Powerscourt. He designed the conservatory at Killruddery, Bangor Castle, now the town hall, in Co. Down, and Dartrey, Co. Monaghan, for Lord Cremorne in the Jacobean style; in his native Scotland he progressed from the Greek Revival style to the Scottish Baronial.

BURTON, DECIMUS (1800–81). The son of a builder he had a successful practice in London partly due to the family friendship with Nash. He built the arch on Constitution Hill and the Colosseum in Regent's Park, London, as well as many other public buildings. In his domestic architecture, he favoured the Greek Revival style and carried out reconstructions and additions to *Áras an Uachtaráin* in the 1840s and 1850s.

CALDBECK, WILLIAM FRANCIS (*c*.1825–72). He built the Bridewell gaol in Newry, Co. Down, the courthouse in Newtownards (1849), and bank buildings all over the country, mainly for the National Bank (later absorbed by the Bank of Ireland). He was also employed on ecclesiastical works around Drogheda and built several rows of houses in Dublin. Caldbeck had few commissions for wealthy clients, but is credited with the service wing at Emo Court. His account book from 1844 to 1860 has survived.

CARROLL, JAMES RAWSON (1820–1911). He came from Dublin and worked in partnership with Frederick Batchelor. He built the Assize Courts at Sligo in 1879 and added a tower to the stable court at Tullynally in 1860. He designed Classiebawn, Co. Sligo, for Lord Palmerston, the Richmond Surgical Hospital, Dublin, and the Limerick workhouse, besides additions to the Great Southern Hotel, Killarney, which cost £40,000 in 1901.

CASTLE, RICHARD (*c*.1690–1751). He was born in Hesse-Cassel of a Huguenot family and after a career as an army engineer, he came to Ireland in 1728. He was employed by Sir Edward Lovett Pearce on the Parliament House. Inheriting Pearce's practice, he designed the Rotunda Hospital, Leinster House, both in Dublin, and many of the most important country houses including Russborough, Carton, Powerscourt and Westport.

CHAMBERS, SIR WILLIAM (1723–96). Although he never came to Ireland, Chambers had a powerful Irish patron in the first Earl of Charlemont for whom he designed Charlemont House, Dublin, overlooking Rutland (now Parnell) Square, today the Hugh Lane Gallery of Modern Art. The Marino Casino at Clontarf was built for the same client; the design was originally conceived as an end pavilion for Harewood, Yorkshire. His pupil, James Gandon, designed or worked on many of the major public buildings in Dublin.

CLEMENTS, NATHANIEL (1705–77). By 22 he was a member of Parliament, becoming Deputy Vice-Treasurer, and Deputy Paymaster-General of Ireland. An associate of Luke Gardiner, together they organized the building of Henrietta Street, Dublin. Clements leased land and built houses in Sackville Street and was closely associated with Richard Castle. Castle and Clements became Gardiner's architects and contractors after Lovett Pearce's death. On being appointed Ranger of Phoenix Park in 1751 he built himself a Palladian villa which, much enlarged, is now *Áras an Uachtaráin*. The Knight of Glin attributes to him a number of houses in the Dublin area, including Beauparc, and Lodge Park, Co. Kildare, which was built for Hugh Henry in 1775–7.

COOLEY, THOMAS (*c*.1740–84). After an English apprenticeship he settled in Dublin having won the competition for the Royal Exchange there, now the City Hall. In 1775 he was appointed chief architect to the Government. He also worked in Armagh for Primate Robinson building the Archbishop's Palace, the Royal School and the Public Library. His country houses include Caledon, Co. Tyrone.

COTTINGHAM, LEWIS NOCKALLS (1787–1847). Known mainly for substantial restoration of church buildings in England. The almost complete rebuilding of Armagh Cathedral (1834–7) was one of his major works in Ireland. An admirer of Gothic architecture, he was employed by the Earl of Dunraven during the building of Adare Manor.

CRACE, JOHN GREGORY (1809–89). A member of the famous nineteenth-century interior-decorating and furniture firm which worked for the Prince Regent. After 1843 Crace, in partnership with A. W. N. Pugin, produced furniture, wallpapers and textiles especially for the Houses of Parliament and the Medieval Court at the Great Exhibition of 1851. Their work in Ireland is found at Lismore Castle and Adare Manor.

CRAMILLION, BARTHOLOMEW (*fl*.1755–72). A plasterworker of unknown origins who came to Dublin in 1755 to work on the decoration of the chapel of the Rotunda Hospital for Dr Mosse. Recent research has attributed to him ceilings at Mespil House, now demolished, which were divided between Dublin Castle and *Áras an Uachtaráin*. He was probably responsible for the ceilings at Belvedere. There is a strong German influence in Cramillion's stucco work.

CURLE, JOHN. (*fl*.1720s). Little is known of this architect. His plans and elevations for the original Castle Coole show him to be a skilled draughtsman. He is mentioned in correspondence in connection with the building of Beaulieu in the 1720s.

DANCE, GEORGE (1741–1825). Studied for six years in Italy and succeeded his father as Clerk of the City Works in London, most competently reorganizing street plans and bridges there. Newgate Prison, now demolished, was his most famous building. In Ireland he added a wing to the north-west end of the mid-eighteenth-century house at Mount Stewart for Lord Londonderry. Dance, whose principal pupil was Sir John Soane, is buried in St Paul's Cathedral.

DAVIS, WHITMORE (*fl*.1780s). The Dublin Evening Post of 5 March, 1789, tells us something of this obscure architect. He is recorded there as proposing to publish his designs for houses such as Caledon (where he seems to have acted as assistant or clerk to Thomas Cooley), Harristown, Co. Kildare, and Charleville. He was patronized by the La Touches and was architect to the Bank of Ireland for a period in the 1780s.

DAY, MARTIN (*fl*.1820–60). Produced two designs for the Dromana Gateway in 1849, one as executed, and also embellished the façade at Dromana. He worked at Johnstown Castle, Co. Wexford, and at Castleboro, Co. Wexford, with Daniel Robertson.

DEANE, SIR THOMAS (1792–1871). He belonged to one of the most prominent Irish architectural dynasties and was based in Cork where he was responsible for the building of Queen's College, now University College. He was the foremost architect/builder in Cork for many years. In 1853 the firm, now joined by Benjamin Woodward and Thomas Newenham Deane (1829–99), moved to Dublin. The partnership of Sir Thomas Deane, Son and Woodward designed the Museum Building in Trinity College, Dublin, and the Kildare Street Club, also in Dublin, as well as the Oxford Museum.

DUCART, DAVIS (died *c*.1784/5). Savoyard architect and canal engineer working mostly in the south-west of Ireland. He built the Limerick Custom House 1765–9 and Castletown Cox from 1767 using Patrick Osborne for the plasterwork as he did at the Mayoralty House in Cork and at Neptune, Blackrock, Co. Dublin. His style is described by the Knight of Glin as 'Baroque-Palladian' and he was the most important country-house builder after the death of Castle.

FAHY (or FAY), OWEN (*fl*.1800–31). A draughtsman known to have worked for Richard Morrison for the first fifteen years of the nineteenth century. His plans are easily recognized by distinctive script and bold black borders. After leaving Morrison he seems to have gone to the well-known Dublin contractors Henry, Mullins and McMahon.

FARRELL, TERENCE R. H. A. (1798–1876). A native of Co. Longford where his grandfather owned stone quarries, he was placed in the modelling school of the Dublin Society. He received instruction from Edward Smyth. In 1828 he set up his own practice. He exhibited from 1826 onwards and carved the Coat of Arms for Barons Court, also the statue of Lowry Cole at Enniskillen, Co. Fermanagh.

FULLER, JAMES FRANKLIN (1835–1924). A native of Kerry he was articled in England to Alfred Waterhouse and others. In 1862 he was appointed architect to the Representative Church Body. He was a sound and competent architect, and built many small churches and asylums. He was architect to the National Bank, and built the Great Southern and Western Hotels at Kenmare and Parknasilla. He designed Kylemore Castle, now Abbey, with S. Ussher Roberts for Mitchell Henry in the 1860s and, in collaboration with George Ashlin, was responsible for additions to Ashford Castle. He was a first-rate genealogist and wrote extensively on this subject.

Gabrielli, Gaspare (*fl.*1805–30). An Italian artist Lord Cloncurry brought to Ireland in 1805 to decorate rooms at Lyons. He was well known in Dublin for his landscape paintings. In 1819 he went to Italy to paint for his Irish patrons and does not appear to have returned.

Galilei, Alessandro (1691–1737). Galilei was probably introduced to 'Speaker' William Conolly, for whom he produced designs for Castletown, by the first Viscount Molesworth. He brought Galilei from Florence to England in 1714, and to Ireland in 1718. Galilei returned to Italy in 1719 so could not have been concerned with the construction of Castletown which began in 1722. He later designed the façade of San Giovanni in Laterano, Rome.

Gandon, James (1743–1823). Born in London, he was a pupil of Sir William Chambers and came to Ireland in 1781 to build the Dublin Custom House. His other great works in Dublin include the Four Courts, the King's Inns and extensions to the Parliament House. His country houses include Abbeville and Emsworth, Co. Dublin, Emo Court, and the farmyard and stable complex at Carrigglas. He was the foremost neo-Classical architect in Ireland.

Gibbs, James (1682–1754). He was a pupil of Carlo Fontana, the leading Baroque architect in Rome. In 1728 he published *A Book of Architecture* which was widely used as an architectural pattern book in England, Ireland and America. He favoured window-surrounds with heavy blocking, known as 'Gibbsian surrounds'. He worked for the Smith-Barrys of Fota Island, at their English residence, Marbury Hall, Cheshire, but never had an Irish commission.

Godwin, E. W. (1833–86). A native of Bristol, he started his practice in 1853 and won the Northampton Town Hall competition in 1861. He moved to London and specialized in stage design and production. He designed Dromore Castle, Co. Limerick, and Glenbeigh Towers, Co. Kerry, as well as studio houses in London. Mark Girouard describes him as one of the most interesting and gifted of Victorian architects but considers his Gothic buildings 'highly impracticable'.

Goodwin, Francis (1784–1835). In private practice he was a very aggressive seeker of commissions and built nine churches throughout the English Midlands between 1820 and 1830, two in the neo-Classical style and the remainder flamboyant Gothic. He was commissioned to build Lissadell for Sir Robert Gore-Booth 1830–5.

Grace, Oliver (*fl.*1750s–90s). An O. Grace entered the Royal Exchange competition of 1769. The Dublin Directory of 1784 lists an O. Grace of 35 Fleet St as 'a projector'. Payments were made to an Oliver Grace for work done for Archbishop Agar in Cashel. An Oliver Grace published an engraving 'View of Sackville Street' in the 1750s dedicated 'To his grace Lionel Duke of Dorset Lord Lieutenant General and Governor Gen of Ireland'. He was responsible for the original house at Lyons.

de Gree, Peter (d.1789). Born in Antwerp, he was a pupil of Martin Joseph Geeraerts, a master of *grisaille* painting. David La Touche brought him to Ireland to decorate No. 52, St Stephen's Green where his painted panels are in green and white to match the marble mantelpiece. Other examples of his work are found at Lucan House in the Wedgwood Room and at Luttrellstown Castle. The latter were formerly at the Oriel Temple, Co. Louth, the residence of 'Speaker' Foster.

Hallam, Benjamin (*fl.c.*1800). A Benjamin Hallam was admitted to the Dublin Society's School for architectural drawing in 1767 where he won premiums in 1769. The same, or a later, Hallam signed drawings for additions to Straffan House in 1808, now in the Irish Architectural Archive.

Hardwick, Philip Charles (1822–92). Born in London he was the son of Philip Hardwick, a prominent architect of institutional buildings, whose outstanding work was the Doric gateway to Euston Station, now demolished. He continued the work of Pugin at Adare Manor in 1862 and designed St John's Catholic Cathedral in Limerick.

Hargrave, Abraham (d.1808). He came from Yorkshire and superintended the erection St Patrick's Bridge in Cork in 1791, later rebuilt by his grandson in 1859–60. He was an extensive contractor, building bridges and quays as well as churches and houses, including Castle Hyde, Fermoy. The fine staircase at Doneraile is attributed to him.

Hoban, James (*c.*1762–1831). Born in Ireland, he worked as an 'artisan' in Dublin before he emigrated to America. He submitted a plan for the President's house which received a first prize of $500 and a gold medal. This was based on Leinster House, Dublin (1745–47), but was reduced to a two-storey design at the request of George Washington.

Hopper, Thomas (1776–1856). Born at Rochester, he worked initially with his father, a measuring surveyor. He carried out alterations to Carlton House at the request of the Prince Regent who admired his work. He was adept at every style and executed designs for alterations to Slane Castle for the 1st Marquess Conyngham, notably the circular ballroom that fortunately survived the recent fire. His greatest work in Ireland was Gosford Castle, Co. Armagh.

Ivory, Thomas (*c.*1732–86). He was born in Cork and was the best of the architects eclipsed by Gandon. He was master of the Dublin Society's Drawing School. His principal works were the Blue Coat School and the Newcomen Bank, Dublin, and the bridges at Carton and Lismore.

Johnston, Francis (1760–1829). A native of Armagh, he lived in Dublin and was appointed architect to the Board of Works in 1805. He built many public buildings including the G.P.O., Dublin. Townley Hall, begun 1794, is a fine example of a neo-Classical country house and his castellated houses include Charleville Forest, Co. Offaly, and Tullynally Castle (Pakenham Hall). His Gothic Revival work includes the Chapel of Dublin Castle (1807–14). He was one of the founders of the Royal Hibernian Academy and its President from 1824 to 1829, designing and building their premises out of his own pocket.

Johnston, John (d.1812). Little is known about Johnston (no connection with Francis Johnston) who worked at Birr Castle for Sir Laurence Parsons, 2nd Earl of Rosse. Mark Girouard suggests that Sir Laurence was his own architect at Birr, his professional assistant being John Johnston, who made working drawings, based on the sketches of his employer. The Protestant Church at Birr, which was started in 1810 or 1811, appears to have been made to Johnston's designs and was completed after his death.

Johnston, Richard (1754–?). Elder brother of the better-known Francis Johnston, he was the architect of the Rotunda Assembly Rooms, now the Gate Theatre, Dublin, and drew the original plans for Castle Coole which were modified by James Wyatt.

King, William (*fl.*1770s). A landscape designer who worked at Florence Court in the 1770s and may also have drawn up plans for the neighbouring gardens at Castle Coole.

Lafranchini, Paulo (1695–1770) and Filippo (1702–79). Born in Ticino, Switzerland, the brothers came to decorate the saloon at Carton in 1739 and worked at 15 houses during their 40 years of activity in Ireland. They have been credited with the introduction of the human figure into plaster decoration and had a profound influence on native Irish stuccodores. Examples of their art may be seen at Riverstown House and Kilshannig, Co. Cork, Russborough and Castletown.

Lanyon, Sir Charles (1813–89). A native of Eastbourne, Sussex, he was articled to Jacob Owen, the engineer and architect of the Irish Board of Works in Dublin in 1832. He became county surveyor of Antrim and spent the rest of his life in Ulster, where he supervised the construction of bridges, railways and roads, as well as designing some of the finest country houses, such as Drenagh, Co. Derry, Dunderave, Co. Antrim, and the flamboyantly Italianate Ballywalter. In the words of C. E. B. Brett: 'His is certainly the greatest name in the development of Belfast.' He was head of the flourishing Belfast firm of Lanyon and Lynn and a prominent public figure.

Lutyens, Sir Edwin (1869–1944). The most important English domestic architect in the first half of the twentieth century. He worked closely with Gertrude Jekyll, the landscape and garden designer. Their work, over a period of twenty years, was marked by the integration of house and garden. In Ireland, Lutyens worked at Heywood, Co. Laois, and Lambay Castle, Co. Dublin, as well as carrying out extensive alterations and additions at Howth Castle.

Lynn, John (?). John Lynn was active in the early nineteenth century in both Sligo and Co. Down. He acted as clerk of works at the building of John Nash's Rockingham and worked on additions and alterations to Strokestown Park in 1819 (in connection with which he is referred to as Mr Lynn, 'an Englishman'). A John Lynn appears as contractor for the new gaol at Downpatrick in the 1820s.

McCarthy, James Joseph (1817–82). Born in Dublin, he studied at the Royal Dublin Society Schools. Known as the 'Irish Pugin', he chose a career as an ecclesiastical architect. He was a Catholic, had strong nationalistic leanings and greatly admired Irish medieval architecture. His domestic practice was small; he designed Cahirmoyle, Co. Limerick, for Edward O'Brien in 1870. His churches include the Catholic Cathedral in Monaghan and the completion of the Catholic Cathedral in Armagh, begun by Thomas Duff.

Morrison, Sir Richard (1767–1849). Born in Co. Cork he was the son of John Morrison, an architect and builder from Midleton. On completion of his studies at the Dublin Society's School, he set up a practice in Clonmel. Archibishop Agar of Cashel commissioned him to construct a tower and spire for the Cathedral. About 1800 he moved to Dublin and established a thriving country-house practice as well as building courthouses and gaols. He also built a number of highly sophisticated villas such as Castlegar, Co. Galway, and Cangort, Co. Offaly. In collaboration with his son, William Vitruvius, who joined his practice in 1809, he worked at Killruddery, Fota Island and Barons Court.

Morrison, William Vitruvius (1794–1838). The second son of Richard Morrison, he was born in Clonmel from a line of architects. He was said to have produced a plan for Ballyheigue Castle, Co. Kerry, when only 15. His brother John described him as being of delicate health, suffering from depression and having a sensitive nature in contrast to his father who was both ambitious and energetic and may have resented his son's ability. He studied abroad spending time in Rome and Paris. In England he learned to admire the Tudor style which he favoured. He was responsible for the designs of Mount Stewart and Barons Court.

Myers, Graham (*fl.*1780–1800). He enlarged Pakenham Hall for the Earl of Longford which is now buried in later Gothic Revival additions and known today as Tullynally Castle. He succeeded his father, Christopher Myers, as executive architect of Trinity College, Dublin. His father was responsible for erecting the Public Theatre, or Examination Hall, there from 1777 to 1800 to the designs of Sir William Chambers while he himself built Chambers's Chapel there in the 1790s.

Nash, John (1752–1835). Best known for his planning of Regent's Park and Regent Street in London in his later years. He established a vast country-house practice, working in the Picturesque style. He was the personal architect of George IV, building the Royal Pavilion, Brighton, in 1815 and working on Buckingham Palace, London, in 1825, later completed by others. In Ireland his work ranged from the Swiss Cottage to Rockingham, Co. Roscommon (burnt 1957), Shanbally Castle, Co. Tipperary (demolished), Lough Cutra Castle, Co. Galway, and Killymoon Castle, Co. Tyrone, besides alterations to Caledon, Co. Tyrone.

Pain, James (*c.*1779–1877) and George Richard (1793–1838). They were sons of an English architectural pattern-book designer. Both were apprenticed to John Nash and came to Ireland to supervise the buildings of Lough Cutra, Co. Galway, which was begun in 1811. James settled in Limerick and George in Cork. They worked together on many projects including Cork Gaol, Mitchelstown Castle, Co. Cork, Strancally Castle, Co. Waterford, and Castle Bernard, Co. Cork. James Pain worked at Adare Manor.

Paxton, Joseph (1803–65). Paxton remodelled Lismore Castle for the 6th Duke of Devonshire in the 1850s partially incorporating the older castle from the twelfth century. He gave it a Victorian solidity designed more to impress than to defend. Paxton started life as a gardener at Chatsworth, Derbyshire, the great country seat of the Dukes of Devonshire, and ended as the eminent architect of the Crystal Palace in London.

Pearce, Sir Edward Lovett (*c.*1699–1733). Studied architecture in Italy 1723–4 and is thought to have been a pupil of his cousin, Sir John Vanbrugh, architect of Blenheim Palace, Oxfordshire. He returned to Dublin in 1724, and succeeded Thomas Burgh as Surveyor of Works and Fortifications in Ireland in 1730 and was knighted in 1732. His works include Bellamont Forest, Cashel Palace, the Parliament House, Dublin, and much of the interior of Castletown. He was Ireland's greatest Palladian architect.

Popje, Henry (*c.*1771–1830). When the 10th Earl of Meath altered Killruddery to the designs of Sir Richard Morrison in 1820, he employed a local stucco plasterer, Henry Popje, who was responsible for the vaulted ceiling in the dining room.

Preston, John (*fl.*1807–25). One of Dublin's leading upholsterers, he completely redecorated Castle Coole in the Regency style between 1807 and 1825 on the instructions of the 2nd Earl of Belmore. He supplied sumptuous curtains with ornate fringes and tassels, elegant gilded tie-backs and furniture in the Grecian manner. The house is as important for its interior decoration as it is for its neo-Classical architecture.

Pugin, A. W. N. (1812–52). A celebrated Gothic Revival architect whose talents extended to the decorative arts such as furniture, stained-glass, vestments, metalwork and embroidery. Pugin was associated with a revival in religious architecture, particularly in relation to the Catholic Church. He was involved in the design of the great halls both at Adare Manor and

Lismore Castle with his partner J. G. Crace. He had a large Irish practice which included Killarney Cathedral and works at Maynooth College.

ROBERTS, SAMUEL USSHER (1813–92). He came from Waterford, and worked as an engineer in Galway. He was a talented Gothic Revival architect and may have had the major role in the designing of Kylemore Castle. He worked at Curraghmore, Co. Waterford, and designed Gurteen le Poer near Clonmel, Co. Tipperary.

ROBERTSON, DANIEL (fl.1825–50). Little is known of his Scottish origins but Robertson seems to have been related to the distinguished Robert Adam, whose mother was a Robertson. He may have been his pupil. He worked in Oxford for several years where he designed the Clarendon Press building in Walton Street. Robertson went to Ireland under a cloud in 1829. He was the architect for Carrigglas in 1837. In 1840 he built Castleboro, Co. Wexford, for Lord Carew and Wells in the same county for Robert Doyne, in the Jacobean style. In 1843 he laid out the gardens at Powerscourt. Lord Powerscourt said that 'he was given to drink and always drew best when he was excited with sherry. He suffered from gout and used to be driven about in a wheel-barrow with a bottle of sherry; while that lasted he was always ready to direct the workmen, but when it was finished he was incapable of working any more'. (Lord Powerscourt, *Description and History of Powerscourt*, 1903)

ROBINSON, SIR WILLIAM (c.1643–1712). Born in England, he was made Surveyor-General of Ireland in 1671. At the instigation of the Duke of Ormonde he designed and built the Royal Hospital at Kilmainham in Dublin. He also built Essex Bridge 1667–8, and Marsh's Library in Dublin, re-designed Dublin Castle after a fire in 1684 and designed Charles Fort, Kinsale. He left Ireland in 1709.

ROSE, JOSEPH, JR (1745–99). Like his father, Rose was an accomplished decorative plasterer. When Joseph Jr returned from Italy in 1766, the family set up in London and executed with great skill most of the work for Robert Adam. They also worked for Sir William Chambers and James Wyatt. Joseph Rose Jr was in charge of the plasterwork at Castle Coole.

ROTHERY FAMILY. Several members of the family involved in building are found in Dublin in the 1680s; John, Isaac and James are found later in Limerick and Clare. Maurice Craig attributes Shannongrove and Riddlestown (both Co. Limerick) to the Rothery family whose masterpiece is Mount Ievers, begun in 1736. John Rothery was the architect-builder; he died in 1736 and an agreement was made with his son Isaac to finish the house. A monument of 1722 in Adare Church, Co. Limerick, is signed, *Rothery fecit*. John Rothery designed the front of Doneraile in 1725.

SANDYS, FRANCIS (?). Sandys the elder was a late-eighteenth-century Dublin architect. An architect of this name entered the Royal Exchange competition of 1768–9, designed some street fountains (such as the Rutland fountain in Merrion Square), and died c.1795. He may be the Francis Sandys who worked at Bellevue, Co. Wicklow, for the La Touches. His son, also Francis, to whom the Knight of Glin attributes Luggala, was patronised by the Earl-Bishop of Derry for whom he supervised the building of Ickworth in Suffolk. Dr McParland believes the younger Sandys's career was largely, or wholly, in England.

SEMPLE, GEORGE (fl.1748–80). His family were deeply involved in building in Dublin during the second half of the eighteenth century. He built St Patrick's Hospital in 1749 and added a spire to St Patrick's Cathedral, Dublin. He designed Headfort, Co. Meath, although the interior is by Robert Adam.

SHANAHAN, MICHAEL (fl.1767–1811). From relatively humble beginnings as a stonemason in Cork, Shanahan, through the patronage of Frederick Augustus Hervey, Earl of Bristol and Bishop of Derry, he became a notable figure in late eighteenth-century Irish architecture. He supervised the construction of the Earl-Bishop's house at Downhill, Co. Derry, and designed the Mussenden Temple beside it. After working for the Earl-Bishop he returned to Cork where he developed his original marble-cutting business. After his glamorous career his old associates in Cork considered him 'too big for his boots'.

SHIEL, JAMES (c.1790–1867). Little is known of this architect of the Morrison school who worked on alterations to Tullynally, in the 1820s, to Dunsany Castle, and to Killeen Castle, Co. Meath.

SMYTH, EDWARD (1749–1812). Born in Co. Meath and in 1811 he became the first head of the Dublin Society School of Modelling. A noted sculptor and pupil of Simon Vierpyl, he is best known for the 14 Riverine Heads on the Custom House. His work appears on most of Gandon's Dublin buildings as well as on those of Francis Johnston.

SOANE, SIR JOHN (1753–1837). Youngest son of a Berkshire builder, he worked as assistant to George Dance. He made the Grand Tour and cut short his travels to return to Downhill in Northern Ireland, where he expected to be given a commission by the Earl-Bishop of Derry, who, in the event, changed his mind. He designed the Academical Institution, Belfast, in 1809. He was commissioned by the Duke of Abercorn to remodel Barons Court in 1791–2, but his work there was soon after destroyed by fire. His career was almost entirely in England, where, by the time of this death, he had established himself as the most original and eminent architect of his generation. His best-known work was the Bank of England, London.

STAPLETON, MICHAEL (fl.1770–1801). He was a native of Dublin and he built and lived in 1 Mountjoy Place, Dublin, until his death in 1801, becoming the major Irish neo-Classical stuccodore as well as an architect. His most important Dublin interiors are at Belvedere House, the chapel of Trinity College, and Powerscourt (town) House which has a room almost identical to one at Lucan House.

STEUART, GEORGE (c.1730–1806). Born in Perthshire and a Gaelic speaker he was patronized by the Dukes of Atholl. In Ireland his only work, at Barons Court, was enveloped by the later work of Soane and the Morrisons.

STUART, JAMES 'ATHENIAN' (1713–88). Born in London. With the support of Lord Charlemont and others he travelled to Greece with Nicholas Revett in 1751, returning to England four years later. On their return they published the first volume of *Antiquities of Athens*. Volumes Two to Four were published posthumously and, like Volume One, were a significant influence on the neo-Classical movement. Stuart designed the Temple of the Winds at Mount Stewart and in London his works include Montagu (later Portman) House, Portman Square, and the restoration of Greenwich Hospital Chapel.

TINSLEY, WILLIAM (1804–85). Born in Clonmel, Co. Tipperary. His family had long associations with building in the area. He worked with James Pain; church design and construction were a major part of his business. He built Grove and Lakefield in the Italian villa style, both in Co. Tipperary. He rebuilt Tullamaine Castle, Co. Tipperary, and remodelled Rockwell (now Rockwell College), Co. Tipperary. He emigrated to America in 1851 where he built up a substantial practice. Examples of his work there include Christchurch, Indianapolis, buildings for the University of Wisconsin and the Institution for the Education of the Blind, Columbus, Ohio.

TRENCH, JOHN TOWNSEND (1834–1900). An amateur architect from Co. Laois and a cousin of John Adair for whom he designed and built Glenveagh Castle, Co. Donegal. He drew an elaborate plan for a street in Arklow which he submitted to Lady Carysfort. His father, William Stewart Trench, a land agent, wrote his memoirs which were illustrated by his son.

VIERPYL, SIMON (c.1725–1810). Sir William Chambers wrote of the work done at the Casino at Marino that it '… was built by Mr Verpyle [sic] with great neatness and taste'. Vierpyl was an English sculptor whose work survives on many public buildings in Dublin including the Royal Exchange (1769), now the City Hall, and the Blue Coat School (1773), presently the headquarters of the Incorporated Law Society. Edward Smyth was his pupil.

VULLIAMY, LEWIS (1791–1871). Born in London, he was articled to Robert Smirke, the architect of the British Museum. Vulliamy entered the Royal Academy School in 1809. He published *Examples of ornamental sculpture in architecture drawn from originals in Greece, Asia Minor and Italy 1818 … 1821*. In Ireland he worked at Emo Court, where in 1834–6 he was responsible for the addition of the portico to the garden front with its massive Ionic columns.

WEST, ROBERT (d.1790). The West family of Dublin were long associated with bricklaying and plastering. Robert West continued the tradition and was the most distinguished of Irish Rococo stuccodores as well as being an architect. He was made Freeman of the City of Dublin in 1752. Among his finest works are 20 Lower Dominick Street and 86 St Stephen's Green, Dublin, now part of Newman House.

WESTMACOTT, RICHARD THE ELDER (1747–1808). An English monumental sculptor, he made chimneypieces for the Admiralty, Woburn Abbey and Castle Coole working with the architect James Wyatt. His son, Sir Richard, is remembered for his elaborate monumental sculptures which found their way to the most distant corners of the British Empire. Richard Sr was given the Royal Appointment of mason for Kensington Palace in 1796 and made chimneypiece tablets for Wedgwood. His most important monument was of James Dutton in Sherborne Church, Gloucestershire.

WHITE, WILLIAM (1825–1900). A British Victorian Gothic Revival architect. Brilliant and eccentric, he practised in Cornwall from 1847 and had a wonderful feeling for stone. His architecture was bold and original and he was a prolific writer, traveller and lecturer. He built many churches in England and cathedrals in Pretoria and Madagascar. His best-known house is Humewood.

WILLIAMSON, Arthur and John (fl.1825–36). Pupils of Francis Johnston, they worked at Emo Court, under Vulliamy in 1834–6. They also designed The Argory, Co. Tyrone, a property of the National Trust.

WOODWARD, BENJAMIN (1816–61). Born in Tullamore, Co. Offaly, his father was a captain in the Royal Meath Militia. Trained as an engineer he was the foremost designer with the firm of Sir Thomas Deane, Son and Woodward of Cork. His work was influenced by John Ruskin. Among his best-known buildings are the Museum Building at Trinity College (1852–7) and the Kildare Street Club (1858–61), both in Dublin. The firm also designed and built the Oxford Museum (1854–60).

WYATT, JAMES (1746–1813). Wyatt's family were well-known builders in Weeford, Staffordshire, in the eighteenth century. He studied architecture in Venice and Rome and favoured the neo-Classical style, though he was equally adept later at the Gothic. In 1796 he succeeded Sir William Chambers as Surveyor-General and Comptroller of the Office of Works. He had a vast practice in England and among his important commissions in Ireland were Abbey Leix in 1773 and Castle Coole in 1790–7.

SELECT BIBLIOGRAPHY

ARCHER, M., *Irish Delftware* (exhib. cat.), Dublin, 1971.

BIANCONI, M. O'C. and WATSON, S. J., *Bianconi, King of the Irish Roads*, Dublin, 1962.

BARRINGTON, T. J., *Discovering Kerry*, Dublin, 1976.

BENCE-JONES, M., *Burke's Guide to Irish Country Houses*, London, 1988.

BENNETT, D., *Irish Georgian Silver*, London, 1972.

BENNETT, D., *The Silver Collection, Trinity College*, Dublin, 1988.

BRETT, C. E. B., *Buildings of Belfast 1700–1914*, London, 1967.

CHILVERS, I. (ed.), *Concise Oxford Dictionary of Art and Artists*, Oxford, 1990.

COLVIN, H., *Biographical Dictionary of British Architects, 1600–1840*, London, 1978.

CONNOLLY, S., *In an Irish House*, London, 1988.

COSTELLO, MURRAY and BEAUMONT, *The Royal Hospital, Kilmainham*, Dublin, 1987.

COURCY DE, C. and MAHER, A., *Fifty Views of Ireland*, National Gallery of Ireland, 1988

CRAIG, M. and GLIN, KNIGHT OF, *Ireland Observed*, Cork, 1970.

CRAIG, M., *Classic Irish Houses of the Middle Size*, London, 1976.

CRAIG, M., *The Architecture of Ireland from the Earliest Times*, London, 1982.

CRAIG, M., *Architecture in Ireland*, Dublin, 1978.

CRAIG, M., *Dublin 1660–1860*, Dublin, 1980.

CROOKSHANK, A and GLIN, KNIGHT OF, *The Painters of Ireland*, London, 1978.

CRUICKSHANK, D., *A Guide to the Georgian Buildings of Britain and Ireland*, London, 1985.

CURRAN, C. P., *Dublin Decorative Plasterwork of the Seventeenth and Eighteenth Centuries*, London, 1967

DE BREFFNY, B. and MOTT, G., *The Churches and Abbeys of Ireland*, London, 1976.

DE BREFFNY, B. and FFOLLIOTT, R., *The Houses of Ireland*, London, 1975.

DE BREFFNY, B., *Castles of Ireland*, London, 1977.

DE BREFFNY, B., *Heritage of Ireland*, London, 1980.

DE BREFFNY, B., *Ireland: A Cultural Encyclopaedia*, London, 1983.

DIXON, R. and MUTHESIUS, S., *Victorian Architecture*, London, 1978.

FITZGERALD, BRIAN, *Emily, Duchess of Leinster*, London, 1949.

FITZGERALD, BRIAN, *Lady Louisa Conolly*, London, 1950.

FLETCHER, SIR BANISTER, *A History of Architecture*, London, 1987.

FOSTER, R. F., *Modern Ireland 1600–1972*, London, 1988.

FOSTER, R. F. (ed.), *The Oxford Illustrated History of Ireland*, Oxford, 1989.

G. P. A., *Arts Review Yearbook*. 'Dublin and the Arts in Ireland'.

GEORGE, M. and BOWE, P., *The Gardens of Ireland*, London, 1986.

GEORGIAN SOCIETY RECORDS, Vols I–V, Dublin, 1909–13.

GIROUARD, M., *The Victorian Country House*, Oxford, 1971.

GRAY, A. S., *Edwardian Architecture*, 1985.

GUINNESS, D., *Georgian Dublin*, London, 1979.

GUINNESS, D., *Portrait of Dublin*, London, 1967.

GUINNESS, D. and RYAN, W., *Irish Houses and Castles*, London, 1971.

GUINNESS, D. and SADLER, J., *Palladio, a Western Progress*, New York, 1976.

HARBISON, P., *Beranger's Views of Ireland*, Dublin, 1991.

HARBISON, P., *Guide to the National Monuments in the Republic of Ireland*, Dublin, 1970.

HARBISON, P., SHEEHY, J. and POTTERTON, H., *Irish Art and Architecture*, London, 1978.

INDIANA UNIVERSITY PRESS, *Life and Works of William Tinsley*, 1953.

IRISH ARCHITECTURAL ARCHIVE, *The Architecture of Richard Morrison and William Vitruvius Morrison*, Dublin, 1989.

Irish Architectural Drawings (exhib. cat.), London, 1965.

IRISH GEORGIAN SOCIETY, *Bulletins*, from 1958, Dublin.

IRISH HERITAGE SERIES BOOKLETS, from 1974, Dublin.

JONES, A., *Biographical Index*. Irish Architectural Archive.

KILLANIN, LORD and DUIGNAN, M. V. *Shell Guide to Ireland*, London, 1962.

KNIGHT OF GLIN, GRIFFIN, D. J., and ROBINSON, N. K., *Vanishing Country Houses of Ireland*, Dublin, 1988.

LARMOUR, P., *Belfast, Architectural Guide*, Belfast, 1987.

LOEBER, R., *A Biographical Dictionary of Architects in Ireland 1600–1720*, London, 1981.

MACNEILL, M., *Maire Rua, Lady of Lemanegh*, Whitegate, 1990.

McDERMOTT, M. J., *Ireland's Architectural Heritage*, Dublin, 1975.

McDONNELL, J., *Irish Eighteenth-Century Stuccowork and its European Sources*, Dublin, 1991.

McPARLAND, E., *A Bibliography of Irish Architectural History*, Irish Historical Studies, no. 102 (Nov. 1988).

McPARLAND, E., *James Gandon*, London, 1985.

MALINS, E. and GLIN, KNIGHT OF, *Lost Demesnes*, London, 1976.

MURPHY, REV. DENIS, S. J., *Cromwell in Ireland*, Dublin, c.1883.

NATIONAL TRUST, THE, Guide Books: *Florence Court*, London, 1979; *Castle Coole*, 1988; *Mount Stewart*, 1986.

O'BRIEN, G. R., *These my Friends and Forebears, the O'Briens of Dromoland*, Whitegate, 1991.

OFFICE OF PUBLIC WORKS, *The History of Glenveagh*, Dublin, 1991.

OFFICE OF PUBLIC WORKS, *The Casino at Marino*, Dublin, 1991.

PLACZEK, A. K. (ed.), *Macmillan Encyclopaedia of Architects*, New York, 1982.

POWER, P. C., *History of South Tipperary*, Cork, 1989.

READERS DIGEST, *The Treasures of Britain*, London, 1968.

SHEEHY, J. and McCARTHY, J. J. *The Gothic Revival in Ireland*, U.A.H.S.

SITWELL, S., *Truffle Hunt*, London, 1953.

STEWART, ANN, *National Gallery of Ireland, Fifty Irish Portraits*, London, 1984.

STRICKLAND, W. G., *A Dictionary of Irish Artists*, Dublin and London, 1913.

SUMMERSON, J., *The Pelican History of Art. Architecture in Britain 1530–1830*, London, 1970.

TEAHAN, J. (ed.), *Irish Decorative Arts, 1550–1928, from the Collections of the National Museum of Ireland*, Dublin, 1990.

ULSTER ARCHITECTURAL HERITAGE, *Ballywalter Park*, Belfast, 1985.

WODEHOUSE, L., *Art and Architecture: A Guide to Information Sources*, Vol. 8 British Architects, 1840–1976.

WYNNE, M., *National Gallery of Ireland, Fifty Irish Painters*, Dublin, 1983.

INDEX